# *Tastefully Yours*

## Savoring Denver's
## Restaurant Past

Pierre Wolfe

2001

book design   *Lee and Jennifer Ballentine*
copyediting   *Jennifer Ballentine*
cover design   *Todd Anderson*
index   *Peggy Swager*
keyboarding   *Verna Frederickson*
proofreading   *Bonnie Beach*

*Tastefully Yours: Savoring Denver's Restaurant Past* is distributed by Professional Book Center, P.O. Box 9249, Denver CO 80209, tastefully@probook.net.

Profits from the sale of this publication have been donated to the Education Fund of the Colorado Restaurant Association.

Library of Congress Cataloging-in-Publication Data is available for this title

ISBN 0-938075-83-7 (deluxe clothbound limited edition)

ISBN 0-938075-84-5 (paperback)

Printed in the United States of America

05  04  03  02  01  1  2  3  4  5

# Contents

*Foreword by Dick Kreck*    *vii*

*Preface*    *ix*

HISTORICAL DENVER DINING SCENE . . . . . . . . . . . . . . . . . . . . . 1

**Alpine Village Inn** . . . . . . . . . . . . . . . . . . . . . . . . . . . . . . . . . . . . . 3

**Apple Tree Shanty** . . . . . . . . . . . . . . . . . . . . . . . . . . . . . . . . . . . . 6

    The Restaurants of Denver: Where You Can Buy
    a Dinner for Fifteen Dollars and One for Fifteen
    Cents. *Colorado Sun, 1892*. . . . . . . . . . . . . . . . . . . . . . . . . . . . . . . . 8

**Baur's Restaurant** . . . . . . . . . . . . . . . . . . . . . . . . . . . . . . . . . . . . . 13

**Brick Oven Beanery** . . . . . . . . . . . . . . . . . . . . . . . . . . . . . . . . . . . 18

    Along the Ziti Trail: Confessions of a Menu
    Snatcher, *by Max Donaldson*. . . . . . . . . . . . . . . . . . . . . . . . . . . . . 21

**Café Giovanni** . . . . . . . . . . . . . . . . . . . . . . . . . . . . . . . . . . . . . . . . 25

**Café Promenade** . . . . . . . . . . . . . . . . . . . . . . . . . . . . . . . . . . . . . . 28

    Some of the Slangy Orders That Bother Carnivalists
    Who Eat, *Denver Times, 1901* . . . . . . . . . . . . . . . . . . . . . . . . . . . 32

**Chateau Pyrenees** . . . . . . . . . . . . . . . . . . . . . . . . . . . . . . . . . . . . . 34

    Palatial Restaurant, *Denver Republican, 1891* . . . . . . . . . . . . . 37

**Cliff Young's Restaurant and Cliff Young the Man** . . . . . . . . . . 39

**The Colorado Mine Company** . . . . . . . . . . . . . . . . . . . . . . . . . . . 45

    235 Fillmore: A Mass Grave for Restaurants. . . . . . . . . . . . . . . 48

**Dudley's** . . . . . . . . . . . . . . . . . . . . . . . . . . . . . . . . . . . . . . . . . . 49

**Golden Ox** . . . . . . . . . . . . . . . . . . . . . . . . . . . . . . . . . . . . . . . . . 52

    Denver's Cheap-Meal District, *Denver Times, 1902* . . . . . . . . 55

**Joe "Awful" Coffee's Ringside Lounge** . . . . . . . . . . . . . . . . . 59

    The Capitol, *Daily Rocky Mountain News, 1869* . . . . . . . . . . 62

**Laffite Restaurant** . . . . . . . . . . . . . . . . . . . . . . . . . . . . . . . . . . . 63

**Lande's** . . . . . . . . . . . . . . . . . . . . . . . . . . . . . . . . . . . . . . . . . . . . 69

    The Man All around You, *Denver Times, 1889* . . . . . . . . . . . . 71

**Leo's Place** . . . . . . . . . . . . . . . . . . . . . . . . . . . . . . . . . . . . . . . . . 74

**Le Profile (also Scotch 'n' Sirloin, Piccadilly, Stephanino,**
    **Los Dos)** . . . . . . . . . . . . . . . . . . . . . . . . . . . . . . . . . . . . . . . . . 78

**Manhattan Café** . . . . . . . . . . . . . . . . . . . . . . . . . . . . . . . . . . . . 82

    Queer Food Concoctions: Dishes in Darkest
    Denver, *Denver Times, 1902* . . . . . . . . . . . . . . . . . . . . . . . . . 85

**Manhattan Restaurant** . . . . . . . . . . . . . . . . . . . . . . . . . . . . . . 89

**McGaa Street Restaurant** . . . . . . . . . . . . . . . . . . . . . . . . . . . . 91

    Vice Ensnares Virtue: Police Break Up the Places
    Where Girls Halt Between, *Denver Times, 1902* . . . . . . . . . . . 94

**Navarre Restaurant** . . . . . . . . . . . . . . . . . . . . . . . . . . . . . . . . . 96

**Normandy French Restaurant** . . . . . . . . . . . . . . . . . . . . . . . . 99

    Her Father's Daughter . . . . . . . . . . . . . . . . . . . . . . . . . . . . . 107

**Ohle's Deli-Restaurant** . . . . . . . . . . . . . . . . . . . . . . . . . . . . . 110

**Patio Restaurant** . . . . . . . . . . . . . . . . . . . . . . . . . . . . . . . . . . . 113

    The Restaurant Hall of Fame . . . . . . . . . . . . . . . . . . . . . . . . 119

**Quorum Restaurant, a.k.a. Pierre's Quorum** . . . . . . . . . . . . . 121

    My Media Career . . . . . . . . . . . . . . . . . . . . . . . . . . . . . . . . . 133

**Rattlesnake Club and Adirondacks** . . . . . . . . . . . . . . . . . . . . 143

    Why Do Restaurants Fail and Disappear? . . . . . . . . . . . . . . 145

**Restaurant Edelweiss** . . . . . . . . . . . . . . . . . . . . . . . . . . . . . . . 146

(The Original) Sam's No. 3 . . . . . . . . . . . . . . . . . . . . . . . . . . . . . . . 147
   Restaurant Critics . . . . . . . . . . . . . . . . . . . . . . . . . . . . . . . . . 153

**The Tiffin** . . . . . . . . . . . . . . . . . . . . . . . . . . . . . . . . . . . . . . . . 156

**Top of the Rockies** . . . . . . . . . . . . . . . . . . . . . . . . . . . . . . . . . . 159
   A Smorgasbord of Eateries . . . . . . . . . . . . . . . . . . . . . . . . . . 162

**Wilscam's (also Hungry Farmer, Dutchman,
Original Broker, pti)** . . . . . . . . . . . . . . . . . . . . . . . . . . . . . . . 169
   Looking Back, It Wasn't about
   the Food, *by Nancy Clark* . . . . . . . . . . . . . . . . . . . . . . . . . . . 174

GENE AMOLE: THE FRUSTRATED CHEF . . . . . . . . . . . . . . . . . . 177

RECIPES FROM CURRENT RESTAURANTS . . . . . . . . . . . . . . . . 191
   *Barolo Grill*   *191*
   *Bruno's Italian Bistro*   *193*
   *Buckhorn Exchange*   *195*
   *Chez Walter*   *196*
   *Chinook Tavern*   *198*
   *Flagstaff House Restaurant*   *200*
   *The Fort*   *202*
   *Fourth Story Restaurant*   *204*
   *Institute of Culinary Arts/Art Institute of Colorado*   *205*
   *Inverness Hotel & Golf Club*   *209*
   *Loews Giorgio Hotel*   *214*
   *Mel's Restaurant and Bar*   *216*
   *Panzano*   *218*
   *Papillon Café*   *223*
   *Radex*   *225*
   *Rose's Café*   *226*
   *Sam's No. 3*   *227*
   *Tante Louise*   *228*
   *240 Union*   *229*
   *Vasil's Euro-Grille*   *230*
   *Yanni's*   *232*

**Index** . . . . . . . . . . . . . . . . . . . . . . . . . . . . . . . . . . . . . . . . . . 235

# Foreword

When many of the pioneers arrived in the 1850s in what would become the city of Denver at the confluence of the South Platte River and Cherry Creek, the first thing they did was devour their mode of transportation.

The same oxen that helped haul the travelers and their goods across the plains were slaughtered and eaten. Their thousand-mile journey must not have made the hard-working animals tasty fare because a common recipe called for the meat to be seasoned with gunpowder.

In the city's early days, lard and various portions of pigs were considered "good eatin'." Denver's residents were most apt to find prepared food in saloons where lager beer and cheap whiskey were the main attractions and a "free lunch" was little more than a come-on. Later, fine restaurants such as Charpiot's, the Manhattan, and the Navarre offered steaks, oysters, and high-quality, frequently imported, champagnes and wines.

The common man was not forgotten. In 1892, the *Colorado Sun* newspaper noted, "It is a fact that one can get along on 50 cents a day in Denver restaurants. It is also a fact that the menu might not be particularly interesting, except as a novelty. But it can be done." A sample 50-cent daily regimen included a hot roll and coffee for breakfast; soup and "a meat stew (variety doubtful)" for lunch, and a small steak, bread, butter, and potatoes for dinner.

Since then Coloradans' tastes may have been elevated somewhat, but they still like going out to eat. At the dawn of the twenty-first century, there were more than nine thousand restaurants operating in the state, and diners spent more than $19 million a day on food away from home, according to the Colorado Restaurant Association.

He wasn't there at the beginning but no one has seen more of Denver's dining history than Pierre Wolfe, who leased his first restaurant in 1954 and didn't retire from the business until 2000. For more than forty years, he survived the vagaries of an industry that sees businesses come and go like summer rains, and he played host to the famous and the merely hungry with equal enthusiasm.

In *Tastefully Yours,* Wolfe tackles a job lamentable only in the fact that no one thought to do it earlier. From the Alpine Village Inn to Wilscam's and a hundred places in between, Wolfe reaches back to the early days of Denver and recalls the extinct eateries' menus and their specialties and records for posterity the words of their owners. He calls back to our memory notable restaurateurs Buck Scott, Joe Sperte, Tom Wilscam, Heinz Gerstle, the Cook family, Cliff Young, Conrad Trinkaus, and others.

When Pierre closed the Quorum in 1990, we gathered for a gala last supper, and it seemed we had seen the last of the indomitable Alsatian. Since then he has carved a new career as a radio host, world traveler and, now, a chronicler of the city's eateries.

To top off this buffet of historical retrospection, Wolfe provides recipes from some of today's best-known and most popular restaurants. There is Braised Duckling from Barolo Grill, Rack of Colorado Lamb from Flagstaff House, Tuna Carpaccio from Panzano, and even the lowly-but-wonderful Meat Loaf from Sam's No. 3. No gunpowder needed.

Through it all, Wolfe maintains his sense of humor and brings to this history the same eye that made sure the silverware was lined up properly, the wine glasses were just-so, and the customer was treated regally.

—*Dick Kreck*

# Preface

Restaurants are about status and celebrity, power and politics, money and sex. Restaurants are not merely places to eat. Whether bygone haunts or the current rage, restaurants are, or were, part of their patrons' lives. They host wedding anniversaries, birthdays, engagements, political skullduggery, visits by prominent people, movie stars, heads of state, and even those hiding from their spouses while engaged in marital infidelity.

Restaurateurs are confidantes, part of schemes, stage producers of special events, and oftentimes fall guys for the failings of their restaurants, self-indicted or falsely accused.

Restaurants, while very volatile, are popular enterprises, often motivated by big egos, ambitious chefs, or cash-happy investors. Profit margins are frequently minimal, or nonexistent, disregarded and overshadowed by pride of ownership. In many cases, the principals of these restaurant operations are characters who give a city a pronounced notoriety.

This book is a recounting of former well-known, Denver-area restaurants, their menus, specialties, and owners. It also includes recipes from former fine establishments, current restaurants, Denver's own Gene Amole, and some of my own. It is impossible to include all the eateries from years gone by. Among the thousands of restaurants in Denver from as early as the 1860s, I have chosen those restaurants that I felt had great stories to tell, and, as a practical matter, those for which menus and articles were available. My memory and research filled in nicely. I was also very fortunate to have former (but still kicking) restaurateurs and current operators share their stories about their ventures with me—some reprinted here, written by them. Merci! Thank you so very much! No doubt every reader will insist that the very best place ("their" place) has been left out! To you, I say, "If you think you can do better, write your own book!" But for sure, the restaurants described in these pages, in one way or another, had an impact on diners and the culinary culture of Denver.

As to myself, had I to do it over again, I would relive my life as part of Denver's restaurant scene, the same way it started and ended. Despite the fact that restaurants are very difficult businesses, we restaurateurs enjoy fun times in our places, sharing the limelight with competitors and loving most of our patrons. And just in case anyone might think I'm doing this for my own glory, the profits from this project are being donated to the Education Fund of the Colorado Restaurant Association. Assuming, of course, there are profits!

## Acknowledgments

My gratitude and sincere appreciation to my wife, Jean, and to my children, Karen Michelle Herrmann and Ronald Pierre Wolfe and their spouses, for their unswerving support throughout my restaurant career.

There are many friends, family members, restaurateurs, and even total strangers, who were instrumental in my becoming a published author. First, I must credit my friend Jeannie Everett for planting the idea for this book in my head. Max Donaldson contributed an article ("Along the Ziti Trail: Confessions of a Menu Snatcher") as well as his peerless collection of original menus (all snatched). Emory C. Walker Jr. turned up with an amazing collection of matchbooks, a number of which adorn the cover of this book. Barbara Walton, acquisitions specialist at the Denver Public Library, helped me plow through dusty archives of old clippings, menus, and microfiche, and put me in touch with Lou-Jean Holland Rehn, who helped tremendously in the slogging legwork of research. The *Rocky Mountain News* and the *Denver Post* were both very generous in their allowing me to reprint articles and photos from long ago. I also very much appreciate the contribution of recipes from the many fine current restaurants in the Denver area today. If the recipes don't work—call them, not me! Among the many others who contributed ideas and materials:

| | |
|---|---|
| Spiro Sam Armatas | Ann and Larry Mailand |
| Maxine N. Becker | Pat Miller |
| Cecil Burkhard | Franklin G. Murphy |
| Crista Carpenter | Ed Novak |
| Nancy Clark | Kathleen O'Brien |
| Morris Crawford | Saul Rosenfeld |
| Tom Cygnar | Robert and Marilyn Savre |
| Duco Debuyzer | Buck and Cindy Scott |
| Clark Fine | Greg and Shannon Sperte |
| Aileen Groen | Ron and Jean Sylling |
| Gail Halper | Conrad Trinkaus |
| R. T. Hopkins | Jo Tweed |
| Father Robert J. Kinkel | Tom Wilscam |
| Kees Janse-Kok | James R. Wiseman |
| Donna Johnson | Dorothy Witulsky |
| Wayne Johnson | Marcia A. Wolf |
| Pat Hanna Kuehl | Larry Wright |
| Jacques La Flecke | Sandra Yangas |
| Chris Leppek | Cliff Young |
| Mel and Janie Master | |

Without these friends and colleagues, and constant encouragement from family and friends, I would probably never have finished this book. But after a year and a half, there is finally proof that I've managed it. Call it a monument to those who toiled in the restaurant field, loving and hating it all at the same time.

But without Jennifer and Lee Ballentine of Professional Book Center, there would only be a pile of clippings, photos, articles, and memories. Jennifer and Lee's organizational, technical, and editorial skills were invaluable. They not only provided logistical support but encouraged me to finish my task, whenever doubts crept into my mind as to the value of such a book. They often dispelled such thoughts by saying, "Your book will be great!" To my editor, Dick Kreck, himself a published author, my gratitude and thanks for years of friendship and support. To Gene Amole, the longtime voice of

KVOD and dabbling chef, thanks for allowing me to reprint some of your favorite recipes. And finally, to those thousands of former patrons of my restaurants, friends and strangers who have eagerly awaited *Tastefully Yours*—Merci Beaucoup!

> *Food sustains us, but our very essence is enriched because it delights and surprises us. What better art can there be than one that transforms the mundane into the magnificent?*
>
> *What greater pleasures can there be than a meal that excites our eyes with color and texture, that stirs our appetites with its aromas, that fills us with exquisite flavors, and leaves a lingering reminder of its delights on our palates, then nourishes us for our endeavors?*
>
> —Art Institute of Colorado

Jean and Pierre Wolfe, 2001. *Wolfe collection.*

# Historical Denver Dining Scene

In doing my research to discover the activities of Denver's restaurants in the late nineteenth and early twentieth centuries, I found an astonishing amount of material on microfilm as well as original newspaper articles at the downtown Denver Public Library. With the help of Barbara Walton, Acquisitions Specialist at the library, and Lou-Jean Holland Rehn, my invaluable researcher, I launched enthusiastically into the stories of my adopted hometown's dining scene. Like a kid in a candy store, I cradled the material, made copies and indulged in the fascinating recounts about eating, dining, restaurant offerings, menus, and the rise and fall of these establishments.

One headline that caught my eye (how could I miss it?) from the *Denver Times* reads as follows: "Palatial Hotels, Cafes, Etc. Experienced and Genial Hosts for Comfort and Pleasure of the People—Hotels for All Classes in Plenty—Restaurants and Cafes Without Number and Many Delightful Places of Rest and Refreshment in Denver and Vicinity." . . . Does this make sense?

Throughout this book, you'll find some of the articles I found, retyped from the original newspaper sources. Together, they give a fascinating glimpse of early Denver's movers and shakers, her eateries and watering holes, and fine dining on the frontier. Read on and enjoy. But remember, the opinions and words used to express them are entirely those of their long-dead writers! Here are some other tidbits:

In 1866, you would have heard that Fred Charpiot had returned from Europe and was buying the International Restaurant. He promised the "Choiciest Delicacies" as well as a select stock of liquor and wine. Charpiot, a year later, announced that he had opened the French Restaurant on Blake Street, opposite the Elephant Corral.

At the same time, you could have found the People's Restaurant, John J. Reithmann, proprietor. Reithmann also owned and operated the Empire Bakery on Blake Street between F and G streets. In 1867, also on Blake Street, which must have been restaurant row, there was "McNasser's Restaurant, Serving Fresh Oysters, Game, and Trout."

Three years later, in 1870, many early Denverites dropped into the Denver City Dining Room on Larimer between G and H streets "for Ladies and Gentlemen." George T. Breed, the proprietor, bragged about his hot rolls and also offered oysters any style. In 1875, wandering down 15th Street and stopping at number 312, you might have discovered James Cella's Restaurant & Oyster House, with dining in privacy, if desired.

From some of the writeups we get an idea about some of the menu items and their prices. Oysters are still very popular and one might wonder why? No matter where or what the name of the restaurant, the oyster was heralded: "The Fattest and Most Lushcious Oysters are Served in the Most Tempting Style" proclaimed the Saddle Rock at 245 17th Street. What's with the oysters? My editor, Dick Kreck, proposed that their popularity could be due to nostalgia by those having migrated from the East to Denver. But I question their freshness, considering that these oysters were most likely coming from the East and had to be transported to Colorado by train. That's a long trip! Maybe they should have served Rocky Mountain Oysters!

John E. Seeley's establishment on 249 15th Street offered regular dinners for 30 cents. Other menu items included broiled Makinaw Trout (20 cents), Porterhouse Steak (35 cents; with mushrooms, 50 cents), Frog Saddles Fried (30 cents), Mutton Chops (15 cents), Tripe (15 cents), Quail on Toast (40 cents), but Teal Duck on Toast was just 25 cents, a bargain compared to a Mushroom Omelette at 35 cents.

In 1881, a new restaurant opened, the Restaurant De L'Opera, by proprietors Mr. Bourgougnon and C. Barthes, two experienced caterers. Mr. Bourgougnon had been employed by the House of Delmonico as a steward in New York and C. Barthes as chief cook for the great hotel keepers of America, the Lelands. This was indeed an elegant restaurant by all accounts—oysters again a specialty.

The Vienna Café, 372 Curtis Street, opened on October 18, 1881. The proprietors were certainly aware of the power of publicity. On Monday night, they entertained the members of the press, with almost every paper represented. By all accounts "a jolly good time was had by all." Marketing mavens do it now—they did it then!

**Alpine Village Inn** ⁓ **1150 South Colorado Boulevard, Denver**

*Gruss Gott:*
*"Ein Mahl ohne Wein, ist wie das Leben ohne Lachen"*
*(A meal without wine is life without laughter)*

This charming German restaurant served some of the best Bavarian fare in Denver.

My wife, Jean, and I enjoyed a pre-wedding evening with my mother-in-law at the Alpine Village Inn. We like German food! Good memories! Gute Erinnerungen!

Specialities of the house included:

| | |
|---|---|
| Alpine Topf (pot of pork and beef cutlet) | $3.50 |
| Fleischrouladen (rolled beef) | $3.75 |
| Wienerschnitzel | $3.25 |
| Kassler Rippchen (smoked pork loin) | $3.25 |
| Sauerbraten with German Potato Pancakes | $3.25 |
| Gebackener Lamm Schenkel (lamb shanks) | $3.00 |

For a special party: Whole Roast Suckling Pig

Desserts:

| | |
|---|---|
| Appelstrudel | $.75 |
| German Cheesecake | $.45 |

To drink, the Inn offered Lowenbrau beer, Deinhart, Liebfraumilch, and Blue Nun.

If you had visited the Alpine Village Inn, you would surely remember the girl servers in Bavarian dresses and the young lads, your waiters, in lederhosen (what else?). The place reeked with Bavarian Alpine allure: kerosene lamps, a very old cuckoo clock from Heidelberg, and beersteins. The perfect setting for a Bavarian-German restaurant.

In 1963, Pat Hanna of the *Rocky Mountain News* wrote:

# A Treat in Bavarian Style Dining

Going to dinner at the Alpine Village Inn, . . . , is like visiting the stage set for a German operetta. It's all so Rudolf Friml-ly.

First there's the fresh-faced girls in Bavarian dresses, voluminous lace aprons and starched white pointed hats. Then there's the friendly young waiters in lederhosen, white shirts, white knee sox and alpine hats. You almost expect them to polka from table to table in the big round dining room.

Ach, what a dining room! Paneled white . . . exposed beams . . . an enormous brick fireplace glittering with gleaming copper.

Sparkling red crystal kerosene lamps hang from the beamed roof, casting a rosy glow on the guests below. Steins, old plates and paintings of burgomasters parade along the wall.

Each table has its own snowy linen, red hurricane lamps and glowing red glasses. It's all cozy comfort, Bavarian style. . . .

Jack and Kaye [Roth] are co-owners of the Alpine with Ray and Pauline Dambach. . . . The Roths met the Dambachs in Las Vegas where the latter had another Alpine Inn.

The Roths were so impressed with the Las Vegas restaurant they set out to reconstruct the place in Denver. . . .

Tablehopping at the Alpine you're likely to find the Abe Perlmutter family (builders of Northglenn); impresario Saul Caston and his secretary, Miss Helen Black; Judge Edward C. Day, the M. H. Robineau family and Helen Bonfils.

—Excerpted from *Rocky Mountain News*, May 10, 1963; with permission

In case you're hankering for food like the Alpine Village Inn used to serve, here's my recipe for Wienerschnitzel:

# Wienerschnitzel

*4 servings*

Although Wiener means Vienna, every "typically" German restaurant serves this dish. And so did the Alpine Village.

| | |
|---|---|
| 1 pound of veal scallops,<br>    4 ounces per person,<br>    pounded very thin<br>½ cup of flour<br>salt & pepper,<br>    mixed into the flour | 3 large eggs, lightly beaten<br>1 cup white bread crumbs<br>3 tablespoons butter<br>3 tablespoons corn oil<br>capers<br>lemon slices |

1. Dip the pounded veal scallops into flour, beaten eggs, then bread crumbs.

2. Pat the breaded scallops on both sides.

3. Heat cooking fats in a large skillet, and when sufficiently hot add veal scallops, two at a time, and brown them about 3 minutes on each side.

4. Garnish with capers and lemon slices. Serve at once.

The perfectly cooked schnitzels should have brown and crisp coating that lifts away from the meat.

**Apple Tree Shanty  ∿  8710 East Colfax, Denver**

*Our Philosophy: Since 1949, our menu has evolved using this basic rationale. Our facility is small and limits the number of items we can offer while still maintaining our high standards. Thus we are called a "specialty restaurant." We think of each item on our menu as a "specialty." Our foods are simple but all are made with much care and attention. All the recipes and methods are uniquely our own, most are closely held secrets. . . .We are best known for our barbequed items and "Secret Sauce." . . . We bake our own pies and ginger-bread here, from our own recipes, even our ice cream is special. We strive to maintain these standards, we try to give the best possible value to our guests. Our portion sizes and prices are designed to allow you to enjoy our little res-taurant at a reasonable price. . . .We are here to serve you.*
*—Apple Tree Folks*
*(excerpted from menu, 1974)*

The Apple Tree Shanty was founded in 1949. This much-loved res-taurant was converted from a small residence and included a gar-den—an outdoor area enclosed to allow seating there all year long. "Simple food blessed with love and attention," stated the menu.

Apple Tree Shanty girls, your servers, were dressed in traditional Dutch garb and were well informed and attentive. This was a very popular restaurant for a long time! The original charm of the place was diminished by enlargement and other cosmetic changes.

Among the restaurant's specialties:

| | |
|---|---|
| Barbecued Pork Spareribs | $8.95 |
| Smoke Roasted Chicken | $7.95 |
| Pork 'N Secret Sauce | $7.95 |
| Steaks | $12.95 |

Apple Tree dinners included hot apple muffins, salad, their "famous baked potato," apple and cheese slaw or a pot of hickory-smoked beans.

## Apple Tree Entrées

Roast Top Round of Beef au jus ............................................. $7<sup>50</sup>
Tender, lean slices with plenty of those juices!

Roast Pork 'N Secret Sauce ................................................ 7<sup>50</sup>
"Leg-of-Pork," tender and lean, slowly smoke-roasted in our special ovens.

"Plum-Good" Ham Dinner................................................... 7<sup>50</sup>
The finest ham available, sliced and served with our "plum-good" sauce.

Barbequed Pork Spareribs ................................................ 8<sup>50</sup>
Our most popular item for many years. Specially seasoned and smoke-roasted in our own way! Served with "Secret Sauce."

Smoke-Roasted Chicken...................................................... 7<sup>50</sup>
Especially juicy, seasoned and smoke-roasted. If you like our spareribs, you'll like this too!

Child's Portion Dinners .................................................... 4<sup>50</sup>
Choose from any of the five items above. Please, only children 12 years and under. Does not include the Apple Tree Salad.

*After a good dinner, one can forgive anybody, even one's own relations.*

—*Oscar Wilde*

# The Restaurants of Denver: Where You Can Buy a Dinner for Fifteen Dollars and One for Fifteen Cents

### *Colorado Sun,* January 17, 1892

Denver doesn't eat at home—that is, the great, big bustling part of Denver. It rustles around when meal time comes and goes to this place or that, wherever appetite and the condition of the pocketbook warrant. With the majority, and particularly those who are employed on salary and have no home—there are more of these than you would guess in Denver—it is invariably a question of finance. Perhaps the newspaper man is a good example of how a person on salary runs the gamut of Denver restaurants. Did you ever "keep cases" on a newspaper man's appetite—for food—and how and where he satisfies it? You can tell the state of his pocketbook from where he eats. He is a regular gastronomic barometer. Let me give you a list, counting from salary day:

| | |
|---|---|
| Monday | Tortoni's |
| Tuesday | Smith's |
| Wednesday | Somebody's café |
| Thursday | Cook's |
| Friday | The Creamerie |
| Saturday | Somebody's coffee house |
| Sunday | ? |

This is a very fair example, being a record of personal experiences. It is not to be supposed that it is a record of every newspaper man—some, as is well known, have untold wealth as a result of frequent dabbles in mining stocks, and stay at the Monday notch all the time. There are, too, those who have acquired a taste for economic restaurants and live on a standard scale and put money in the bank. But I am referring to newspaper men, not journalists. Some, too, have a boarding house, but with these we are not to deal.

The newspaper man is a good type of the average person who "dines out" all the time. There is a collection of yawning mouths, if not stomachs, at every Denver restaurant three times a day, and sometimes all day.

The proprietor of a well-known restaurant was asked the other day how much a man could live on in Denver and eat three meals in twenty-four hours. He was very prompt in this reply: "If he has $50 a day to spend he can eat very comfortably—he can do the same with 50 cents; or, at least, keep from starving." Fifty dollars a day means wine, a chateaubriand, some more wine, a juicy waiter's fee, and about anything else you can think of.

It is a fact that one can get along on 50 cents a day at Denver restaurants. It is also a fact that the menu might not be particularly interesting, except as a novelty. But it can be done. The same person who volunteered the first information made out of a bill of fare for a man living on 50 cents a day. It was as follows:

Breakfast: Hot roll—with butter, 5 cents. Coffee, 5 cents.

Lunch: Soup, 10 cents. A meat stew (variety doubtful),
    10 cents.

Dinner: A small steak, 15 cents, including bread, butter and
    potatoes, Coffee or tea, 5 cents.

Or he might diversify the menu on occasion by taking cakes for breakfast, or, by going without soup at lunch and coffee at breakfast, might have a somewhat more elaborate steak and some vegetables at dinner. There are any number of ways of changing a 50-cent diet if you study the bill of fare.

For 75 cents a day one may really get along very well in Denver. There are some admirable 25-cent meal houses—any number of them—all over the city. Here is a sample every-day dinner menu from one:

Soup

Fish          Boiled Beef and Cabbage

Roast Lamb        Roast Beef

Mashed or Boiled Potatoes

Cauliflower        Asparagus

Apple Pie    Fritters    Pudding

Coffee    Tea    Milk

There is no need of starving at a 25-cent restaurant, especially when the menu, as given above, is varied by roast chicken or turkey on Sundays and vegetables and fruits in season. The proprietor of one of these popular restaurants explained why he could get such a variety before his guests at such a price. "In the first place," said he, "we always buy wholesale—frequently and especially as concerns vegetables—direct from the first hands; that is, the grower. We are careful in buying . . . even in large quantities. As to meats, it is no uncommon thing to get a large lot of fair beef at 10 or even 8 cents a pound—meat that the housewife pays 18 or 20 cents for. This is, of course, a pretty low rate. And a pound of beef goes a long way in a restaurant like ours where the meats served, although of several varieties, are small in individual quantities."

One restaurant proprietor, who was reckless enough to estimate what he made on one 25-cent meal, gave the following figures: For an individual the meats served him would amount in value to 6 cents; vegetables 2 cents; pie and pudding, 1 cent; coffee, soup and incidentals, a fraction each, amounting altogether to about 2 cents. Therefore, he gives 11 cents and receives 25, and it is not too much to suppose that even this amount might be reduced. Another 25-cent restaurant keeper claimed that he didn't make 4 cents on an individual meal. Still, another acknowledged to profit of about half.

Denver is profuse in lunch counters, and they are probably more popular than anything else. There are any number of good ones, too. They are patronized by some of the best people of the city, for they are the invariable resort of the business man at noon-time. It is no uncommon thing to see a Colorado millionaire or two at the Creamerie, the Boston, the Brunswick, and other convenient and speedy lunch-rooms in the heart of the business district.

The proprietor of one of these lunch houses said that between 400 and 500 people patronized his place every day, and very frequently he had been called upon to wait on 800.

The bill of fare includes almost everything in market, with "specials" for the luncheons. Millionaires, brokers, clerks and business men seldom go beyond a luncheon costing 80 cents. There is a quiet but earnest demand for ham and eggs, and such plebian but satisfying food at noon, while many are content simply with a bowl of soup.

You may see this sign in the oddest of places, all over town:

BUSINESS MEN'S LUNCH, 12 to 2.

This is a "specialty" nearly everywhere. Beer and noon-time lunch are inseparable with a great many, and hence the crowd flocks to the "Rathskeller," "the Opera House vaults," "the Side Line," and a number of like places of which these are representative. The luncheons are really admirable, and calculated to fire the heart of the bohemian with joy. You may get soup, potatoes, weiner wurst and sauer kraut—this is a favorite—roast beef or roast pork, and your glass of beer.

All this, too, for the sum of 15 or 20 cents.

These last are strictly for men, however. Ladies who are downtown on shopping expeditions usually take a run into Glendinning's, the Chesapeake, Pella's, the Woman's Exchange or cozy places of a like character, where oysters are the feature. And, apropos of oyster houses, there are some very excellent ones in Denver where little else is served, and where the bivalves are usually as fresh almost as at the seashore. It would puzzle you, were you the greatest oyster fiend on earth, to think up a dish that the cooks at these places could not prepare for you.

Up on Seventeenth street there is a charming little French restaurant, probably the only one in the city, where you are sure to meet someone from the Denver French colony at any meal time. You get a taste of garlic there that carries you right back to bots and boulevardes and cafes. This unique little place is so small as to need a search for discovery, but to him who has a French palate is never forgotten when once found.

Tortoni's, a representative Western restaurant, is unique in itself, with prices equally unique. It would probably tax one's memory to think of what he could not get here. The same would about apply to Smith's, Nelson's and probably four other restaurants.

Forty- and fifty-cent restaurants predominate in Denver. The menus here are usually semi-elaborate, with good service. They are apt to be found on the more quiet streets, such as the Albert, uptown, or Gevens's, or the Oxford, or twenty others nearer the business center.

The Denver waiter is cosmopolitan. He comes and goes from and to the four corners of the earth. Wages vary. Where "no fees" are the rule, they range from $10 to $20 a week, according to the standing of the restaurant. A waiter at Tortoni's was trapped into an acknowledgement that he made from $2 to $4 a day on fees. In some restaurants, fees are strictly prohibited.

White male waiters predominate in Denver, and are acknowledged by a majority of restaurant men to be more satisfactory than any others. Colored waiters are in the minority. The 25-cent restaurant believes in the waiter girl of whom much might be written. The latter are paid from $6 to $14 a week.

A conservative estimate is that there are 250 restaurants in Denver. Of course every grade and nearly every nationality is represented. From the French restaurant referred to, it is but a matter of a few blocks to one distinctively Italian, while if one were traveling on Blake street he might be induced to drop into Sam Joe Yang's restaurant, which is distinctively Chinese.

They are a curious study, these public eating houses, from the most modest to the most pretentious, and life may here be observed in its downs as well as ups. Denver is right in line with other cities in the way of restaurants.

# RESTAURANTS
# OF DENVER

**Baur's Restaurant** ∽ **1512 Curtis Street and Cherry Creek Mall**

The colorful history of Denver's one-time oldest confectionary company has been told in many published articles. Here's just part of the story, from a house publication, the *Baur's Beacon*:

Otto Baur was the son of Dr. John Joseph Baur of Tamaqua, Pennsylvania, a distinguished physician who gave his skill without thought of compensation to the poorly paid coal miners. Dr. Baur and his wife, Pauline (Kohler) Baur, in 1853 brought to America their large family from Germany where Otto was born October 15, 1846, at Wurtenberg. In 1862, when sixteen years of age, Otto went to Pottsville, Pennsylvania, where his brother-in-law, John Henry Jacobs, who had married Clara Baur, Otto's sister, had opened a bakery. Here Otto spent three and a half years learning the confectionery business. The first two years his wage was ten dollars a week; the third year this was increased to sixteen dollars.

He was employed as a confectioner in New York City when, in April 1867, Dr. Baur called him home to escort his daughter, Thusnelda, and her four small children to Denver where Thusnelda's husband, Julius F. Stockdorf, had gone the year before and was now proprietor of the Pennsylvania House, a hotel on Blake Street, between E and F (now Fourteenth and Fifteenth) streets, and across from the Elephant Corral, famous end-of-the-journey inn, stable, and auction house for the sale of merchandise freighted across the plains by ox-trains.

The Baur's candy store (right) on Curtis Street as it appeared in the late 1800s. Reproduced from the *Baur's Beacon,* vol. 3, no. 9, n.d.

Two friends, seeking greater opportunity than offered in the East, accompanied young Baur. The crowded stagecoach taken at North Platte, Nebraska, rail's end, was chased by Indians. The coach immediately following was attacked and passengers wounded and killed. Denver was reached May 5, Otto delivering in good health his sister and the children of Julius Stockdorf. The lad, enthused by tales of riches made in the mines and borne out by fortunes changing hands nightly in the glittering Palace gambling hall in the same block with his brother-in-law's hotel, and the prodigal spending in shops, wrote his father his decision to remain in the West.

Next door to the Pennsylvania House was the City Bakery, which opened January 2, 1859 and was Denver's first bakery and restaurant. Here he at once obtained work at forty dollars a month. The expenses of the long trip had exhausted his purse, and he was five dollars in debt to one of his companions. With his first wage he paid the loan and bought the cheapest pair of blue jeans he could find, for ten dollars. . . .

[After several failed ventures in Denver and New Mexico, by 1870 Baur] was employed in the Jacob Schueler confectionery store on Larimer Street, baking the finer cakes and making the ice cream. Determining again to go into business for himself he formed a partnership with James Colwell, a bookkeeper, who furnished the capital, a modest sum, Baur representing the production end and skill. The

The "modernistic" candy counter at the May Company, Baur's store.
Reproduced from the *Baur's Beacon,* vol. 3, no. 9, n.d.

firm of Colwell and Baur rented a store, two floors and basement, at the corner of G (16th) Street and Lawrence for the bakers, confectionery and catering business. Otto brought from Pennsylvania a young brother to assist him.

The firm prospered. Baur was Denver's first caterer, and hostesses kept him busy from the start serving dinners and parties. The small hotels of that day contracted with him for entire banquets. Baur's candies and cakes led in popular favor. In 1871 he invented the ice cream soda when a regular morning customer for cream charged with seltzer water came in before the dairyman had made delivery. He induced the disappointed merchant to try a glass of ice cream into which the charged water was spurted. The customer relished it so much, he advertised the new drink to such an extent that soon Baur was serving hundreds of ice cream sodas flavored with fruit juices every day, and the drink became an institution throughout the nation before the end of 1872.

In 1874, the long established and larger Schueler business was purchased and consolidated with Colwell and Baur. Baur bought out Colwell, who went to Cheyenne to establish a business of his own. In 1876, Otto Baur married Marie Kuner, daughter of Jacob Kuner, founder of the Kuner Pickle Company, [later] the Kuner-Empson Company. In 1878, a young Kentuckian arrived, Theodore L. Meier, who had been employed by leading confectioners and caterers in New

Baur's main store fountain—famous for many years. Reproduced from the *Baur's Beacon*, vol. 3, no. 9, n.d.

York, Boston, and other large cities. Now Otto Baur could relax; in 1885 with Mrs. Baur, he toured Europe. In 1891, after seventeen years at the Larimer Street location, the old Schueler store to which Colwell and Baur had moved after buying that business, the Baur Company moved to No. 1512 Curtis Street shortly after Meier had been made an officer of the firm.

The following year, John Joseph (Joe) Jacobs, Baur's nephew, and the son of John Henry Jacobs, who was Otto Baur's first business associate, came from Hazleton, Pennsylvania, where he was born in 1872, to Denver at his uncle's behest to learn the business. By this time Baur's candies, famous throughout the United States, were shipped in large quantities to foreign countries. Originations furnished new adventures to eye and to taste and coined new confection names. The catering department served not only the fashionables at events and on occasions that made social history in Denver and Colorado, but Baur banquets for notables visiting Denver and for large civic as well as society affairs were an integral part of the brilliant entertaining characterizing the rich "Queen City of the Plains" that boasted more millionaires and more wealth per capita than any city of comparable size in the world. . . .

In the 1920s, the restaurant was added, at once becoming fashionable and popular despite the fact that Denver already was celebrated for its fine restaurants. The beautiful Pompeian Room, the tea room, and the English room with its wainscoted walls, hunting prints, and mellow light through mullioned windows came in time. This room has been popular with business and professional men for lunch and groups of friends have daily met at their own tables very much in the custom of clubs and of the famous "round table" at New York's old Mouquin's. With Denver's old families, the custom of lunching at Baur's is a tradition even unto the third generation of the socially prominent. . . .

Who remembers the opening of the then ultra-modern Baur's Restaurant in the old Cherry Creek Mall? One million bucks was an enormous amount of money to be spent on a restaurant, especially in 1955. This restaurant featured the latest innovations in food serving, exquisite ambience, and a capacity of 450 patrons. Along with ultra-chic furnishings, the restaurant featured an electric-eye water-glass-filling system used by waitresses for very efficient water refill service. In addition, the restaurant employed the forerunner of today's touch food-ordering system—the Tel Autograph—which allowed servers to order food without going to the kitchen. Cell phones, often used in restaurants today to the annoyance of diners, were yet to be invented, but Baur's had their precursors installed at every table. Along with the Denver Dry Goods Tea Room, Baur's was *the* place to go. Among Baur's distinguished alumni is John Ott, brother to Eddie Ott, who ran the Aviation Country Club, one period of the Navarre, and Eddie Ott's Sherman Plaza.

Baur's Restaurant prospered for a number of years. Will McFarland, former owner of the Denver Buffalo Company, admitted to me that he bought Baur's and, in his own words, "I ruined Baur's restaurant and the corporation."

There is an honest man!!

*Author's Note:* My wife, Jean, craved Baur's chocolate MIJA pie (made with butter and almond toffee) and lunched at Baur's frequently—before she met me!

**Brick Oven Beanery** ∼ **1007 East Colfax Avenue, Denver**

This restaurant was for a decade East Colfax Avenue's home-cooking legend. Remember muffaletto sandwiches, their famous meat loaf, turkey, and pot roast—comfort food at its best, or "Convenient Food, Convenient Fun," as the menu proclaimed.

Among popular Brick Oven Beanery offerings:

| | |
|---|---|
| Turkey, Country Corn Gravy | $3.65 |
| Country Ham Platter | $5.25 |
| Cherry raisin sauce and an assortment of muffaletto sandwiches | $2.45–4.75 |

The Brick Oven Beanery was one of (the "Gabby Gourmet") Pat Miller's favorite hangouts. Pat and Mark Miller were very friendly with owner Ross Johnson, and Pat promoted this East Colfax neighborhood place as a quiet haven in her frequent broadcasts.

What follows is Pat Miller's tribute to the Brick Oven Beanery:

What is that place where the parking lot is full, there's a line outside to get in, and everyone leaves with a smile on his or her face? That's the Brick Oven Beanery, or so it was when it was alive and well. A concept way ahead of its time, fresh fast food prepared to order as you pass through the line is what happened, complete with caring

## CONVENIENT FOOD, CONVENIENT FUN

### SANDWICHES

CHEWY FRESH BAKED BREAD, HAND CARVED MEAT, SWEET RED ONION AND ROMAINE LETTUCE.

CHOICE OF:

**TURKEY** - HOMEMADE MAYONNAISE

**BEEF** - HORSERADISH MAYONNAISE

**HAM** - CHERRIED COARSE GROUND MUSTARD

**VEGIE**

HARD COOKED EGG & CHEESE

**TEXAS CHOPPED BBQ BRISKET**

SMOKEY SAUCE

**LARGE $2.45      JUMBO $4.65**

SAY CHEESE FOR 25¢ (SWISS)

**REUBEN HAMWICH**

SPICY KRAUT AND SWISS CHEESE

**LARGE $2.65      JUMBO $4.75**

### DIETING

**CARVED LEAN TURKEY** SLICED TOMATO AND APPLE NUT COTTAGE CHEESE. FRESH BREAD IF YOU LIKE

**$3.45**

### HOT SANDWICHES

SERVED OPEN FACE WITH DRESSING AND POTATOES.

**TURKEY** - COUNTRY CORN GRAVY

**BEEF** - BURGUNDY MUSHROOM SAUCE

**$3.65**

### AMERICA'S HOLIDAY PLATTERS

OUR **DAILY ROASTS** ARE HAND CARVED AND SERVED WITH A **BREAD AND SALAD BASKET** (CREAMY COLE SLAW OR BEANERY SALAD), HAND MASHED POTATOES AND SAGE NUT DRESSING.

**TRADITIONAL TURKEY DINNER**

COUNTRY CORN GRAVY

**ENGLISH ROAST BEEF PLATTER**

BURGUNDY MUSHROOM SAUCE

**COUNTRY HAM PLATTER**

CHERRY RAISIN SAUCE

WELL WORTH

**$5.25**

* PLATTERS CAN BE ORDERED **PICNIC STYLE** WITH BEANS AND POTATO SALAD.

### SIDE DISHES

**RUM POT BEANS**

BEANS AND MEATS SLOW BAKED IN RUM, SPICES AND MOLASSES

**POTATO, EGG AND OLIVE SALAD**

UNSKINNED POTATOES, HARD COOKED EGG, CELERY, RIPE OLIVES IN FRESH MAYONNAISE

**HAND MASHED POTATOES**

SKIN ON

WITH REAL CREAM COUNTRY GRAVY

**APPLE NUT COTTAGE CHEESE**

CURD CHEESE, CELERY, TART APPLES AND WALNUTS

**SAGE NUT DRESSING**

CRUMBLED FRESH BREAD, NUTS AND CELERY

**CREAMY COLE SLAW**

HOMEMADE MAYONNAISE AND SOUR CREAM

### 95¢ EACH

### EXTRAORDINARY CHICKEN

A **HALF** MARINATED IN FRESH CITRUS JUICES AND SPICES WITH A BREAD AND SALAD BASKET, POTATOES & SAGE NUT DRESSING

**$4.25**

and wonderful ownership and staff that was personable and efficient. Owner Ross Johnson made every person who entered feel that he or she was the only customer and all personal requests were accommodated immediately. Dave Peters, his right-hand man, did all the recipes and made sure that every bit of food was perfect. The staff often came from a less-than-wonderful background but proved that if given a super environment, they performed like college-trained help.

The food was first rate. How well we remember the muffaletto sandwich, the turkey, lamb, beef, barbecue served on thick, delicious rolls. Chili with chicken or vegetarian, delicious coleslaw, homemade soups, sliced brisket, and that most famous citrus-marinated half chicken kept the crowds coming. The big favorite was the turkey dinner with stuffing and mashed potatoes. Brownies, sundaes, strawberry shortcake, and tarts sweetened the meal. Oh, how I wish for those recipes so we could make those dishes today! And the prices—so reasonable that return visits were often.

I would love to once again visit with the ladies who arrived every Sunday after church wearing their best chapeaux and carrying a bouquet of flowers for their table. How is the gentleman who needed much help and was served by Ross personally? Annie, our favorite employee, chatted caringly as she fixed your order behind the counter. Thanks to the folks at the Beanery, she could finally support her children and even spend time with them.

I remember my father's first visit to BOB's. He had doubts about a serve-yourself eatery that quickly changed to compliments and applause for the amazing food and service. Although it never happened, he then thought he should purchase a franchise. The Brick Oven is no more, but as you drive by Colfax and Downing, memories flow of happy times shared by all.

Despite Pat's efforts, the restaurant was sold to Ed Hoagland, who had plans to move the Beanery to Cherry Creek North and open other Beaneries. Ed did not have the "life-saving" formula for his place. May he rest in peace. Ross Johnson died in April 2000.

> *If pale beans bubble for you in a red*
> *earthenware pot*
> *You can oft decline the dinners of*
> *sumptuous hosts.*
>
> —*Martial*

# Along the Ziti Trail:
# Confessions of a Menu Snatcher

## By Max Donaldson

Restaurant owners, beware! I steal menus.

Oh, yes. I keep my driving speed at the posted limits, and I have never been convicted of a felony or any other misdeeds tending to designate me as a miscreant. What I am saying is, I try my best to toe the line in this world. Except, except when in a restaurant. I have been known to plead for, pirate, even purloin a prized menu for my worldwide collection. But not just any old menu—I do have certain criteria.

I target menus that are colorful and creative. Generally, I'm not interested in a typed-page, insert menu unless the holder itself is unique, such as the carved mahogany holder from the Old Lighthouse, whose front and back menu boards are fastened with hammered copper hinges.

I started collecting menus by accident in the early 1970s when a friend brought over a ceramic, "little brown jug" from a restaurant with its bill of fare handpainted on the surface. I was intrigued—and thus began my twenty-five-year fascination with collecting menus, which now cover several walls in my home and provide a historical tour of some of the great old restaurants not only from Denver but around the world.

How do I acquire all these menus, you might ask. My methods vary from a straightforward request to the surreptitious and clandestine. When I spy an irresistible menu, I first ask if I can have a word with management to explain my desire to add to my collection. Being well-groomed and a rather decent sort, I can usually coax a donation about seventy percent of the time. I've even resorted to showing

Polaroid pictures of my collection to substantiate my sincerity. I then go one step further and ask the owner, manager, or chef to sign and date the menu, for added value.

If this strategy fails, I then have to consider what sort of subversion would work best to liberate my intended prize. It's pretty easy if I'm with a party of several people. Once the orders are scribbled down and the menus are collected by our waiter, mine is already under my butt, and I am sitting on it! This is successful because rarely does a waiter count menus, plus, we have the advantage of jumbling them up when everyone hands them back at the same time. Or, I may ask the waiter to bring back a menu so I can "have another look" at what's for dessert.

On other occasions, I use my jacket by tucking the emancipated menu just under the back of my belt, poking up between the shoulder blades, safely hidden from view. I can't tell you how many times my dinner companions have later exclaimed on seeing my newest acquisition, "Gee Max, I never even saw you take that!"

Menus can be concealed in folded newspapers or slipped into briefcases or valises. I marvel at the miracle of gravity as many a menu has slid into the handbag of an innocent lady friend dining with me. Another thing—many restaurants place all their menus by the front door, in a stack, on a shelf, or behind a bracket. Easy pickin's for a guy like me.

There's no such thing as a typical menu in my collection. They may be printed on paper, cardboard, metal, glass, leather, or wood. Many of them are real works of art featuring photographs, paintings, etching or sketches of nature, landscapes, beautiful women, historical events, and cartoon caricatures.

Menus from exotic ports of call all over the world have made their way back to my collection—Russia, Norway, China, Pakistan, New Guinea, Switzerland, Northern Ireland, Puerto Rico, Mexico, Canada—some I have visited, some I haven't. Friends know of my obsession, so I have confederates learning the art of menu appropriation. Instead of sending me postcards from their travels, they bring me . . . you guessed it.

The name of an English restaurant asks the culinary question, "Have U E 10?" Another menu from the United Kingdom is autographed by a member of Parliament. Also in the governmental category, I have a nifty menu from the House of Representatives in Washington, D.C.

One corner wall of my collection features transportation menus for meals served on trains, cruise ships, and first-class airlines, including Air Africa, Air Nuigini (yes, that's how they spell it), British Airways, Lufthansa, Saudi Air, and the Concorde SST. Cruise ships are famous for their lavish food service, and I always save space in my luggage for souvenir menus from any seaward journeys.

America used to travel by train, and all the rail systems had wonderful dining cars for the traveler to savor. My collection contains menus from the Norfolk & Western, Baltimore & Ohio, New York Central, Chicago & Northwestern, and the Chesapeake & Ohio lines. I treasure a Fred Harvey menu from the old Santa Fe Railroad, printed in February 1944 during the waning days of World War II. I understand that any soldier or sailor in uniform, carrying orders, could ride the rail system for free. To promote patriotism and conversation between civilians and our uniformed personnel, menus showed illustrations of the various military ranks. One stripe indicated a rank of ensign, whereas three bars let you know you were speaking to a commander in the U.S. Navy.

By the way, a tossed salad on the Santa Fe in those days fetched the handsome price of 35 cents, which you can bet was about forty percent higher than in your average, neighborhood café. These magnificent railroad cars of the past provided an elegant and memorable dining experience with heavy, silver service settings, flowers, and layered linen tablecloths.

When I review some of my old hometown, Denver menus, nostalgia really sets in. Who can forget the Taylor Supper Club, whose menu at one time spotlighted musicians Al Fike, Kenny Smith, and Frankie Burg on the cover? Can you recall eating at the Alpine Village Inn or the unique Grain Exchange? Did you take your prom date to see the spectacular view from the Top of the Rockies? You probably listened to the pilot-to-tower communications at the French farmhouse called the 94th Aero Squadron. An early menu from the venerable Normandy Restaurant offered Le Beefsteak au Poivre Grillee at a staggering $5.75, the most expensive item on the menu! A glass of Cabernet would set you back an additional 90 cents.

Some of the never-to-be-forgotten restaurants of Denver's past seem to come alive with their old menus and once again I'm walking under the windmill at Hans Brinker's or admiring the antique automobiles at Duesenburg's. I'd bet many downtown workers enjoyed a quick, tasty lunch at Simms or the Magic Pan. A menu for My Friends in Evergreen shows two "gentlemen" slugging it out on the fender of an old roadster. And rumor has it that the Stonescape Restaurant at the old Wolhurst Mansion, long-since burned down, was a favorite rendezvous for politicos, who were said to meet for a discrete liaison, away from the public eye.

Yes, I do have my favorites. Surprisingly, one of my greatest treasures is only a copy made from an ancient mimeograph machine during the 1940s. It's from Denver's first Christmas Festival in the 1800s. I don't know what the original menu was made of and the ink on my copy is slowly breaking down and it's getting difficult to read. But these must have been some rugged folk with mighty hearty appetites. The menu featured some unusual entrees such as mountain sheep, venison, buffalo, and grizzly bear! To wash it down, you could choose from such popular beverages as hockheimer, cherry bounce, and Taos lightning (introduced by Uncle Dick Wootten of Raton Pass fame, before the name Tequila came into common usage in Denver).

So, yes, I admit that I'm a menu snatcher. Hey, I can hardly wait to investigate another restaurant. And not for just for the ziti on the menu, either!

*Next to eating good dinners, a healthy*
*man with a benevolent turn of mind,*
*must like, I think, to read about them.*

—*William M. Thackeray*

**CAFÉ**

*Giovanni*

Café Giovanni ✧ 1515 Market Street, Denver

If ever there was a popularly acclaimed restaurant in town, it was Café Giovanni, which debuted in 1980. Working wonders in the kitchen was Jack Leone, graduate of Michigan State University, Hotel and Restaurant Management School. Jack worked his kitchen with a passion, transforming the mundane into the magnificent. Team partner and wife, Jan Leone, researched recipes, made soups (her specialty), and created desserts and salads for the restaurant. This pair of culinarians quickly transformed Giovanni into the "darling" in-place, where "trendetties" wanted to be seen and see. Here now are excerpts from one of Café Giovanni's menus:

| | |
|---|---|
| Sauté of Wild Mushrooms and Bacon | $7.00 |
| Sausage Stuffed Roast of Pork | $18.50 |
| Fresh Lobster Soufflé | $22.00 |
| Caramel Praline Soufflé | $4.50 |

Before the Leones created Café Giovanni in lower downtown Denver, the building was used for a meat-packing house in the late nineteenth century. The transformation of this space into a restaurant took a couple of years, and the Leones worked very hard to create one of Denver's most magnificent eateries. Café Giovanni functioned on three levels. From Market Street, you would enter the lounge area with high ceilings and a mirrored bar. At the foot of the steps you were greeted warmly by Jan Leone at the maitre d' stand, and then directed to the dining areas above. Jan also acted as dining

## Veal Janette

thinly sliced scallops of Provimi veal and tender shrimp
sauteed in butter, white wine and cream...finished with imported
capers, dill and Dijon mustard

$22.50

## Roast Rack of Lamb with Fresh Rosemary

an individual rack of spring lamb marinated
in olive oil, garlic, fresh rosemary and lemon...served with
a lightly minted lamb sauce and bouquet of
fresh field vegetables

$25.00

## Veal with Wild Mushrooms and Cream

thin pounded veal in a sauce of brandy, cream,
garlic, butter and assorted fresh wild mushrooms,
seasoned with fresh thyme

$22.50

## Fresh Lobster Souffle

delicate lobster meat from Maine
baked into a spectacular souffle and served with
a rich sauce made from lobster, shrimp,
cream and pale dry sherry

$22.00

room manager of the restaurant at night. The room facing Market Street was my favorite. Dark green booths, wooden chairs, tapestries, and a beautiful fireplace. Complementing the food was the professional service.

Later, Al Fresco was born next door to Café Giovanni. The setting and food were contemporary Italian, with an astounding three story–high pizza oven. The menu was more like a trattoria–pizza restaurant, a far cry from west Denver's venerable spaghetti joints. For some time, Al Fresco had no peers.

In January of 1993 both operations closed their doors after dazzling diners with inventive, freshly prepared food, using the finest ingredients. The closures were attributed to personal reasons and a general business downtrend in Denver. Today, Jan Leone operates her own namesake restaurant at Colfax and Marion.

This may not be how Jan would prepare it, but here's my recipe for Frozen Praline Soufflé:

## Frozen Praline Soufflé

*8 servings*

| | |
|---|---|
| 1 quart butter pecan ice cream | ¼ cup Kahlúa |
| 5 egg yolks | 3 cups whipping cream |
| ⅔ cup sugar | 2 teaspoons vanilla |
| ⅓ cup caramel sauce, plus extra for topping | ½ cup chopped filberts |

1. Take 8 pieces of wax paper, 12×6 inches, and fold in half lengthwise to they measure 12×3 inches. Wrap them around 8, 6-ounce ramekins so they extend 2 inches above the top of the dish and secure with tape. Place one scoop of butter pecan ice cream in each dish. Put in freezer.

2. Place 5 egg yolks in mixer bowl and whip until light and fluffy. Set aside.

3. Mix sugar in sauce pan with 4 teaspoons of water. Boil until mixture reaches 250 degrees.

4. With mixer on low speed, gradually add the sugar to the egg yolks. When all the sugar is in, return to high speed until mixture has cooled to room temperature. Add caramel sauce and Kahlúa and whip for 1 minute. Set aside.

5. Whip cream with vanilla until stiff. Fold the egg yolk and sugar mixture into the whipping cream and add the chopped filberts. Divide into the 8 ramekins and freeze for at least 4 hours. Remove paper collars, unmold, and serve with hot caramel sauce.

**Café Promenade** ⟳
**1430 Larimer Street, Denver**

New York City was the place where two future Denver restaurateurs—Tish Kllanxhja and Mario Lalli—met. Both left their musical and culinary footprints on our city.

In 1952, Tish and Mario undertook the adventure of driving to Aspen, Colorado, a four-day trip, upon the urging of Joe Masala of Aspen. Masala was one of the leading jazz clarinetists and songwriters of those days. The purpose of this trip was to explore the possibility of opening a night club with operatic singing. The result: Mario's of Aspen.

This story, however, is about the Café Promenade. Tish, a total novice in the restaurant business, became more acquainted with operating a restaurant after Aspen. He managed Henrici's for a while and later became manager of the University Club from 1960 to 1980. In 1965, the developers of Larimer Square, Dana Crawford and Charles Callaway, approached Tish to open a restaurant to give the area a boost. Now Tish needed a managing partner and permission from the University Club to proceed. He accomplished both.

Then Tish became acquainted with Albanian Fred Muftar, a.k.a. Fred Thomas, who at the time was working at a joint called Eddie's. Fred was the spitting image of King Farouk. They formed a partnership: Tish, Fred, and their chef, Frank Beck. Thus, the Café Promenade was born. Fred Thomas with his salty humor, Tish with his great

Cheese Board

(Sliced at your table - All :75)

| Swiss | Smoked American | Brie |
|---|---|---|
| Edam | Camembert | Tilsit |
| Provolone | Port Salut | Gorgonzola |
| Feta | | Bel Paese |

( Includes the Bread of your choice)

Pastries and Desserts

Sacha 50
Seven Layer 50
Prince Regent 50
Baba au Rum 75
Zuppa Inglese 75
Cheesecake Promenade 60
From the Pastry Tray: your choice 50

Cassata Siciliana 50
Pistachio Ice Cream 50
Mocha Ice Cream 50
Apple Ice 40
Champagne Ice 40

5

SUPPER

(served from 6:00 p.m until 11:30 p.m)

Hors d'oeuvres

Half Dozen Eastern Oysters
or Clams (in season) 1.25
Fresh Beluga Caviar 4.00
Langouste Cocktail, Sauce Piquante 1.50
Half Dozen Escargots, Bourguignonne 2.00
Prosciutto and Melon (or other
fresh fruit) 1.25
Antipasto Platter Promenade 2.00

Soups

Jellied Consommé 50
Consommé à la Russe 1.25
Chilled Borscht, Polonaise 50
Chilled Minestrone 50
Oxtail Promenade or Soup du Jour 50

6

voice, and chef Frank's good food made Café Promenade a great success. While Fred Thomas managed the restaurant, Tish continued his duties at the University Club and at the same time acted as adviser to the Promenade. Tish did not have a great deal of culinary experience, but wine was a different story. Tish produced a great wine list for the Promenade and entertained the patrons of the restaurant with his operatic renditions. John Wolfe of KVOD radio had a small booth built in the restaurant and did interviews and classical music from the Promenade.

Some of the luncheon specialties, offered by the Promenade in 1977:

| | |
|---|---|
| Braised Oxtails à la Mode | $3.25 |
| Vienna Goulash | $3.50 |
| Chicken Paprika | $3.00 |
| Ragout of Veal Parisienne | $3.50 |

For Supper:

| | |
|---|---|
| Veal Scallopine al Marsala | $4.00 |
| Frog Legs Sauté, Maison | $4.25 |

*Rocky Mountain News* writer Marjorie Barrett wrote about the Promenade in October of 1966: "For many [the Promenade] will be a rendezvous supper spot, a congenial gathering point after a concert, a theater performance, or as a topper to a quiet evening with friends."

The oil bust years of 1984 to 1987 saw a decline of forty percent of the Café Promenade's business. In 1987, Dana Crawford and Charles Callaway, partners in the Oxford Hotel, bought the Promenade but were unable to keep it going.

Café Promenade was sorely missed by many! If you miss the braised oxtails, especially, my recipe for this dish follows. At the time of this writing, Tish is teaching Italian and consults for Trio's Enoteca wine company.

# Braised Oxtails

2 tablespoons, either olive oil or shortening
2 tablespoons flour
salt & pepper
2 pounds oxtail, cut into $1\frac{1}{2}$- to 2-inch pieces
2 small onions, chopped fine
1 carrot, diced
1 small rutabaga, diced
a couple of cloves of garlic, chopped fine
$1\frac{1}{2}$ cups beef broth plus 2 cups water
1 cup of fresh peeled and diced tomatoes (or a can will do)
basil, chopped fine
2 bay leaves

1. Heat the olive oil or shortening in a skillet.

2. Mix salt and pepper with the flour and roll the oxtail pieces in it.

3. Brown the pieces thoroughly in the oil or shortening, turning them until colored on all sides. Transfer to a covered casserole.

4. Brown the onion, carrot, rutabaga, and garlic in the same fat as the oxtails.

5. Pour on the beef broth and water; add tomatoes, basil, and bay leaves.

6. Cook until done, perhaps 3 hours. If you leave the cooked oxtails in their broth until the next day in the refrigerator you can easily remove all fat. If reheated, taste for additional seasoning. You may want to thicken juices with a little cornstarch or arrowroot.

# Some of the Slangy Orders That Bother Carnivalists Who Eat

*Denver Times,* October 2, 1901

A visitor to the Denver carnival entered a down-town restaurant this morning. His hair was mussed and he looked as though he were very much in need of an eye opener. He sat down at the counter and said to the smiling waiter who appeared.

"Give me a cup of strong coffee, and don't have any cream in it, either."

"Java in the dark!" yelled the "hasher."

"Hey there young feller; don't get too flip!" answered the old man who had given the order. "I may not look as well as I did yesterday this time, but By Ginger, I don't look so rocky that I have to take that coffee in the dark. Not by a darned sight." And the old gentleman looked as if he could whip a whole army of waiters.

"You don't understand," replied the waiter, eager to undeceive the irate old gentleman, who evidently thought someone was trying to "kid" him. "You see I called in the dark because you wanted the coffee without cream. If you had said coffee with cream I would have hollered Java in the light." And the waiter smiled reassuringly.

The old gentleman subsided and the waiters all smiled. The ruralite had only happened into one of those restaurants where the orders are called for the man who stands just out of sight behind the curtain which is stretched across to hide the kitchen.

For the benefit of those who are not familiar with the calls as given by the waiters in these restaurants a few pointers are hereby given. Don't faint if you happen into a restaurant and order a bowl of bread and milk, only to hear the waiter yell:

"Graveyard stew!"

He is perfectly innocent and is not trying to "josh" you. That call always means "bread and milk" and the call has nothing to do with the undertaker, although it is suggestive. The call probably originated from people of delicate constitutions ordering the dish so often. It does not mean any harm to you, so don't get mad.

Poached eggs on toast are always "Adam and Eve on a raft" with the restaurant people. By the same token scrambled eggs in hash house parlance is "shipwrecked hen." If you go into one of these places and ask for a ham and egg sandwich it is a 10 to 1 shot that you will hear the waiter call:

"A hog an' a hen with a blanket on!" and from the depths of the mysterious kitchen will come the echo:

"Hog an' a Blanket!"

By and by when your order is ready, you will hear the cook say:

"Hog an' a hen Blanket. Take it away!"

And so on through a long list of orders. Everything on the menu has a different name when applied by the waiter. He calls an order for pork and beans "Continental Blanks." Ham and eggs are "Ham and" and an order for two eggs fried and turned over would be "Fry two in the air." Hash is a "mixup," an order for wheat cakes sounds like a "stack of wheat."

Some of the waiters call "hash" by the up-to-date name of "Duke's Mixture," but it is only the cigarette fiends who do that and if you happen accidentally into that kind of a place it is proper to withdraw in order to show the proprietor that you are accustomed to better fare. More than likely if you order pork chops you will hear the waiter shout, "Ragtime! Shake 'em well." But there is no use in getting angry about it, for that is the only way he has of making the cook understand him. Some cooks are dull, you know, so you must overlook what seems like slang on the part of the waiter.

There are many, many different kinds of calls, and the more eating houses you enter the more you will learn of them. If you don't believe it, just try it a few times, and when you return from a day's trip during which you have visited various restaurants, you will have almost learned a new language.

RESTAURANT

**Chateau Pyrenees  ∽  6338 South Yosemite Circle, Englewood**

Every great city has a special restaurant synonymous with classic elegance. In Denver, that restaurant was the Chateau Pyrenees.

The exterior was reminiscent of a chateau in southern France, with slit windows set into stone walls. The building seemed incongruous against the backdrop of suburban southeast Denver, but inside there was a sense of faraway time and place.

The atmosphere within Chateau Pyrenees could only be described as magnificent. Soft lavender accented the décor, highlighted by an impressive crystal chandelier illuminating the two dining areas. These areas were divided by a raised platform and an ornate grand piano dating from 1874 and styled after Louis XVI, played expertly for listening and dancing. On the walls were original paintings by Marc Chagall and Frank Hopper. Polished waiters in tuxedos moved smartly through the room, heightening the restaurant's special brand of sophistication.

In 1980, Austrian-born Conrad Trinkaus with his wife, Apollonia, purchased Chateau Pyrenees. The cuisine benefited from his twenty-five years' experience at such fabled restaurants and hotels as

## *Entrees*

*(includes the soup du jour or the daily house salad)*

### Grilled Yellow Fin Tuna
*with soy ginger vinaigrette*

HM
12.50

### Fresh Roasted Monkfish
*apple cider vinegar sauce*

HM
9.75

### Fresh Roasted Atlantic Salmon
*with tomatoe coulis*

HM
11.95

### Fresh Sea Bass
*with artichoke hearts*

HM
9.95

### Seafood Brochette
*shrimps, scallops and fish of the day*
*with bell peppers and mushrooms*
*pernod flavored sauce*
9.95

### Grilled Chicken Breast
*with fresh vegetables*

HM
9.50

### Roasted Rocky Junior
*fresh free range chicken with tarragon jus*

HM
9.95

### Veal Scallopini
*with piccata sauce*
11.95

### Tournedos of Beef Tenderloin
*marchand de vin*
12.95

### Colorado Trio of Lamb Chops
*with thyme sauce*
13.50

George V and Plaza Athenee in Paris, Hilton Hotel in Berlin, British Hotel Corp. in London, and other first-class restaurants in Europe, and the Four Seasons and the Forum of the XII Caesar in New York.

Conrad changed the menu from the old all-French style to a more modern, continental selection, such as Dover Sole and Lobster Medallions with Yams. The most popular dinner entrées were Medallions Pyrenees, Medallions of Beef Tenderloins with Wild Mushrooms and Burgundy Sauce, Chateaubriand, and Rack of Lamb, all produced with distinctive appeal to the most discriminating palate.

Over the years Chateau Pyrenees became the place for the rich and famous, power brokers, and business executives. To name a few who visited the restaurant: Gregory Peck, Charlton Heston, Magic Johnson, Jamie Lee Curtis, Robert DeNiro, Ted Turner, Scott Hamilton, Miss USA, Miss Duval . . . and many others.

Chateau Pyrenees was sold at the end of 1995.

*Contributed by Conrad Trinkaus*

*We may live without poetry, music
    and art;
We may live without conscience, and
    live without heart;
We may live without friends; we may
    live without books;
But civilized man cannot live without
    cooks.*

—*Earl of Lytton*

# Palatial Restaurant

*Denver Republican,* February 1, 1891

*The Arcade Restaurant Company Will Open Monday, February 2.*

*Some Facts Concerning This Palace of a Place—The Brightest and Most Attractive Dining-Room in Denver—Conveniently Located and Calculated to Be a Great Success.*

The Arcade Restaurant Company will give Denver a rare treat on Monday in opening to the public at 1613 Larimer street one of the grandest epicurean retreats to be found anywhere in the United States. The gentlemen connected with this palace of a place have spared neither pains nor money to make it first-class in every respect and from an inspection it cannot help but bring forth expressions of pleasure and satisfaction. This restaurant is new in every sense of the word and as bright as one of Uncle Sam's silver dollars direct from the mint.

The tiling is a most attractive feature of the concern, being of the newest and most beautiful designs, and the decorations are all of oil and most exquisite. The dining room is a perfect gem of a room, with costly mahogany tables of latest patterns and covered by the cleanest and whitest linen imaginable, with table settings, glassware and china most attractive. The mirrors surrounding these apartments hardly have their equal anywhere in brightness and massiveness, and the place is lighted by both gas and electricity, and the chandeliers can be pronounced very fine. It is the intention to furnish the best of services. Politeness and attention will be insisted on to every one who patronize the house, where they will also find oysters, game and fish at all seasons of the year, delicacies of all kinds and cookery to please the most fastidious, immense ice chests filled with ice, to keep all kinds of meats and game fresh and fruits cool and palatable, is a matter of no little importance. The ice box in question is divided into apartments and is said to hold at least 3,000 pounds of ice. The store-rooms are all large and airy and well filled with things to tickle the palate.

The kitchens are separate and apart from the dining-rooms, so that there is no possible chance whatever for greasy and foul smells arising while you are enjoying your meal. The dishes—all of china— were ordered especially for the Arcade and bear that name on each and every piece. The glass and silverware department is most convenient and well supplied with the best of goods in this line that the market affords. The drip coffee-urns are calculated to furnish the best coffee to be gotten in Denver.

The proprietors seemed to take great pride in their stock of liquors stored in their cellars, and claim as to quality and quantity they stand at the top of the heap here. Forty barrels of Hermitage '82 whisky were pointed out, also several barrels of rye, 1882–3, and some back to 1875, also wines of all imported brands. Monday morning the restaurant will be opened, and these gentlemen deserve and no doubt will meet with unbounded success in their undertaking, as it is a long-felt want at last filled.

*Americans are just beginning to regard food the way the French always have. Dinner is not what you do in the evening before something else. Dinner is the evening.*

—*Art Buchwald*

## Cliff Young's Restaurant and Cliff Young the Man
### 700 East 17th Avenue, Denver

Well-educated, entrepreneurial, philosophical, athletic, and stylish. An elitist, who served the carriage trade with an uncanny gift of surrounding himself with great culinary talent, well-trained service personnel, but above all, eager investors—that is Cliff Young the man.

With thirty-four years of restaurant experience behind it, there is no doubt that Cliff Young's Restaurant was a rousing success! Cliff made a lasting impact on Denver's culinary scene. His ingratiating personality was reflected in no small way in the stylish, personal service he offered at Cliff Young's.

Cliff made his first serious restaurant commitment as maitre d' at the Profile Room, later renamed Le Profile. He served some of Denver's high-profile, upscale clientele, which connected him well for future endeavors—from would-be writer, poetry book reviewer, and student of philosophy, chemistry, and literature to manager of Hudson's. Hudson's was a basement operation, but it afforded Cliff the opportunity to graduate from maitre d' to general manager, and it was the overture to his magnum opus: Cliff Young's, which opened in 1984. Judging by long lines on snowy nights and rave reviews by Michael Carlton and Alan Katz, Cliff Young's restaurant was a rousing success. Stan Richards, a Denver businessman, loaned Cliff the money, and together they also purchased the bar across the street to the west, a hangout for drunks, soon to be known as the 17th Avenue Grill.

While Cliff Young's flourished along with the opulent Amethyst Room and neighboring Ruby's nightclub, both Cliff and his partner

# Entrées

Roasted Colorado Rack of Lamb with Apricot Mustard, Brioche and Lamb Essence.
**Thirty two Dollars & fifty cents**

Peppered Tuna Charred Rare with Candied Ginger and a Sweet Soy Lemon Butter.
**Twenty four Dollars & fifty cents**

Maine Lobster served over Wilted Spinach and a Saffron Beurre Blanc.
**Market Price**

Oven Roasted Duck served Crisp on a Duo of Roquefort and Lavender Coulis served with a Port Poached Pear and New Potatoes.
**Twenty two Dollars & fifty cents**

Grilled Filet of Beef with Onion Confit, Blueberry Bordelaise Sauce, Roasted Garlic Whipped Potatoes and Parsnip Chips.
**8 oz.. .Twenty five Dollars & fifty cents**
**12 oz. ..Thirty two Dollars & fifty cents**

Applewood and Rosemary Smoked Chicken Breast Stuffed with Avocado, Cilantro and Roasted Red Peppers served over an Exotic Fruit Salsa and Polenta.
**Nineteen Dollars & fifty cents**

Pinwheel of Chilean Sea Bass and Atlantic Salmon with a Saffron Scented Tomato Ragout Served over a Bed of Pistachio Cous Cous and Sautéed Vegetables.
**Twenty four Dollars & fifty cents**

looked toward LoDo for expansion. And thus, Bibelot (French for "trinket") was born, in the space of the now-defunct Café Promenade at 1424 Larimer Street. Described as a "diamond in the rough," Bibelot's lifespan was short. Whatever the intent by designers James Pfister and Marc Roth, with much usage of faux, Bibelot's ambiance had mixed appeal despite the talents of chef Jack Goldsmith's work in the kitchen.

I never quite discovered the reason for Bibelot's failure, but the restaurant closed. Cliff Young now found himself saddled with a large debt. Had Cliff lost his Midas touch? It was this unfortunate state of affairs that forced Cliff to sell his flagship restaurant, Cliff Young's, and Doug Spedding, of Spedding Chevrolet, bought the place. This ownership did not last very long; enter Stew Jackson, owner of the Denver Burglar Alarm Co., now the Stew Jackson Burglar Alarm Co., and owner of the Woody Herman Band. Stew had known Cliff since the latter's days at the Profile Room, and he also played the saxophone at Ruby's nightclub. Stew always enjoyed good food and the finer things in life. The reason for buying Cliff Young's, according to Stew: "It made sense to me to have some place to trade favors, to pamper my clients." Stew Jackson, the successful businessman, did not always see eye to eye with Cliff Young, the idealist. So the relationship ended with Cliff's departure. Without Cliff's personal attention to the restaurant, and with the opening of Vino Vino and Dante Bichette's along 17th Avenue, this venture was on a declining path. "You really need one vision behind one restaurant," Cliff said, and with his departure, the vision for Cliff Young's became blurred.

As I mentioned earlier, the extraordinary talents in Cliff Young's kitchen impacted the Denver dining scene. Jack Goldsmith, along with sous chef Sally Witham, created signature entrées. The Rack of Lamb, the Salmon with Macadamia Five Citrus Butter, tuna, BBQ shrimp, totally American haute cuisine that Denver had not previously seen, except perhaps at Duesenberg. A few years later, enter Dave Query—owner of Q's, Jax, and Zolo Grill. According to Cliff, "Dave is a bona fide culinary genius and a terrific businessman," who dropped the food cost at Cliff Young's substantially without sacrificing quality. Dave's Curried Skatewing and his tuna recipes are still replicated all over town. Then came the Sean Brasel era. (Sean is currently at Touch in Miami's South Beach.) Sean, former sous chef for Dave Query, continued with great food at Cliff Young's.

Now appeared on the scene James Van Dyke, the brilliant food scholar, who brought Japanese American fusion to Cliff Young's. Venison Grand Veneur on a Bed of Soy Noodle Cake, Duckling Nostallion Crepes. Even though these were very unusual combinations—Cliff used to say, "People don't give a damn how you get there"—the food pleased the crowd.

At this point in Cliff's career, he had no desire to take any more risks; therefore he began a new page in his culinary endeavors. Now Cliff turned to consulting. One of the key figures who still looms prominently in Cliff's consulting work is Bobby Rifkin. Names like the Turn of the Century, The Dove, The Palm, Mama Mia, and, more recently, the Pacific Cabaret, connected the two, whose working relationship still blossoms today. Bobby Rifkin was never known as a restaurateur but as a club operator. Shotgun Willie's and the Diamond Cabaret are his Denver operations. Bobby Rifkin's latest venture is the aforementioned Touch.

Always expect the unexpected from Cliff Young, but who would have believed that Cliff and his wife, Sharon Gomez Young, would move to Beaune, France, and be engaged in a totally unique project with Americans doing business in Burgundy, France? Domain Montagny is a small-scale, luxury hotel, which opened in the spring of 2001. Here Cliff sold shares to friends and investors, retaining controlling interest. Go visit him, and taste winemaker Terry Leighton's Kalin Bourgogne.

Cliff delightfully agreed to contribute some of his own story:

Now, I came up the old-fashioned way, the European way. I entered the Broadmoor as a busboy–apprentice in order to earn some cash to assist my studies at the Colorado College as a philosophy student. I always say that the only quicker way into the restaurant business than one philosophy degree is two—and that's what I had, Phi Beta Kappa and Woodrow Wilson Fellow. While philosophy has always concerned me and never let me alone, the restaurant business has been my life. From busboy to backwaiter, to table captain, to room captain, to maitre d', to general manager, and finally proprietor of five restaurants and clubs.

What a glorious ride. So many personal and private customer memories that may not be told. And so many public tales of which I offer a few:

- Liz Taylor—"Eggs in space." A very lucid way to voice a complaint.
- Mick Jagger for midnight dinner. Trout to start and well-done, thin New York steak with dry mustard for the

main plate. The German chef at first refused to cook this "elephant ear." Still my most vibrant memory.

- Robert Redford flirting with my wife, the maitre d'; joy for all.
- Oscar de la Renta. My pastry chef replicated his logo in chocolate for the dessert plates. Mr. de la Renta so very pleased.
- Ken Bunn, sculptor, requested the "Star-Spangled Banner" from the violinist. A table of twelve leaps to their feet. Bill Husted and I are having a cigar by the fire. They are the American Gold Medal Hockey Team!
- All nine members of the Supreme Court for dinner.
- Michael Carlton, the food critic for the *Denver Post*. I was in Los Angeles when he came in. His headline read, "Cliff Young's Is the Perfect Restaurant." Chilled face and soul, as I read it in the newspaper the morning after my return.
- Dear Raymond Burr, our most devoted celebrity and friend. He called me to design a Steak Tartar after his surgery. No garlic, onion, mustard, or Worcestershire. I did it with three strong cheeses and red wine. His death was near, and I miss him still. I went to the funeral and sat with "Della." We both wept.

And a thousand more celebrity stories. And ten thousand stories of regular customers who feel that restaurateurs are extended family, because we are there for so many important occasions; and we make the memory if we do it right.

In the 1970s, all the restaurants in Denver offered the same menu. Veal Oscar, Tournedos Henry the Fourth. Who did it best? Mr. Wolfe? Le Profile? Strombergs? Mon Petit? There was no espresso and little fresh fish in Denver until 1978. Enter Café Giovanni, Dudley's Duesenberg, Cliff Young's, and the Rattlesnake Club. Food in Denver changed forever. The 1980s were extraordinary for fine dining. Now enter the casual bistro of the 1990s and the steak houses take over fine dining. I got to see it all.

Now in 2001, after thirty years of giving and receiving more, I live in Burgundy, France, with my wife. I love . . . the land, the past, the future, and the present. My Sharrie and my four kids. My two grandkids. My dear mother. All of us have been under the spell of the magic made by my restaurants and their guests. All the memories.

Thank you, God, for letting me serve in this vibrant, unforgettable, risky, and totally beloved industry. Bon appétit for life to all my clients of thirty years and the years to come.

## Filet Mignon of Tuna with Sweet Soy and Ginger Butter
*4 servings*

4, 6-ounce yellowfin tuna filets (cut as square as possible)
1 ounce Japanese togarashi seasoning
4 shallots
1 cup Chardonnay
2 ounces heavy cream
1 pound butter
6 ounces peeled fresh ginger, julienned

2 tablespoons sugar
4 ounces Japanese plum wine
1 small bottle Indonesian kecup manis
1 head Belgian endive, julienned
4 leaves obba shizo
4 ounces Tabiko caviar

1. Season the yellowfin filets liberally with Japanese togarashi. Sprinkle with salt and sear in a smoking-hot sauté pan or very hot grill to desired temperature.

2. Chop 4 shallots, add Chardonnay, reduce until 2 tablespoons of liquid are left.

3. Add heavy cream, reduce until thick and slowly add butter in pieces over a low heat.

4. Season the sauce with salt, pepper, and lemon juice.

5. Place ginger in a sauce pan with sugar and plum wine and cook slowly until almost no liquid is left.

6. Spoon butter sauce onto plate, drizzle kecup manis and place filet of tuna on top; sprinkle the border with julienned endive; top tuna with 1 tablespoon of ginger and garnish to one side with a leaf of shizo and a spoonful of caviar.

# THE COLORADO MINE COMPANY

**Colorado Mine Company** ⌇ **4490 East Virginia, Glendale**

This faithful reproduction of an 1880s mine tipple was one of the hottest spots in town. Suave Buck Scott ran the place with his beautiful wife, Cindy, the hostess with the mostest.

The female employees in the dining rooms and bar areas were handpicked by Cindy and heartily approved of by patrons for their female attributes. Taxi loads of out-of-town visitors, dropped off by handsomely rewarded drivers, were unloaded at the Mine's door. See and be seen, guys on the prowl, girls enjoying the attention bestowed upon them, Roger Wolf at the keyboard, Tom Murphy on the guitar. Only premium brands of liquor were served—twelve-year-old Chivas Regal, Boodles Gin, Stolichnaya, and Wild Turkey. But the food at the Mine was a feast fit for a king. My wife, Jean, and I spent many an evening with Cindy and Buck. I loved his Prime Rib, a cut big enough to feed two offensive linemen of the Broncos.

A very popular menu, it would still be a hit today. Specialties:

| | |
|---|---|
| Colorado Prime Rib (large cut) | $11.95 |
| New York Strip | $11.95 |
| Prime Filet Mignon | $12.95 |
| Alaskan King Crab and Lobster Tail | $17.95 |
| Dover Sole | $12.95 |

Buck Scott contributed his own story:

I met Saul Davidson in an elevator in early 1968 and within a short time, we had decided to look for a suitable inexpensive site. I was able to find a perfect location on a seldom used street called Virginia in Glendale, next to a sewage treatment plant, overlooking the pond they pump the processed waste into.

The rest is history. It took me two years of starts and stops to get it built, at a cost of $237,000. We lived in a trailer on the site, and the night we opened, I borrowed $200 from my bartender's wife to make change.

Opening night was fantastic—it was like people had been waiting for years for us to open. We had such a great collection of characters working for us. Roger Wolf, whom I had hired two years earlier, playing the piano as well as Billy Wallace and Bobby Green. Curtis Calhoon, Jimmy Lambatos, and the greatest, Nick Andurlakis, cooking. My pal, John Kaskela, in the bar with Steve Pasoe, a Cork and Cleaver owner, doing the training. Bill Burgess and the wonderful Jeffrey Bainter. Cindy and Romona Brooke ran the dining room, with a fabulous collection of women to staff the restaurant.

Between the staff and the wonderful collection of Cops, Robbers, Business People and Celebrities, we had eighteen years of excitement and great memories. Our great reward is having met all the *fabulous* people that were our customers, and the great and lasting friendships that continue to enrich our lives. Some of the celebrities we entertained were Elvis dressed as a police captain, Patti Page, Mario Andretti, John Denver, Clint Eastwood, Sandra Locke, Woody Allen, Robert Redford, Telly Savalas, Richard Roundtree, Cathy Lee Crosby, Arthur Ashe, Jackie Cooper, Ginger Rogers, Jacqueline Bisset, Nell Carter, The Rolling Stones, The Eagles, Vic Damone, The Monkees and Joe Namath.

In addition to the great food, the Mine served a varied selection of specialty drinks with creative names such as Dust Cutter, Blasting Powder, The Zamboanga Hummer, and The Mind Shaft.

A unique way of saving the cost of matches was Buck's idea of "bumming" boxes of matches from all fine restaurants around town and handing them out to their surprised customers. Takes a lot of self-confidence to do this!

So whatever spelled the demise of this gangbuster restaurant? Buck and Cindy decided to slow down after twenty years of operating the Mine but had no one to take over. It was time to go—

Here are a couple of true Colorado cuisine recipes of my own:

## Chateaubriand of Buffalo
*3 to 4 servings*

Remove all silver skin and fat from buffalo tenderloin. Cut 2-pound steak from top end. Season with white pepper and garlic. Sear top and bottom over high heat. Continue to cook over medium heat until desired temperature. Slice to $\frac{1}{4}$-inch thickness. Garnish with assorted fresh vegetables and béarnaise sauce or with Rocky Mountain Oysters (recipe follows).

## Rocky Mountain Oysters
*3 to 4 servings*

Parboil peeled "bull fries" in lightly salted water until firm. Rinse in cold water. Slice into 1-inch pieces. Dip in beaten egg. Dredge in flour seasoned with cinnamon (10 parts flour to 1 part cinnamon). Deep fry in oil at 325 degrees until batter is crisp. Drain on towel. Serve immediately with Chateaubriand of Buffalo.

# 235 Fillmore:
# A Mass Grave for Restaurants

Try where others failed! After all, you know so much more about running a successful restaurant than your predecessors. Your ideas and menus are unique, you also stole someone else's chef, who is a genius, and then you bought the place right—just small cosmetic changes to be made—a new name, lots of enthusiasm and, above all, egocentric, eager investors, who would just love to tell someone that they own the joint!

235 Fillmore Street in Cherry Creek North has hosted numerous restaurants over the years. All the principals of these bygone establishments had a fair amount of experience in running restaurants and in most cases a loyal following. And, "We know how to get good publicity"!

Well, then, how come they all failed—and at the same location? Particularly as the current operator, Mel Master of Mel's Restaurant and Bar, is extremely successful! My assumption: many of the causes that I discuss in my writings as to why restaurants fail could be the explanation. What appears certain in this case is this: it is not the location!

Here are the restaurants that once operated at 235 Fillmore:

| | |
|---|---|
| Café Bonaparte | Ramon's |
| Continental Broker | Abalone |
| Eugene's | Chianti's |
| Craig Morton's | 235 Fillmore |

May they rest in peace!

**Dudley's ～ 1120 East 6th Avenue, Denver**

Take a quart of Mel Master, stir vigorously, gently add a pint and a half of Janie Master; in a separate bowl, place a hefty amount of Blair Taylor, seasoned with two ounces of Thom Wise, with final assembly by chefs Orville Knight and Fred Bramhall. Cook for nine years at high temperature, and you have the most successful recipe that created Dudley's. "Some of Denver's veteran restaurateurs thought that these young entrepreneurs were great fools and that Denver was not sophisticated enough to support an unpretentious restaurant that charged $50 to $100 for dinner for two," claimed *Denver* magazine.

Dudley's, while it lasted, always tasted good!!

Melvin Master and his wife, Janie, grew up in Surrey, England. In 1969, Mel worked as a wine merchant in France, while Janie spent time at "hard labor" honing her cooking skills with such great culinarians as Paul Bocuse, the Troisgros Brothers in Roanne, and Roger Verge of the Moulin de Mougin in the south of France.

When the Masters moved to Denver in 1975, Janie launched Master Chef Cooking School where the "Gabby Gourmet" Pat Miller was a pupil. Then Janie met up with that shy character, J. B. French, and opened Les Jardins in the Denver Tech Center. Mel in the meantime had met up with hotshot wine salesman, Blair Taylor, who also had experience in the restaurant business. Financed by a Canadian

## Entrées

| | |
|---|---|
| Selle d'Agneau Duxelle en Feuilleté | 21⁰⁰ |
| Suprême de Caneton, Zinfandel et Champignon Sauvage | 18⁰⁰ |
| Côte du Veau aux Poivrons Rouge et Poivre Vert | 23⁰⁰ |
| Fettuccine à la façon du Chef | 14⁵⁰ |
| Suprême du Poulet farci, Sauce Beurre Basilic | 15⁰⁰ |
| Poisson du Marché | S.P. |
| Selle de Porc aux Olives Pumate et Madeira | 17⁰⁰ |
| Ris du Veau aux Pois et Pernod | 15⁰⁰ |
| Escalopes du Veau aux Noisettes et Armagnac | 23⁰⁰ |
| Specialités Saisonieres | S.P. |
| Selle d'Agneau Crepinettes | 21⁵⁰ |

partner, together they opened Fleurie's on Hampden, which closed after a falling out with the Canadian.

In 1977, the die was cast, and the cast was assembled to bring about the birth of Dudley's. Wildly successful and outrageously popular, it was no showcase in its interior design. Converted from a seedy establishment called the Eden East, next to Safeway on 6th Avenue, "We put snakeskin on the walls, and my straw hats and silk evening clothes were nailed to the walls to cover up the horrid wallpaper," said Janie Master. Francophile and oilman Tom Jordan, who had served one term in the Colorado legislature and later launched the Jordan Winery, helped finance the venture.

Dudley's was the cat's meow, *le plus courant,* the hottest place in town. Trendetties converged and imbibed, lusting for the latest culinary creations. All that under the watchful eye of Blair Taylor and waiter–host and partner, Thom Wise.

Here are some of those menu delights that would please the most discriminating diners of today:

| | |
|---|---|
| Côte du Veau aux Poivrons Rouge et Poivre Vert | $23.00 |
| Selle de Porc aux Olives Pumate et Madeira | $17.00 |
| Salmon à la Sauce Menthe, Cerfeuil et Lillet | $21.00 |
| Capellini à la Façon du Chef | $15.00 |

In conversation with Blair Taylor, he emphasized that Dudley's all-French menu gave the wait staff the opportunity to talk about the food, how it was prepared, and they could do it in a fashion that made diners very, very hungry.

After the Masters sold their interest in Dudley's in order to help launch the Jordan Winery in California, Blair Taylor continued to operate the restaurant. This successful venture ran out of gas as a result of the oil bust in Colorado. Then Blair Taylor created Chives in July of 1986, in the same location as Dudley's, after closing for only forty-five days—"The fastest forty-five days of my life," he said.

At this writing, Blair Taylor operates the very popular Barolo Grill. Mel and Janie Master operate one of Denver's finest—Mel's Restaurant and Bar in Cherry Creek North—with the help of their son, Charles.

*Cooking is like love. It should be entered into with abandon or not at all.*

*—Harriet van Horne*

**Golden Ox**

Pat Hanna's 1963 article (

# Golden Ox

There are steaks . . . and there are steaks. They don't come any better anywhere than they do at the Golden Ox. Ask the man who has eaten one.

The Ox décor is about as Western as you can get. Paneled walls. Carpeting with a branding iron motif. Big golden ox heads flanking a yoke on the wall. There are even spurs in the center of the lighting fixtures. And everything's in a kind of golden haze.

In the bar, even the drinks have a western flair. There's the Little Dogie (really a kind of duded up Bacardi), the Cowboy Punch, (a potent mixture of brandy, rum, bourbon and fruit), the Ranchers Cocktail (rum, apple jack and lemon juice) and Desert Gold (port, crème de cacao and cream—for the ladies).

The night we were there, manager Randy Browder admitted he'd never had the courage to tackle one of the Cowboy Punches—so my escort did and reported it a "real fine little drink."

As for me, I'll stay with the martinis. . . .

There are three Golden Oxes—the first, in Kansas City, opened in 1949. That's where Randy, a University of Denver hotel management alum, got his ground work. Then, in 1960, Randy came back to Denver to open the Golden Ox here. About six months ago, the third Ox opened in Washington, D.C. The menus are the same in all three.

While we were lingering over cocktails, I asked for some pointers to pass on to home steak chefs. Randy . . . says he has learned a thing or three during his years in the steak house business.

"First, if you're cooking over charcoal, keep turning the steaks. Keep the outside from burning while you're trying to get the inside the way you want it. You can tell how done it is by feeling the meat, either with a finger or a fork. The firmer the meat is, the more well done it is. If it springs back, it's rare."

Then the young restaurateur shook his head sadly at the thought of those who call for their meat well done.

"Never order an expensive steak well done. When it's well done you lose the juice and most of the taste—and that's what you're paying for. Most of our orders are for medium or medium rare. We even had one man who ate strip sirloin, absolutely raw. What's more, he came back for another one the same way!"

You have your choice of five different steaks at the Golden Ox. . . . The Strip Sirloin is the pride of the house.

When it came time to go into the 2-tiered dining room, we paused by the grill, just to inhale the marvelous aroma of the sizzling meat. Nobody . . . but nobody . . . could hold down an appetite under conditions such as those. As each steak comes from the grill, the waiter is called by number over a public address system. Insurance that the customer will get his steak while it's still at its best.

Both my friend and I ordered the strip sirloins—rare for him, medium rare for me. And while we waited for the meat to cook I tackled a shrimp cocktail while he downed marinated herring.

Next came a man-sized salad [and] a basket of wonderful garlic toast.

And then the steaks. Huge, juicy, perfectly cooked, delicious steaks that shared a large plate with a king sized baked potato, swimming in sour cream. My friend went through with the speed of Cooper in orbit—then had the audacity to sit back and make cracks about how, for a woman, I sure had a man-sized appetite! Ah, but that steak was too good to waste on playing at being lady-like!

After all that, I couldn't face dessert—or for that matter, even the thought of it—but my walking-appetite-for-a-companion went for broke and had cheesecake with strawberries, with much coffee. He didn't say much—but the expression on his face was sheer bliss.

Came the time of the reckoning, we found we'd eaten very high on the steer at modest cost. The shrimp cocktail was 85 cents, the herring, 55 cents, the steaks, $3.95 each, and the cheesecake, 50 cents. Total—$9.90.

—Excerpted from the *Rocky Mountain News*, May 31, 1963, with permission

## APPETIZERS

Blue Point Oysters
On a Bed of Ice ..................... 1.75

Fresh Gulf Shrimp Cocktail ..... 1.45

Marinated Herring ................... .75

Chilled Tomato Juice ..... .35

Soup du Jour ..................... .45

French Onion Soup ......... .45

# FROM OUR CHARCOAL BROILER

*All Entrees Are Served With Choice of
Baked Potato or French Fried Potatoes,
Hot Garlic Toast and the Best Salad in Kansas City.*

**KANSAS CITY STRIP** ........................ 5.95
*The Steak That Was Born Here
For the Hearty Eater, A Boneless Sirloin
from Choice Steers, Aged to Perfection*

**GOLDEN OX TOP SIRLOIN** ................ 4.85
*A Choice Aged Sirloin Steak for the
Above Average Appetite*

**FILET MIGNON** ............................. 5.95
*Of the Finest Choice Beef Tenderloin*

**CLUB STEAK** ................................. 4.10
*½ Pound of Aged Sirloin from Choice
Steers — for the Average Appetite*

**FILET and LOBSTER COMBINATION** ...... 6.75
*with Lemon Butter
If You're Undecided, Try This Great Specialty*

## ON THE SIDE

French Fried Onion Rings ................................. .75

Danish Blue Cheese Dressing .......................... .35

Sour Cream and Chives (Cup) ......................... .35

Vegetable du Jour .............................................. .45

# Denver's Cheap-Meal District

## *Denver Times,* January 26, 1902

The old saying that "One-half the world does not know how the other half lives" may be illustrated by a trip down on Larimer or Blake streets where most of the cheap lodging houses and restaurants are located. Here may be found numerous 10-cent restaurants where one may obtain a full meal for a dime.

That a meal may be purchased for 10 cents will not be a matter of much surprise to many who have seen the signboards out, but the quality of the food might to those who have never tried it. Let some of you who live in palatial mansions and dine on costly viands served by soft-voiced waiters whose footfalls are unheard as they tread the Brussels carpet clad in showy liveries, go and see the difference in the service; you who employ a high salaried chef to concoct toothsome dishes and whose plate and cut glass would buy a home for the laboring man whom you find eating in the cheap restaurants, go and try the food there. On — street may be seen a signboard standing before the door of a restaurant reading:

"A cup of coffee and three doughnuts or rolls for 10 cents."

"Three eggs, any style, with potatoes, bread, butter, tea or coffee for 10 cents, with a plate of hot cakes free."

"The biggest meal in town for 10 cents."

### *Resent Good Clothes*

That sounds promising and you enter. The place is no better and no worse than dozens of others. A motley assortment of poor men are seated at the various tables and hoarse-voiced waiters, clad in black alpaca jackets and dirty white aprons, are rushing around, rattling dishes and bawling orders to the cook in the rear. The tables are covered with oilcloth that is sticky with the sloppings of previous patrons. The floor is covered with sawdust and the woodwork is grimy with the accumulated grease and tobacco spit of months. A pimply-faced waiter bolts for your table and, with a swipe of a dirty rag, pretends to wipe off the table immediately before you, but in reality simply smearing the leavings over a little larger surface, and with offensive haste inquires [about] your order. He acts as though you were a low interloper who had committed a crime in interrupting him while telling an obscene story to another waiter, a blear-eyed chap with a villainous scar across his cheek, and that his only thought was to get you out of the way as soon as possible. Your delay in reading the bill of fare seems to arouse his ire and he exclaims impatiently, "Wot'll you have? I can't wait all day on yer." Receiving an order for steak and eggs he bawls out in stentorian tones: "One plainer and three with their eyes open."

"One plainer and three with their eyes open" is echoed by the cook as he deftly flips a small steak and the contents of a saucer into their respective frying pans which stand smoking on the vast range. In less time than one would imagine possible the waiter returns with the dishes piled up on his arm. These he scoots across the table with startling velocity and utter disregard for the raiment of the patron. Good clothes seem to be his special aversion and he eyes the wearer of them with a supercilious air that plainly says: "Another swell gone busted."

The steak is tough, the potatoes cold, the bread fairly good, but the butter must be labeled to distinguish it from lard, either in taste or looks: the coffee is—well, it is something new to your palate. In short, you who have been used to good food cannot eat a single article set before you.

## A Blessing to Some

But there are others who are not so fastidious. Heavy-faced laborers and sodden specimens of humanity, in whose faces the bloat of dissipation and evil associations show but too plainly, with here and there a face and figure that suggests better days, munch away in silence and devour every vestige of the food brought them. Many of these men live on 10-cent meals regularly. They are the unfortunate ones who cannot afford any better and the 10-cent restaurants are a matter of necessity to them. The 10-cent "joints" fill a place in the world and save many a poor man from going hungry. In these restaurants you can get a 5-cent lunch, consisting of coffee and doughnuts or rolls, or you can pay as much as you wish for short order articles, but the cooking and the service is all the same.

## Secret of the Business

The question of how these houses can afford to put up such a quantity of food is a subject of much conjecture, but when we consider that only the cheapest of food is purchased, and that at wholesale prices, and that every scrap of uneaten food is used over and over again, the meat and potatoes as hash and the broken bits of bread in puddings, the matter explains itself. For 10 cents they give a piece of steak weighing three or four ounces, which costs them 8 or 9 cents a pound. The potatoes are first served boiled with the jackets on. About two-thirds of these go back to the kitchen and are sent out again as fried potatoes. The scraps of these, which are generally unpalatable, are mixed with the smaller scraps of meat and set out as hash. The larger pieces of meat are used in making meat pies. The waiters must be swift and able to carry a number of orders at one trip, one waiter serving as many as four are expected in establishments of a more pretentious character. Many of these restaurants serve from 100 to 200 persons at a meal, and if there is a profit of 1 cent on each order after paying for food, rent and help the owners, consider that they are making money.

## Swells Eat Free Lunch

There is another source of cheap eating for the man whose pocketbook is in a bad state of depletion. That is the free lunch counters connected with many of the saloons. Here you go in and buy a glass of beer and are at liberty to help yourself to a reasonable amount of the lunch which is kept ready and hot on a table or end of the bar. This lunch generally consists of roast beef, sometimes roast turkey, rye bread, cheese, hot tamales and baked beans. They must be eaten with the fingers, while the patron of the free lunch stands before the "trough" or marches around the room. Strange to say, there are practically but two classes who frequent the free lunch counters—the professional spongers and bummers and the business men or young blades of the town. The latter come in for a glass of beer and dally over its drinking while they sample the viands set before them. It is not done through any desire to save the money necessary to buy a good meal, but rather to take advantage of the opportunity to get something for nothing, or perhaps to induce an appetite for a regular meal. The middle classes as a rule do not pay any attention to the free lunch counter.

### Cheap Lodgings

Along in line with the 10-cent meals come the 10 and 17-cent lodging houses, whose cots are ranged along in rooms of twenty-five or thirty and lodging may be had for 10 cents.

Some houses partition off with curtains or cheap lumber a large room into a score of two apartments and advertise single "rooms" for 15 cents. These partitions are about eight feet high of the thinnest lumber or canvas and the noises of sleeping men and incessant slamming of doors and talking by incomers all night are anything but conducive to slumber. The cots are cheap affairs filled with straw and the bedding consists of a straw pillow and a couple of highwater comforters that reach from the chin to the ankles. The offices of these lodging houses are generally used as public rooms by the guests of evenings and are packed full of men smoking, drinking, playing cards or telling ribald stories that make the place sound like a bedlam.

*Automat—The first restaurant to make it possible for the poor man to enjoy food served under glass.*

*—Fred Allen*

DOUBLE MARTINI
OR
DOUBLE MANHATTAN
70¢

*Joe "Awful" Coffee*

*welcomes you to the popular*

**RINGSIDE LOUNGE**

1120 SEVENTEENTH ST., DENVER, COLORADO
KE. 4-2818        KE. 4-9912

## Joe "Awful" Coffee's Ringside Lounge ⁓
### 1120 17th Street, Denver

According to the biography on the lounge menu, Joe "The Battling Newsboy of Pueblo" started his boxing career at fifteen, whipping "Kid Plank" for the flyweight championship of Colorado. In 1920, he captured the state championship in the bantam class and by 1922, he beat Don "Terror" Long for the Colorado featherweight championship. Before entering the restaurant business, he graduated from Denver University, where he also was boxing coach and football trainer, worked as boxing promoter and official, and served as contract manager for the May Co.

It is perhaps a relief to know that the moniker "Awful" referred to his reputation as a boxer, and not his reputation as a restaurateur. Joe served up a wide variety of basic fare for the business lunch and evening crowd—cold plates with potato salad, hot and cold sandwiches, sides and salads, and a basic offering of entrées: Spaghetti with Chicken Ravioli ($.90), Breaded Veal Cutlets ($1.50), Grilled Virginia Ham Steak with Pineapple Rings ($1.50), and Roast Prime Ribs of Beef au Jus ($2.75).

Chris Leppek, in his article for the *Intermountain Jewish News*, profiled this colorful Denver character and his eatery:

# The Life and Times of Joe 'Awful' Coffee

They just don't make 'em like Joe "Awful" Coffee anymore. The times are different, for one thing. The people are different too.

And Coffee himself? Well, they must have broken the mold after they cast him. He's pretty much one-of-a-kind.

He's the kind of guy whose punches were once known and feared by some of America's best boxers, a good many of whom ended up with their backs on the mat, trying to see through stars.

They didn't call him "Awful" for nothing.

He grew up on Pueblo's mean streets, back when they really were mean, when a kid selling newspapers on the corner often had to fight to protect his turf.

Joe learned to fight well indeed for that very practical reason. Well enough, in fact, to become a pro boxer and to train, when just a teenager, with the legendary Jack Dempsey. And, in short order, to become a regional champ. . . .

Sure, Coffee was a little guy. Still is. But don't tell that to the boxers he beat, nor to those who beat him. They knew how hard Coffee was to knock down. Very few of them managed it.

And you can't apply the word "little" to Joe Coffee's heart. He grew up tough and he fought like a tiger, but he's got a heart as broad as his jabs were fierce.

The father of three children of his own . . . he's always loved kids, especially kids who are poor or disadvantaged in any way. Coffee always had a special place in his heart . . . for children who are retarded, like his daughter Barbara.

Years after he hung up his gloves, when Coffee was a big-time restaurant operator in Denver, he used to interrupt his many guests and direct their attention to some eight or nine-year-old kid. . . . He put the child in the spotlight and asked for applause. . .

"Let your conscience be your guide," Coffee would say, and the guests would gladly dig deep into purses and wallets. Usually, the kid would go home to North Denver or Globeville or Five Points or the West Side with an amazing sum of money in his pocket. Money that he could help his family with. Just like Coffee once did.

—Excerpted from *Intermountain Jewish News,* Mar. 6, 1992, with permission

## ...Choice Sea Foods

Alaskan Smoked Salmon, Potato Salad .... .85
Grilled Red Salmon Steak ........ *1.25* ~~1.00~~
Fried Halibut, Lemon Butter ...... *1.25* ~~1.00~~
Chef's Special Shrimp Louie Salad ........ 1.50
Fried Eastern Oysters with Tartar Sauce ... ~~1.25~~ *1.50*
Colorado Mountain Trout, Pan Fried ....... 1.50
French Fried Jumbo Shrimp, Tartar Sauce .. 1.40
French Dip Eastern Scallops, Tartar Sauce.. 1.25
Broiled Live Eastern Lobster .................. 2.50
Crabmeat Louie ................... *1.50* ~~1.15~~
Crabmeat Salad ................................ 1.00
Lobster Tails .................................. 1.65
Cracked Crab .................................. 1.65

## Delicious Desserts

| | | | |
|---|---|---|---|
| Plums | .20 | Pineapple Slices | .20 |
| Peaches | .20 | Assorted Pies *20* ~~.15~~ | |
| Pears | .20 | Ice Cream | .15 |
| Figs | .20 | Sundaes | .20 |
| Apricots | .20 | | |

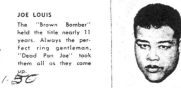

### Drinks

De War's Scotch ........................ .50
Alexander — Gin or Brandy ....... .75
Stinger ................................. .75
"Coffee's" Special Cocktail.......... .65
Vodka Collins ......................... .50
Singapore Sling ...................... .75
B & B Imported ....................... .75
B & B Domestic ....................... .60
Pink Lady ............................. .75
Grasshopper .......................... .75
Vodka Martini (Single) ............... .45
Vodka Martini (Double) ............. .75
Gimler ................................ .60
Dram Buie ............................ .65
King Alfonso ......................... .60
Cointreau — Imported ............... .60
Cointreau — Domestic .............. .50
Zombie ............................... 1.00

**JACK DEMPSEY**
The "Manassa Mauler" from Colorado, one of the greatest of champions, was popular for his weaving, bobbing, slam-bang style of fighting.

**JOE LOUIS**
The "Brown Bomber" held the title nearly 11 years. Always the perfect ring gentleman, "Dead Pan Joe" took them all as they came up.

**ROCKY MARCIANO**
The "Brockton Blockbuster" is probably the hardest hitter in the game today. Won heavyweight crown from Joe Walcott by a KO in the 13th round in December, 1952.

**SUGAR RAY ROBINSON**
Perhaps the greatest ringman of the present day. Held both welter and middleweight crowns at one time or other. Retired after losing to Maxim in 14th round from heat exhaustion in June, 1952.

**BENNY LEONARD**
The perfect boxer, Benny held the lightweight championship for years. Due to his great boxing skill he retired without a mark on his face.

# The Capitol

*Daily Rocky Mountain News,*
December 31, 1869

Yesterday we visited for the first time the newly established "French Restaurant" and Oyster Saloon called "The Capitol," No. 35 Larimer street, 2d door west of F street, Mr. Louis Charpiot, proprietor, and can safely say without flattering the proprietor, that it is the neatest and most elegant establishment of that kind in Denver. The restaurant department is arranged in the eastern style with little rooms or stalls, which can comfortably seat six persons. These are all provided with mirrors and at the entrance with curtains, the latter to be raised or lowered at the pleasure of the occupant. The room is carpeted and well lighted up by two large chandeliers. The bar and cellar contain the choicest native and foreign wines and liquors. The oysters are the best and freshest in this market, and of the culinary art of the establishment passers by might have formed an idea by examining the different dishes displayed at the windows and expressly prepared for the supper and accommodation of visitors at to-night's *Turner's Ball* at Cole's Hall. Attendants are respectfully invited to give him a call, one and all. Bills of fare and wine lists will be posted in the cloak rooms as well as in the dance hall. It is the intention of Mr. Charpiot to manage the Capitol in such a manner that the most scrupulous *pater-familias* shall not hesitate to visit his establishment at any time with his family, and to keep the best of everything the season affords, at reasonable prices. In fact, Mr. Louis Charpiot has supplied Denver with a place of resort for ladies and gents, the want of which has been long felt here, and therefore richly deserves the patronage of the public, which we trust the "Capitol" will meet with. Give him a call, and judge for yourselves.

Laffite Restaurant ⌒ 14th and
Larimer Streets, Denver

When I first met Joseph Sperte in 1951 he was the manager of Green Gables Country Club. As a matter of fact, I actually worked for Joe for about three months at Green Gables, filling in for one of his chefs, who was on sick leave. Joe was tough to work for, just as demanding as the members of the club!

But I owe my first chef's job to Joe Sperte, who recommended me to Jim Blankenship, then owner of the Patio Lamaze, at the southeast corner of Belleview and South Santa Fe Drive in Littleton. More on this later. . . .

It was at Green Gables Country Club that Joe Sperte became well acquainted with Marvin Cook, of the venerable Cook family of Denver. The Cooks owned properties such as Ben Cook Plumbing at 14th and Larimer streets (destined to become Laffite Restaurant). They also owned the Stanley Plaza and the Gotham Hotel at 11th and Grant. Later, these locations became the homes of two very popular and well-respected restaurants. Can you guess?

This, however, is the story of Joseph Sperte, who, along with his son, Roger, operated the highly successful Laffite, which opened in December of 1960.

It is at this point that I want to thank Greg and Shannon Sperte of Oregon, who, through a story by Dick Kreck of the *Denver Post,* contacted me and loaned me a family treasure—namely their family photo album and stories, as well as clippings that are the foundation of this article. Greg Sperte is the grandson of Joseph Sperte and son of Roger Sperte. Shannon is Greg's spouse.

The following is a story that is part of the above-mentioned album.

The Cooks owned a building used for storage by Ben Cook Plumbing Supply Company. Located at the corner of 14th and Larimer, it was near the site of Denver's first covered-wagon settlement. Later, gambling saloons and bordellos abounded in the area as miners came into town with their golden nuggets. Denver slowly developed to the southeast. The Brown Palace Hotel became society's meeting place; the main thoroughfares were Broadway running north and south and Colfax east and west, all the way to the mountains. The Broadway Theater in the Hotel Metropole and the Blue Parrot Restaurant were at the dividing line between the business section and Capitol Hill, the site of Denver's first mansions. Soon, Larimer Street became Denver's skid row.

Marvin and Joe decided Denver could support [a] first-class restaurant, this one to specialize in fresh fish entrées. On a trip to New Orleans, the partners studied décor and cooking styles and then embarked on a total renovation of the narrow, three-story, old supply warehouse. Even the newspapers predicted doom; after all, who in their right mind would venture into Denver's skid row for lunch, let alone after dark? All new business development was headed "up the hill" with only Central Bank and Luby Chevrolet (directly across from the proposed Laffite site) courageously maintaining their lower downtown identity.

Laffite opened with a roar. Valet parking was provided—a first in Denver—and car after car pulled alongside the restaurant as patrons hurried inside and parking attendants took care of the vehicles. Heavy red-flocked wallpaper, wood stained to black, semi-circular booths in red leather lined the walls. A small bar with approximately twelve bar stools, cloak room, restrooms, and the kitchen were on the main level. A wide stairway in the center led to the oyster bar, which featured an exposed wine cellar and piano bar. Carpet that looked like plank flooring surprised many as they thought they were stepping onto a hard floor.

Joe (left) and Roger Sperte.
*Courtesy, Greg Sperte.*

The Laffite became the talk of the town. Even the ladies' room with its metal stalls and golden swan faucets became a must-see for the men as well as women. One determined patron even removed a gold toilet paper holder as a souvenir. If additional help was needed to scrub pots and pans or mop the kitchen floor during the busy evenings, Roger simply walked out onto Larimer Street and offered a few hours of work to a yet-sober wanderer. People would call in on Thursday night for a Saturday evening reservation to be told the first available time was at 10 or 10:30!

Joseph Sperte, or Papa Joe as people would call him, was a tough, cigar-smoking, hard-drinking restaurateur. But no one could deny the fact that while Joe operated Laffite, during and after the partnership with Marvin Cook, the restaurant was an unqualified success. Some writers described the décor as opulent, reminiscent of the elegance of New Orleans' fine-dining gourmet rooms. Others thought it fit the trend during the late 1950s and 1960s when restaurants used a lot of red color for décor, not unlike the Red Slipper in the Cherry Creek Inn, managed by Frank Turner.

Major attractions of Laffite's oyster bar, renamed the Rogue's Room, were drinks with swashbuckling names like the Velvet Dagger, Blue Beard, or Crimson Cutlass with its own souvenir glass. A variety of entertainment was provided nightly including the D'lighters and Denver's favorite, Jimmy Roberts, at the piano. Jimmy made people happy and he made them laugh.

Laffite was known as a seafood house and flew in live lobsters twice weekly and also brought in fresh seafood from both coasts frequently. Many classic French preparations were in evidence on the menu. Joe was quoted as saying, "There's a French verse that says, 'It's the sauce that makes the fish'"! Laffite closed during the economic downturn of the 1980s, and newspapers and loyal patrons lauded the Spertes' accomplishments and lamented the end of an era.

## TABLE D'HOTE DINNER FOR TONIGHT

Relish Tray
Salade Laffite  Pommes du Jour
Fresh Garden Vegetable
New Orleans Hot French Bread
Beverage

★ ★ ★

| | |
|---|---|
| Laffite Sea Food Platter, fried shrimp, smelts, oysters, scallops and Filet of Sole . . . . . . . . . . . 3.90 | Broiled Swordfish Steak, Creole Sauce . . . . . . 3.75 |
| Baked Shrimp, au Vin Blanc Cassolette . . . . . 3.85 | Louisiana Fried Prawns, Two Tone Dressing . . 3.60 |
| Sauteed Smelts Provencale. . . . . . . . . . . . . 3.00 | Broiled Filet of Salmon, sauce Bearnaise . . . . . 3.50 |
| Fresh Rainbow Trout Belle Meuniere . . . . . . . 3.65 | Filet of Sole Bonne Femme . . . . . . . . . . . . 3.85 |
| Filet de Sole, Champagne fine . . . . . . . . . . 3.25 | Broiled Filet of Halibut Steak Cambaceres . . . 3.65 |
| Curried Seafood Madras . . . . . . . . . . . . . . 3.75 | La Bouillabaisse, Cote d'Azur . . . . . . . . . . 3.90 |
| Maine Lobster Thermidore . . . . . . . . . . . . . 4.75 | Les Petite Cuisses of Frog Legs Provencale . . . 4.25 |
| Danish Petite Broiled Lobsters, la sause du Patron . . . . . . . . . . . . . . . 4.50 | Broiled Alaskan King Crab Legs, Bourgignonne Butter . . . . . . . . . . . . . . . 4.25 |
| Broiled African Lobster Tail, sause Maison . . . 4.50 | Louisiana Shrimp De Jongle . . . . . . . . . . 3.75 |
| Maine Lobster Newburg . . . . . . . . . . . . . . 4.50 | Linguine with Clams Poulette . . . . . . . . . . . 3.25 |
| Louisiana Shrimp, stuffed with Crab Meat . . . . 3.65 | Monterey Abalone Steak saute Bercy . . . . . . . 4.10 |
| Le Pompano en Papillote . . . . . . . . . . . . . 3.90 | Shad Roe, sauteed with bacon, fine herbs and capers on toast points . . . . . . 3.85 |
| Filets of Pompano, Lobster sauce . . . . . . . . 4.65 | Le Crab Meat au gratin Mornay . . . . . . . 3.90 |
| Authentic English Dover Sole, saute . . . . . . . 4.45 | Broiled Florida Red Snapper, Maitre d'Hotel . 3.75 |
| Filet of Sole a la Marguery . . . . . . . . . . . . 4.25 | Lake Superior White Fish Saute Amandine . . 3.50 |

For fans of Laffite's fare, here are some recipes:

## Homard (Lobster) au Court-Bouillon
*4 servings*

| | |
|---|---|
| 2 tablespoons butter | 2 sprigs parsley |
| 1 large onion, chopped fine | 6 peppercorns |
| 1 large carrot, chopped fine | 2 cloves |
| 3 stalks celery, chopped fine | 2 tablespoons dry |
| 2 quarts water | white wine |
| 1 bay leaf | 4, 1½-pound live lobsters |

1. Melt butter in sauce pan and cook onion, carrot, celery until brown. Add water, bay leaf tied with parsley sprigs, peppercorns, and cloves.

2. Add wine and bring to a boil. Cover the pan tightly and simmer for 30 minutes or longer. Strain and cool before using.

3. Plunge the live lobsters into boiling court-bouillon. To serve hot, boil for 20 to 25 minutes. Split the bodies lengthwise, removing the dark vein along the back and the small sac behind the head, and crack the claws. Place lobster, cut side up, on a serving dish and serve with lemon quarters and melted butter.

4. To serve cold, boil the lobsters for about 15 minutes and cool them in the court-bouillon for another 15 minutes. Chill and serve with mayonnaise or Russian dressing, lemon wedges, and capers.

## The Greatest Bouillabaisse
*12 servings*

Bouillabaisse had its origin on the Mediterranean Sea coast when fishermen's wives made a soup of the unsold portions of the catch. America has a different variety of seafoods, but the principle is the same. Our bouillabaisse is made from an assortment of fish such as mackerel, eel, and snapper, as well as lobster and other shellfish. We serve the liquor in a tureen, the fish on a platter, and then the diner may blend the soup and fish according to his or her own taste.

| | |
|---|---|
| 2, 2-pound lobsters | 3 garlic cloves |
| 1½ pounds striped bass or sea bass | 2 tablespoons chopped parsley |
| 3 pounds red snapper or mackerel | 2 tablespoons chopped fennel |
| 2 dozen shrimp, shelled | ½ teaspoon saffron |
| 2 dozen mussels | 1 bay leaf, crumbled |
| 2 dozen clams | ½ teaspoon thyme |
| ½ cup chopped carrot | 1 tablespoon salt |
| 3 leeks, chopped | fresh ground pepper |
| ¾ cup chopped onion | ½ cup butter, melted |
| ½ cup olive oil | 12 slices French bread |
| 4 cups canned tomatoes | |

1. Cut up lobster, leaving shell on. Cut bass and snapper or mackerel into 1-inch slices. Scrub mussels and clams thoroughly to remove all outside sand and grit.

2. Sauté carrot, leeks, and onion in olive oil for 10 minutes in a large pot. Add tomatoes, 2 minced garlic cloves and other seasonings.

3. Add lobster and 2 quarts water and bring soup to boil. Reduce heat and simmer for 15 minutes. Add bass and snapper and cook for 10 minutes. Add shrimp, mussels, and clams and cook for 20 minutes or until shells open. (Discard any mussels or clams that do not open.)

4. Mix butter and 1 crushed garlic clove. Spread some on one side of French bread slices and toast, buttered side up, in the broiler under moderate heat until brown. Turn slices, spread with rest of butter and toast the other side. Serve the toast with the bouillabaisse.

**Lande's**  ～  **3130 East Colfax Avenue, Denver**

I arrived in Denver in the fall of 1950 and Lande's restaurant was very popular. Later the site was taken over by the Golden Ox. The menu heralded: "A Place for the Discriminating."

Whomever I asked, mainly old-time Denverites, to describe Lande's, it went like this: "Oh yes, I remember Lande's—nice place"; "We went any number of times to Lande's—good food"; "I can't remember what it looked like . . . "; "Was that the place that became the Golden Ox?"; "Who can remember 1939? Lande's?"

Lande's all-time favorites:

| | |
|---|---|
| Beef tenderloin à la Stroganoff | $2.75 |
| Pepper Steak en Casserole | $2.25 |
| London Golden Duck | $1.25 |
| Casserole of Chicken Livers | $2.50 |
| Real Southern Fried Chicken | $2.25 |

Dinner:

Your choice of: Shrimp Cocktail, Watermelon Cup, Cream of Celery, Fresh Jellied Consommé, Relish and Juices

Salads: Iceberg Head Lettuce or Minced Beet Salad

| | |
|---|---|
| Broiled Filet Mignon with Mushroom Sauce | $.85 |
| Grilled T-Bone Dinner | $.90 |
| Creamed Chicken in Casserole | $.65 |
| Fried Calf Liver with Onion or Bacon | $.65 |

Accompanying starches and vegetables (steamed cabbage, buttered beets) and desserts (Chocolate Nut Sundae, Liederkranz, Roquefort or Camembert Cheese with Crackers) were included.

Lande's offered many more entrées on different days, but all in the same price range during the 1930s and early 1940s. Their variety of foods was amazing!

# DINNER

Shrimp Cocktail      Pineapple Juice      Tomato Juice
Fruit Cup      Grapefruit Juice
Watermelon Cup      Cantaloupe Cup
Orange Ice      Relish

Cream of Celery Soup —Fresh Jellied Consommé

| | |
|---|---:|
| Cold Virginia Baked Ham and Turkey Plate | .75 |
| Creamed Chicken en Casserole | .65 |
| Breaded Veal Cutlets in Tomato Sauce | .65 |
| Breaded Deep Sea Scallops, Tartar Sauce | .65 |
| Assorted Cold Meats, Potato Salad | .75 |
| Fried Calf's Liver with Onions or Bacon | .65 |
| Broiled Tenderloin Steak en Mushroom Sauce | .75 |
| Broiled Fillet Mignon with Mushroom Sauce | .85 |
| Southern Fried Spring Chicken, County Gravy | .75 |
| Grilled T-Bone Steak Dinner | .90 |
| Broiled Short Cut Steak, French Fried Potatoes | .80 |

Hot Bread

Steamed Cabbage      Buttered Red Beets
Cream Whipped Potatoes      Candied Yams

Iceberg Head Lettuce or Minced Beet Salad

Chocolate nut Sundae
Liederkranz, Roquefort or Camembert Cheese with Crackers
Fresh Fruit Cup
Orange Ice      Iced Honey Dew Melon

# The Man All around You

## *Denver Times,* January 19, 1889

*He Who Takes Your Order and Yells it Wildly.*

*Many Kinds of Waiters.*

*Where They Come From and How They Have a Tough Time of It in Their Hash Slinging Occupations.*

The waiters of Denver are a class by themselves, and yet there are hundreds of them who are unacquainted with hundreds of others, and the order possesses an aristocracy quite as exclusive as is known in other professions. The majority of the waiters are white, and the hotels, with one exception, employ white help of this sort.

The hotel waiter is, of course, the autocrat of all the waiters, and his possibilities for fees are excellent, which, together with the good living furnished by the average hotel give him an air distingue, by which he is readily discovered from the medium or cheap restaurant waiter, and which places him a good many degrees above the coffee and cake saloon waiter, who, from associating with the poorer classes, loses much of the politeness which he originally possesses as a part of this stock in trade.

The hotel waiter is generally a married man of thirty or thereabouts, who understands his business, and who, as a rule, is steady and methodical, saving his "tips" and fees to buy shoes for his large family of infants, and who attends to his business and makes a study of being attentive and obliging.

The restaurant waiter is not so conservative as his confrere in the hotel business, is, as a rule, younger, and is less careful as to how he serves the customers of the place.

To be sure, a restaurant has always a few regular customers, but many of those who patronize the place never enter it but once, and the waiter is not going to run his legs off to oblige a man whom, in all probability, he will never see again.

The feeing system is almost unknown in Denver, except at the most exclusive restaurants, and as a consequence the waiters receive better pay. The waiters receive as a rule about $80 a month and board. The restaurant waiter is, as a rule, a young man, and although many follow the business as a profession, the majority are waiters, not from choice, but from necessity. The youth who finds himself stranded in the far West without money or friends, can take a waiter's position, and they are generally more plentiful than any others.

The dishes, crockery, etc., broken by the waiter, must always be paid for by the breaker. Constant practice in carrying great quantities of dishes renders the waiter skillful, but a glass too much or a plate to one side and the whole business falls to the ground, and a week's salary is frequently smashed to atoms.

The waiter in the cheapest restaurants, or "beaneries," as they are called, is a character. His only aim in Life is to abbreviate the order given him by the guest, and mystify the hungry individual with a jargon of his own. For instance, a man orders ham and eggs, and a cup of coffee without milk. The waiter yells as loud as he can to the cook in the other end of the establishment: "One in the dark,"—that's the coffee; "ham and"—that's the rest of the order. A rare beefsteak is a "slaughter in the pan," while milk toast rejoices in "graveyard stew," probably because it is generally used by sick persons.

Poached eggs are "Adam and Eve afloat in mid ocean." Sausage is "once on the bark," and buckwheat cakes, "once on the buck." Everything is brevity, and the more so the better.

The toughest waiter of all is probably the man who waits on his own table and does his own cooking. He runs the cheapest restaurant of all and his tough customers have to be treated in a tough manner or they wouldn't feel at home.

This is the man who glares at his guests and asks them what they want with a sneer and frown on this face, who gets a reply to his question in the same style and who fairly hurls things at you. Napkins are an unknown luxury here, and the man who would eat with his fork would not be tolerated.

The waiter as a rule is a man who works hard; who has to attend to the wants of hundreds of people who are all hungry and consequently ill-natured. His disposition becomes soured and he has made up his mind that the only way to get along is to pretend to be deaf and do his work in as perfunctory a manner as possible.

There are over three hundred waiters in Denver and they are of all nationalities. The St. James Hotel employs colored waiters, who have a union of their own. Charpiot's hotel will have nothing but Frenchmen. The Markham has Irish waiters and the other hotels and restaurants employ, as a rule, no special nationality.

*When you find a waiter who is a waiter*
*and not an actor, musician, or poet,*
*you've found a jewel.*

*—André Soltner*

**Leo's Place** 〜 **16th and Broadway, Denver**

Leo Goto arrived in Denver from California when his Japanese American family was ordered inland after Pearl Harbor. Leo was just a small boy when his family settled between Fort Lupton and Brighton, where his father managed a small farm. East High School and Denver University gave Goto a fine education. Chris Leppek, in his article "Culinary Artist," tells more of his story:

## Culinary Artist: Leo Goto

. . . Later . . . Goto went to work as a dishwasher in order to pay for his own education, which culminated with a BS in business administration and an MBA from DU.

His first restaurant job was at a place called the Outrigger, located in the now-demolished Cosmopolitan Hotel on Broadway.

"The chef at that time was a man named Jimmy Chin," Goto recalls. "This was in the early '50s, when there was still a lot of animosity between the Chinese and Japanese, but he took a strong liking to me and gave me my first cooking and food preparation lessons."

Goto learned quickly, but he was not destined to wash dishes, nor to cook, for very long. When he turned 18, there was an opening for maitre d' at the Outrigger.

"Jimmy said, 'This guy laughs too much and smiles too much so we ought to put him at the door.'"

Thus was born a long-term job at the Cosmo, which was to cement Goto's lifelong involvement in the restaurant business. Before long, the Outrigger had become Trader Vic's, a tropical theme restaurant which became a huge hit in Denver during the 1950s.

"That was when people were still drinking," Goto recalls with a nostalgic smile, "and they weren't worried about cholesterol."

The always affable Goto learned a lot from the many businessmen who frequented Trader Vic's. By the time he was 24, Goto was named manager of the restaurant, and before long was assigned to establish satellite Trader Vic's establishment, under management contracts, in Portland, Houston, and London, all of which saw success similar to the Denver original. He also helped establish the Senor Pico chain of Mexican theme restaurants.

By 1968, Goto was ready to branch out on his own, forming a partnership with longtime buddy Howard Torgove and Larry Atler. "We started our partnership with a handshake," says Goto, adding that he has no qualms about calling them his best friends.

The trio's first venture was Leo's Place, which, with a great downtown Denver location and a décor taken in part from Denver's historic Turf Bar, became a huge success. Leo's Place, under the management of its namesake, might have lasted for decades but urban renewal finally forced its closure in 1980.

—Excerpted from *Intermountain Jewish News*, Oct. 21, 1994, p.2-B, with permission

"The trio" are still in partnership at the Wellshire Inn on South Colorado Boulevard.

My wife, Jean, and I first met Leo at the Outrigger Room in the now-demolished Cosmopolitan Hotel. He always greeted us with his great smile, and was always good for a laugh. This was in the 1950s when I was still at the Patio Restaurant in Littleton. Many a Saturday night when things were calming down at the Normandy and later the Quorum, we and our wives would meet at the Outrigger and later at Trader Vic's for late-night snacks and a few Mai Tais and Harvey Wallbangers. Those were the drinking days!

# FAR EASTERN SPECIALTIES

Entrees complete with Today's Special Soup, choice of Our Spinach or Garden Salad, appropriate accompaniments and beverage.

**PRECIOUS DUCK**
Boned and pressed with exotic spices and waterchestnut flour — with our special plum sauce. Marvelous ............................................................... **7.95**

**CHOW CHOW**
A steamy concoction of fresh Japanese vegetables served over Pan Fried Noodles and your choice of thinly sliced Beef, Chicken, Pork or Shrimp ..................... **5.75**

**CHICKEN WITH ALMONDS**
Sliced Chicken with diced vegetables steamed in a rich broth and sprinkled with almonds. A delectable choice ......................................................... **5.95**

**CHICKEN TERIYAKI**
Golden Breast of Chicken topped with our subtle Teriyaki sauce ................ **6.25**

**PEKING DUCK**
W. L. Wong's magnificent version of the Mandrin roast duck, complemented by our Chinese Plum Sauce ............................................................ **10.25**

**SWEET AND SOUR BREAST OF CHICKEN**
Sauteed to a golden crisp, topped with our pungent sauce and freshly crushed almonds. Good! .............................................................................. **7.25**

This bit from the Leo's Place menu gives a flavor of the ambience:

The setting is one of quiet elegance, surrounded by a wealth of richly crafted items that adorned the homes and businesses where Denver's early history was made. They were discriminatingly collected to create a unique gathering place with an ambience of pleasure and leisure. . . .

The well-worn, but definitely elegant, black and white marble checkerboard floor came to view when 12 layers of flooring were taken up. No one knew the balconies or the ornate tin ceiling existed; they were hidden by a dropped ceiling. The warmly hued brick wall appeared when the wallpaper disappeared.

To complement the mellow background, we knew we needed to collect unique memorabilia that would give Leo's Place a sense of history and create an appropriate setting for superb dining. . . .

Churches, mansions, and antique dealers were the mother lode for the stained class windows. . . . The light fixtures came from several well-known locations. The rock crystal chandeliers in the main dining room are from the old Baur's on 15th and Curtis Streets. . . . The hanging lights over the bar came from the majestic white marble Federal Reserve Bank on 17th Street. . . .

The beautiful hand-painted porcelain sink in the ladies' room came from Belgium and is over 100 years old. The wooden arches framing the entry to the intimate Bamboo Room, and the matching arched windows and back door came from a Capitol Hill mansion. . . . The ornate hardware is from the demolished Cooper Building. The French Lion etchings are over 200 years old. The four gilded crouching lions atop the booths are hand-carved, and originally were on a Brunswick Championship Pool Table. We found them . . . right here in the Mile High City!

The exterior lights above the front door are from the Colorado State Capitol. Four of Denver's original street lamps are at the curb. . . .

Leo's Place closed on Saint Patrick's Day, 1980.

*He that eateth well, drinketh well;*
*he that drinketh well, sleepeth well;*
*he that sleepeth well, sinneth not;*
*he that sinneth not goeth straight*
*through Purgatory to Paradise.*

—*William Lithgow*

Le Profile  ~  1560 Sherman Street, Denver
(also, Scotch 'n' Sirloin  ~  Piccadilly  ~
Stephanino  ~  Los Dos)

By the sheer number of restaurants, operated by Cook family members, and the high regard in which they were held, they play an important role in Denver's restaurant history. Attorney-turned-entrepreneur Marvin Cook and his three sons, Tony, Kenneth, and Michael, operated some of the most popular eateries and watering holes in the city.

In 1955, Marvin Cook and Joe Sperte, then manager of Green Gables Country Club, formed a partnership to open and operate fine dining restaurants in Denver. Thus, in 1955 the Profile Room opened, soon to become one of the premier dining spots in the city. The underground parking garage of the Stanley Plaza Apartments was converted to house the Profile Room. The restaurant offered continental cuisine and tableside service, and with its proximity to the State Capitol, the Profile Room quickly became a favorite with Denver's society as well with legislators, accompanied by a flock of lobbyists, who most happily picked up the tabs. After a disastrous fire, saved only by the concrete walls of the parking garage, the Profile Room was redecorated and given a new name—Le Profile.

Noteworthy too is that Cliff Young was the dining room manager of Le Profile for ten years and cut his teeth in this establishment.

Le Profile favorites:

| | |
|---|---|
| Crepes "Profile," stuffed with Seafood Specialty | $1.50 |
| Roast Prime Ribs of Beef with Yorkshire Pudding | $5.75 |
| Supreme of Chicken Doré Kiev | $4.50 |
| Buisson of Frog Legs Belle Provence | $4.75 |
| Curried Sea Food Madras | $4.75 |
| Crown Rack of Lamb (for 4) | $25.00 |

Joe Sperte and son, Roger, along with Marvin Cook and sons were very successful in operating the restaurant and, in 1959, they decided to convert part of another of the Cook properties, namely the Gotham Hotel at 12th and Grant, into the Scotch 'n' Sirloin. Here was the classic forerunner of today's steakhouses. It was also a great watering hole for state legislators, surrounded by hordes of lobbyists. Not to be outdone were media types and ad agency gurus.

They feasted on a fine bill of fare, and one did not have to ask, "Where's the beef?"! Tournedos were a specialty, prepared numerous ways (au Poivre, aux Champignons, Oscar) for about eight dollars.

The location of the Scotch was near the Capitol in the midst of Denver's old Gold Coast, where gold and silver barons built monumental estates, in celebration of their new-found wealth. A couple of recipes from the Scotch are included in this section. The restaurant closed in 1987.

In 1960, in the former Cook's Plumbing building at 14th and Larimer streets, Laffite was born. But the partnership of Cook and Sperte came to a separation in the mid-1960s after ten years of business arrangements. The split gave Joseph and Roger Sperte sole ownership of the Laffite, and Tony Cook took over management of the Gotham Hotel, including the Scotch 'n' Sirloin as well as the Stanley Plaza, which housed Le Profile.

At the time, many of Denver's restaurateurs thought that the Spertes had picked a bad location. Larimer Street was Denver's Skid Row and "LoDo" had yet to be developed. The Spertes proved everyone wrong and, when devoting full time to Laffite, were highly successful, as you will read in the Laffite part of this book (page 63).

In 1967, Lowry's Prime Rib of Los Angeles became the inspiration for the Piccadilly. The site was the Denver Bank building at 17th and Broadway. The Cooks operated this hangout for those on the hunt, but also for persons seeking prime rib served from a specially designed silver cart. Also featured was the spinning salad bowl, nested in ice to assure freshness. Piccadilly Sherry Dressing, an acclaimed original, was the perfect complement.

To quote from the Piccadilly menu, "We chose the name, Piccadilly, to suit the English in us. The preparation of our prime ribs in the Yorkshire manner is, of course, English. Our location at the hub of downtown activity is similar to Piccadilly Circus in London."

Besides the prime rib, house specialties included:

| | |
|---|---|
| Quiche Lorraine | $3.50 |
| Fish 'n' Chips | $3.50 |
| Eggs Casanova | $3.95 |
| French Pepper Steak | $9.50 |
| Barbecued Back Ribs—Maui Style | $6.95 |
| Broiled South African Lobster Tail | (Market Price) |

Marvin Cook was not quite finished expanding. In late 1969, he transformed a bar in Brooks Tower into a restaurant and bar that became known as Marvelous Marv's, a.k.a. Marv's Folly.

Stephanino, a northern Italian restaurant later converted to Los Dos on East Colfax Avenue and Milwaukee, rounded out the Cook family operations. Le Profile, also known as T. Michael's Le Profil, was around the corner from my Quorum Restaurant. While in fierce competition throughout the years, we also cooperated for publicity reasons as seen in a dated photo of Tony Cook and myself. At this writing, Michael Cook, ex-restaurateur, is a very successful stock-

Tony Cook (left) and a chef from Le Profile and Pierre (right) and a chef from the Quorum. *Courtesy, Tony Cook.*

broker, and I owe him my sincere thanks for material provided by him and for his personal help in getting facts for this article.

(P.S. to Michael: The Quorum lasted a little longer than your Profile!)

## Scotch 'n' Sirloin Salad Dressing

1 raw egg
1 cup olive oil
¼ cup wine vinegar
¼ pound Roquefort cheese
1 teaspoon finely chopped
　tarragon leaves
pinch of finely chopped
　chervil leaves
salt & fresh ground pepper to taste

pinch of English mustard
1 teaspoon Worcestershire
　sauce
3 tablespoons finely chopped
　parsley
½ teaspoon paprika
1 hard-boiled egg,
　chopped

1. Break egg in mixing bowl or blender and beat well.

2. Add oil and vinegar slowly and continue to beat; blend in Roquefort cheese and remaining ingredients.

3. Sprinkle the salad greens with hard-boiled egg; add dressing.

# Manhattan Café

**Manhattan Café  ~  16th and Market Streets, Denver**

The restaurant scene in Denver during the 1970s was one of fern bars (Zach's), cutesie themes (Northwoods Inn, Alpine Village Inn, Apple Tree Shanty) and some downtown oldies (Gaiety, Roosevelt Grill, the Albany, and one not-so-old favorite of many, Leo's Place).

It was about this time, after having been a waiter, bartender, and manager at various Denver operations during and after completing law school, that Larry Wright decided it was time to bring a New York City–style restaurant to Denver; thus began the roots of the Manhattan Café in lower downtown at 16th and Market streets. Wright had spent a couple of years in New York and missed the small, swank, and casually upscale houses of the Upper West and Upper East sides, Chelsea, Greenwich Village, and Gramercy Park areas.

In an 1893, renovated building owned by Wright and friends, he commenced the opening of a place that had a long, solid cherry bar on the side of the walk-down level; black and white tile floors; Halofone original lighting; bottle green stools, booths, and lower walls; light peach upper walls and ceilings; a piano at the entry with nightly music. Fresh seafood was the focus as Seattle Fish was half a block away and deliveries came by push cart. Colorado lamb, Black Angus beef, and free-range poultry were also featured. Ten to twelve wines by the glass were offered—the Manhattan was one of the first restaurants to do that in Denver. A large bouquet of fresh flowers sat at the end of the bar—another first in Denver.

With a liquor license in hand, the owners commenced construction at a furious pace in November of 1979, and the grand opening occurred on Saint Patrick's Day, March 17, 1980. As fate would have it, Leo's Place closed at the same time so RTD could take over the old

Cory Hotel for a turnaround mall station. The sad patrons of Leo's Place heard of the Manhattan and down they came—stockbrokers, attorneys, 17th Streeters. Business was terrific from the start. The Manhattan was the first to do fine dining—with a chef from the Culinary Institute of America in Hyde Park, New York—in the lower downtown area. The table clothes were fine old rose damask from the Denver Country Club after they changed décor. The art was focused on New York City—Central Park, the Chrysler Building, and the Dakota, with a few pieces of Erté as well.

Customers included Jack Lemmon, who spent an hour with Wright at the bar one night because Lemmon and his wife were having a tiff! Table 15 was his favorite on his multiple visits while in town performing. Another name of note, Debbie Reynolds, was performing at the Elitch Theatre and frequented the Manhattan Café. Table 6 was her choice—hidden around a corner and quite private. Raymond Burr never came in, perhaps due to the stairs being a challenge to his girth, but he did takeout a few times. Dionne Warwick was in twice and always had her back to the front door. She had to have Table 13!

The real success connection was with the many people and friends who lunched three times a week and did dinner once or twice a week. The *New York Times* twice featured the Manhattan Café over the years in their "What's Happening in Denver" column, saying it was the premier fresh seafood restaurant and one of the five best overall in town.

Because the size was small—eighty seats plus seventeen at the bar—Wright opened a piano bar on the first floor in early 1983 called Ivory's. It was pure Art Deco—murals on the wall of elegant Gatsbyesque parties, a marble-mantled fireplace, a small granite, rosewood, and ebony bar whose idea came from the first-class section of the old flagship Rotterdam of the Holland-American ship line Wright sailed on in the late 1960s. Many champagnes by the glass, single-malt scotches, single-batch bourbons, and specialty drinks allowed the hosts to hold people upstairs while the waitstaff turned downstairs tables for their reservation. Likewise, people could be moved up to the piano lounge to keep the dining turns flowing. This was the most romantic room in Denver; many a proposal occurred in the loveseats in front of the fireplace, including one bow-tied mayor of Aurora. This was that last-stop place after dinner, theater party, or game to hang and listen to Ellyn Rucker (five years), Mark Pressey (two years), and one lovely night with Dave Grusin, who played till dawn.

After nearly thirteen years of operation, Wright sold the Manhattan Café and Ivory's Piano Bar in July 1992.

*Contributed by Larry Wright*

*If a man be sensible and one fine morning, while he is lying in bed, count at the tips of his fingers how many things in this life truly will give him enjoyment, invariably he will find food is the first one.*

*—Lin Yutang*

# Queer Food Concoctions:
# Dishes in Darkest Denver

*Denver Times,* January 12, 1902

Chop suey, Chinese noodles, chile concarne and liverling!

Did you ever eat any of these dishes? There are but few people in the ordinary walks of life who have, and yet there are gallons and gallons of each consumed in Denver every day and night. The people who indulge in these gastronomic curiosities inhabit, for the most part, that section of the city known as the Tenderloin. The dishes are queer combinations and are either the dishes of some foreign country or the result of some culinary nightmare. Many of the people that eat them do not know how or with what they are made, but they are not epicures and the matter worries them little. The places where the mixtures are dispensed are called "joints," but they are not the kind that Carry Nation has had dealings with. There are only two of these joints above Larimer street in this city and these dispense chile concarne, which is getting to be very popular even among the business and domestic people. All the dishes are designed to taste good and to appease the appetite of their consumers. As long as they are up to these requirements, there are no questions asked. So satisfying are they, it is said to be impossible for a man to eat more than one bowl of chinese noodles without feeling overful.

Chile joints are scattered. There are two on Curtis street—one between Seventeenth and Eighteenth, conducted by a Mrs. Ellis, and one at Nineteenth and Curtis streets, conducted by J. N. McCrary. These places admit only white customers, but others in the city do not draw the color line.

There are many chile joints along Larimer street between Seventeenth and Twenty-eighth streets. They are crowded during the day, but the most business is done at night, when the places are thronged with people of all classes and colors. The places keep open all night and never at any hour lack patronage.

## Chile-Concarne

Chile concarne is a native of Mexico and is as ancient as that country. It is a kind of soup, made from beef, beans and chile peppers. The beef is cut into small squares and boiled into a broth: the beans are of the brown Mexican kind and are cooked separately and added after the broth is done. Chile enough to make it smart and burn is cooked in the broth. The whole is of a reddish-brown color and hot enough to make the uninitiated cry for water. There is a very appropriate name that has been given it by those who have tasted it. They jokingly call it "hell-fire stew." It is served in small bowls at 5 cents per bowl. One would think, upon seeing a bowl of chile for the first time that he could eat a dozen dishes; however, he will find that one or two at the most will appease the most vicious appetite.

Liverling is a new dish and is said to have originated in Denver. It is served in all the chile joints along Larimer street, and is said to be getting very popular. It is made of liver, white beans, onions and potatoes. The material is ground into a pulp, and cooked in water until it is a consistent jelly-like mass. When served it looks like apple butter. It is eaten mostly by colored people and is sometimes made more rich by the addition of a little fat bacon.

A liverling and chile joint is usually provided with a long counter and high stools. The dishes are served at the counter and are prepared behind a partition or in a kitchen that is not open for the inspection of the public. Men, women and children sit at the counter together and eat with tin spoons. They never remove their wraps and usually eat fast and ravenously. The price is 5 cents a dish.

The uptown joints for white people are styled parlors, and boast of several tables besides the counters. There are also private dining booths for ladies. Both the Curtis street places are clean, nicely furnished and have phonographs which grind out popular airs while you eat. Many people employed in offices and stores have acquired the chile habit and may be seen in the parlors daily. Liverling is not served in either Ellis or McCrary's parlors.

## In Chinatown

It is in the Chinese joints where the unusual and unique are met, and where all classes of society are wont to mingle. Noodles and chop suey attract hundreds—some on account of hunger, others on account of curiosity. The noodle-joints are in the heart of Chinatown. To reach them one must go through a dark passage between buildings on Market street between Twentieth and Twenty-first or through a dark alley between Market and Blake on Twenty-first street. There are many of them and each displays a sign bearing Chinese characters and the inscription in English: "Chop Suey and Chinese Noodles." The joints are usually found upstairs in buildings, the basements of which are devoted to the smoking of the dream pipe. Unless you are "wise" to the opium habit you can never get in on the ground floor. Any one can go upstairs where the dishes are served. The joint that does the biggest business is that of "Doc," a Chinese who formerly kept a Chinese doctor's office on Larimer street. He has several Chinese cooks who are said to be artists at preparing the dishes and his place has a reputation for cleanliness and courtesy. "Doc" says that chop suey is a stew of pork or chicken with eggs. It is covered with a dressing which resembles the frosting on a cake and is seasoned with Chinese nut oil. It ranges in price from 15 cents to $1 a bowl, the price depending upon the manner of its preparation and the materials used.

## Chinese Noodles

Chinese noodles are thinner than any other noodles. The dough is made of a mixture of rice and wheat flour. It is rolled out very thin. When the dough is rolled out so it covers a great deal of surface, it is rolled into a big spiral bundle, from which the noodles are cut. The cutting is done with a knife as big as a butcher's cleaver, and in such a manner that there are only two ends to a bowlful of noodles. If you could untangle the noodle in one bowl it would reach for several blocks. The dish is eaten by the Chinese with chopsticks and there are many Americans who have mastered the sharpened sticks, so that they can throw the noodles into their mouths as fast as they can swallow them. When the noodles are served they are covered with a layer of baked pork, chicken or egg. If the layer is pork or egg, or pork and egg, the price is 10 cents. When the layer is chicken the price is 25 cents. With every bowl a pot of tea is served. This tea is always the same, never stronger or weaker, never hotter or colder, but always of the purest, most appetizing flavor imaginable. The noodles are unseasoned and unflavored. A tiny dish of nut oil is served with the noodles and with this you may season them to taste. The bowls in which they are served are about twice the size of those in which you get chile, and in the bottom is placed a layer of Chinese onions.

A taste for all these dishes must be acquired, but when once acquired it amounts almost to a habit. When a man learns to eat noodles, a half-bowl usually tests his capacity, but after he has eaten them for a few weeks he can master a bowl. Two bowls is the record. No one except the Chinese themselves has ever been known to eat more than two bowls of the mess.

"Doc's" place is reached by a narrow stairway which runs from the alley. There is a turn in the stairway and after this is passed a glimpse of the cashier's desk is to be had. It is built like a counter and is covered with Chinese lottery drawings and writing materials. Behind it presides "Doc's" wife, who is considered, with one exception, the most beautiful Chinese woman in Denver. She collects the dimes and quarters after you have eaten. She has a good eye to business and has never been known to let anyone get away without paying.

When the top of the stairs is reached the whole dining room may be seen. There are tables and chairs strewn around regardless of order and in one end of the place is a stove. Chinamen in loose, greasy blouses and bare necks and shoulders are pitter-pattering about. They take your order in English and translate it into Chinese for the benefit of the cooks.

This place at one time was lighted with kerosene lamps and swinging Chinese lanterns, but "Doc" is progressive, so he had incandescents installed. They swing from the ceiling and are utilized by the industrious spiders as a foundation for their webs. "Doc" has a mania for clocks and there are clocks of all varieties hanging about the walls and perched on shelves. Some are running and some are not.

The Manhattan Restaurant OYSTERS . SEA FOODS . FISH

## Manhattan Restaurant  ⟋  1635 Larimer Street, Denver

I arrived in Denver in 1950, and as I inquired about the restaurant scene, the Manhattan Restaurant would often be mentioned as one of those great restaurants of the past. To quote Barry Morrison (*Denver Post*, 1966): "The Manhattan Restaurant was probably Denver's most famous steak house."

The restaurant was operated by an Englishman, Richard Pinhorn, from 1896–1922, located at 1635 Larimer Street. Pinhorn's policy: "The best possible food at the lowest possible price." After Pinhorn's death in 1922, the restaurant continued to operate under various owners until 1951. I was so busy building my career in 1950 to 1951 that I never quite made to the Manhattan. But the menu is priceless—almost literally!

Once upon a time, for 70 cents, you could get choice of tomato juice or fruit cup, small combination salad, plain steak charcoal broiled, French fried or shoestring potatoes, ripe kadota figs, pie, chocolate sundae or jello, hard rolls and butter, and coffee! And, if you were feeling really adventurous, you could substitute two lamb chops or a Spanish omelet for the steak.

Draught beer, notably Denver's own Tivoli Bock, was served "at the traditional time" for 5 or 10 cents, and you could dress up your dinner with a huge variety of side vegetables such as young radishes ($.10), minced onions ($.15), canned asparagus ($.30), or spinach with egg ($.15). Fruits, relishes, pastry, potatoes, sandwiches, and dairy dishes (bowl of cream, $.25) were equally plentiful.

# Bill of Fare

**Salad Dressing with Meat Orders 5 Cents Extra**
NO SERVICE LESS THAN 10c PER PERSON

## STEAKS, CHOPS, ETC.

| | |
|---|---|
| Plain Steak .45 | Lamb Chops (1) .25 |
| Short Cut Steak .55 | Lamb Chops (2) .45 |
| Sirloin Steak .80 | Lamb Chops (3) .60 |
| Tenderloin Steak .80 | Half Spring Chicken to order .50 |
| T-Bone Steak, for 1 or 2 1.30 | Half Spring Chicken a la Maryland .75 |
| Porterhouse, for 2 or 3 persons 2.25 | Bowl of Creole .40 |
| Family Porterhouse, served for 3 | Link Sausage .30 |
| or 4 persons (40 min., well done | Pork Chops (1) .25 |
| 50 min.) 3.00 | Pork Chops (2) .45 |
| Salisbury Steak .35 | Veal Cutlets .35 |
| Hamburger .35 | Veal Cutlets, Breaded .45 |
| Steaks with Spanish, extra .10 | Veal Cutlets, Breaded, Tomato |
| Bowl of Spanish .25 | Sauce .50 |
| Steaks with Onions, extra .15 | Liver and Bacon .40 |
| Steaks Stripped with Bacon, extra .10 | Liver and Onions .40 |
| Mushrooms with Steaks, extra .40 | Fried Calf's Liver .30 |
| Steaks a la Bordelaise, extra .25 | Fried Green Ham .35 |
| Steak Chicken Fried 10c Extra | Fried Bacon .35 |
| Orders Breaded, extra .10 | Welsh Rarebit .50 |
| Steaks Planked, per person, extra, .50 | Fried Tomatoes .35 |
| English Lamb Chop with Kidney, | Wilted Lettuce .25 |
| (30 min.) .80 | Cream Gravy .10 |

**Bread and Butter served with all Meat orders**

## EGGS AND OMELETS, ETC.

| | |
|---|---|
| Boiled Eggs (2) .15 | Half Portion Bacon and 1 Egg .25 |
| Fried Eggs (2) .15 | Spanish Omelet .35 |
| Shirred Eggs (2) .20 | Plain Omelet .20 |
| Scrambled Eggs (2) .15 | Parsley Omelet .25 |
| Poached Eggs, Plain (2) .20 | Ham Omelet .30 |
| Poached Eggs on Toast (2) .25 | Onion Omelet .30 |
| Poached Eggs, Vienna .45 | Jelly Omelet .30 |
| Ham and Eggs, Fried .35 | Cheese Omelet .30 |
| Half Portion Ham and 1 Egg .25 | Asparagus Omelet .45 |
| Bacon and Eggs Fried .35 | Mushroom Omelet .60 |

**Coffee or Milk 5 cents extra with all orders**

*As everybody knows, there is only one
infallible recipe for the perfect omelet:
your own.*

—*Elizabeth David*

# *McGaa Street Restaurant*

**McGaa Street Restaurant** ～ **1751–1761 Market Street, Denver**

The reason for featuring the story of this restaurant are the historical facts featured on the inside page of the restaurant's menu. To me, this was one of many priceless discoveries made during research at Denver's Public Library, and it says as much about Denver as it does about the McGaa Street Restaurant. It is reproduced verbatim here:

McGaa Street was the original name of Market Street. Named after William Denver McGaa, the first white child born in the region. [*Editor's note:* most other historical accounts suggest the street was named after William McGaa, senior, not his son.] McGaa, who was called Denver, was born March 8, 1859 at the S.E. corner of what is now 14th & Lawrence Streets.

McGaa's father, William, was born and educated in Dublin, Ireland. William McGaa was one of the first settlers of the newly founded (Sept. 24, 1858) town of St. Charles, which was located on the north side of Cherry Creek at Lawrence Street and 14th to Wynkoop Street northeast to about 21st Street.

The town was named St. Charles by Charles Nichols, who led a party of gold miners from Lawrence, Kansas, to the area. Soon the Nichols party left the area and returned home, planning to return in the spring. On November 1, 1858, gold-seekers settling on the south side of Cherry Creek founded the town of Auraria. (Auraria means "gold" or "golden" in Latin.) (Gold was first discovered in Cherry Creek in 1850 by Green Russell.) On Nov. 16, 1858 General William Larimer rode into Auraria leading a group of miners from Leavenworth, Kansas. Larimer found that the best land had already been taken, and so, in the middle of the night, he waded across Cherry

Creek and laid claim to the ground previously claimed by the St. Charles Company.

Gen. Larimer, a clever politician, named the town Denver, in honor of the governor of the Kansas Territory, James William Denver. Larimer was hoping for future considerations from the governor. The towns of Auraria and Denver soon became rivals. Cherry Creek divided them, though they developed a single street system. On April 23, 1859, William Byers founded the first newspaper in the region, the *Rocky Mountain News.* In order to sell his paper in both camps, Byers set up his office on stilts in Cherry Creek.

The unification of Auraria and Denver was effected on April 5, 1860, with a moonlight celebration on the newly completed Larimer Street bridge. The name of Denver was mutually agreed upon.

In 1866, McGaa Street was changed to Holladay Street in honor of Ben Holladay, owner of the Holladay Stage Lines, which was located at 15th (F) & McGaa (Holladay) Street. Later Holladay sold the stage lines to Wells Fargo.

Holladay Street from the 1700 to 2100 block was known in the 1880s as "The Row," which was the name given to the Red Light District. Friends of Holladay petitioned to have the name changed, not wishing to see the name of their honorable friend tarnished. Because many of the city's markets were located nearby, the name was changed to Market Street in 1889. Many of the plushest "Parlors" in the west were located on this historic street.

The first permanent building at this location (1751–1761 Market Street) was built in 1886 and was known as the European Hotel. It was a three-story building.

Records dating back to 1924 show that a grocery store was located at 1761 Market. In 1926 the Midway Hotel was located at 1759½ Market. In 1939 the name was changed to New Wyoming Hotel until 1948, when the top two stories of the building were torn down and the hotel closed.

Also in 1926, at 1755 Market, the Blythe Restaurant was opened. The restaurant closed in 1930. The famous Windsor Hotel stables were located in the rear of the building at 18th and Blake Street. In 1929 and 1930 the Liberal Church Mission was located at 1759 Market Street. In 1930 Richlow Manufacturing Company came into being, making syrups and candies, and located at 1751 Market. By 1950, Richlow occupied 1751–1759 Market Street until 1975.

## House Specialties
[*Includes trip to the soup and salad bar*]
### McGaa Steak Sandwich
*A tender Rib Eye marinated in a special House Sauce and broiled to perfection. Served with choice of steak fries, baked beans or side of spaghetti.*
**$3.50**
### Homemade Spaghetti
*With sausage or meat balls, as you like it.*
**$2.50**
### Fettucine Alfredo
Flat-wide egg noodles, coated with a light cream, cheese and egg sauce.
**$3.50**
### Braciole Plate
Italian delight rolled veal covered with our own recipe tomato sauce
**$4.00**
### Tortillini
For those with gourmet tastes. Served in the best restaurants in Rome.
**$4.00**

In 1934 at 1761 Market, Samuel Sileo opened a dance hall and restaurant. Sileo sold to Rudolph Kludge (Kludge Restaurant) in 1938.

In 1940 James Bertoni purchased the restaurant and renamed it the "Jail House Bar." The bar attracted some of Denver's most elite society. It contained wooden cells (booths), which lovely ladies let you in and out of with a huge wooden key. A door-man dressed as a jail guard stood at the entrance-way.

In 1950, the bar was sold again, and was named Lou's Restaurant & Bar. In 1951 the bar was called Helen's Bar, and in 1953, Marty's Bar & Restaurant. The bar was named "Gandi Dance" in 1959. In 1963, it was sold once again and was called Ross' Lounge.

In 1964, the location at 1761 was called the Banjo Club. Stripteasers were the main attraction for ten years. The club name was changed to Satan's in 1974 with strippers again the main attraction. The unique backbar is reportedly the second oldest in Colorado.

# Vice Ensnares Virtue:
# Police Break Up the Places
# Where Girls Halt Between

## *Denver Times,* May 17, 1902

*Restaurants Where Women Buy Drinks Must Take Out Licenses
and the Public Dancing Halls Must Close*

The fashionable restaurant which serves liquors to its patrons must take out a liquor license just the same as a saloon. The fire and police board made this order yesterday and probably half a dozen places will have to toe the mark.

The first restaurant notified was a swell eating house on Champa street. This is one of the most popular restaurants in the city. Beer and wines have been served with meals, but the place has never had a liquor license. Under the new order of the board the proprietors will either have to pay a license fee of $600 a year or stop serving liquors at meals. They have until tonight to decide what action they will take.

There are other restaurants which have not the reputation that this one has that may have to close when the order is enforced. Some of these are much worse than the lowest dive in the city. Under the guise of respectability they cater to a better class than is seen in the lower part of Denver, but they are responsible for more sin than any of the out and out winerooms. They keep on hand a stock of liquors and beers and serve them just as a saloon man would, only with a little more style. Women and girls, attracted to these places by their fine furnishings, take their first drink in them. Evil-minded men make them a headquarters.

Forced to secure a regular saloon license, it will be difficult to most of these places to exist, for then they will be placed on a par with the saloon, and the patrons of these restaurants do not go to saloons.

The police board has also decided to close the dance halls operated by "professors" after 9 o'clock each night. The fact that a number of young girls have been picked up on the street late at night drunk has forced this action to be taken. There are a number of so-called dancing academies in the city which are nothing more nor less than common dance halls. Dances are held two or three times each week, and the music can be heard until daylight. Women and girls are admitted free, but the men are required to pay a small fee. There is sin in these places.

Only a few nights ago a policeman found a girl 17 years old wandering on Larimer street. She was drunk. He was a humane man and after hearing her story sent her home. She had gone to a dancing academy. A young man she met there gave her beer. Then while her brain was affected she was forced to drink whisky.

The girl's story was told to the members of the police board and there will be no more sordid tactics at the so-called academies. Of course, legitimate institutions will not be molested.

*Drink! for you know not whence you came, nor why; Drink! for you know not why you go, nor where.*

—*Omar Khayyám*

# NAVARRE

**Navarre Restaurant** ～ **1727 Tremont Place, Denver**

During my working years, 1950 to 1990, we visited the Navarre on a number of occasions—a couple of times when Johnny Ott operated the restaurant, followed by visits during the years of William L. Winter and Peanuts Hucko. My wife, Jean, and I had a great time enjoying our dinners, visiting with Bill Winter and taking in the musical renditions by Peanuts Hucko. The Navarre was very popular, centrally located opposite the Brown Palace, and pleasantly decorated, with a warm atmosphere.

Looking at some of the dinner offerings:

| | |
|---|---|
| Anchovy-Larded, Prime Roast of Veal, with broiled tomatoes and farfel | $5.50 |
| Breast of Chicken, with Lobster Mousseline | $6.25 |
| Oyster Loaf, "The Peacemaker," peculiarly applicable to the Navarre's past, for two persons (This one has me mystified.) | $7.50 |
| Fowl du Jur [Jour], duck, goose, pheasant, quail, whatever the chef fancies in season, with appropriate accompaniments | $8.95 |
| Roast Loin of Colorado Pork, with sweet potato and pear casserole | $4.00 |

WELCOME VISITORS

## Luncheon — 1.10

Served from 11:30 A.M. to 2.30 P.M.
(Served in Private Dining Rooms, 10c Extra)

Choice of One:

Tomato Juice      Pineapple Juice      Menorah Wine
Glass of Sherry, Port, Sauterne, Burgundy or Muscatel

Vegetable Soup

Creamed Fresh Shrimp and Seafood a la Newburg
Fried Fillet of Sole, Tartar Sauce
Chilled Fruit Plate with Cottage Cheese
Minced Ham and Scrambled Eggs
Lamb Curry with Steamed Rice
Browned Roast Beef Hash, Mushroom Sauce
Chicken Giblets Saute, Spanish Rice
Italian Ravioli with Meat Sauce
Braisesd Shortribs with Brown Gravy

Swiss Cheese Sandwich on Rye, Cole Slaw

Hot Baked Ham Sandwich, Bun, Cole Slaw, French Fried Potatoes

Hamburger Sandwich on Bun, French Fried Potatoes, Cole Slaw

American Fried Potatoes           Green Beans

Peaches  or  Chocolate Pudding
or  Ice Cream  or  Pie

Coffee, Milk, Tea, Gingerale, Sweet Soda or Cola

SPECIAL — 1.20

Grilled Salisbury Steak, French Fried Potatoes, Mushroom Sauce

Drink and Dessert

From previous menus and word of mouth, these various Navarre restaurant operations were of high standards. It puzzles me greatly why none of these Navarre editions, from its establishment in 1879, had a lasting quality. Even most recently, the Western Art Museum that occupied 1727 Tremont Place ceased to exist. Is the place haunted?

But it appears that despite culinary achievements, the Navarre is best remembered for its raucous past. Most often mentioned is the rumor that a tunnel connected the venerable Brown Palace Hotel to Navarre across the street, where Messrs. Chase and Chucovich operated the Navarre as a "sporting house": first and second floor for gambling and third and fourth floor were operated as a brothel.

A drawing of the early Navarre, reproduced from the menu. *Courtesy, Denver Public Library collection.*

This excerpt from the Navarre's menu tells more of the story:

Twelve to fourteen grand and glorious years of profitable operation ensued until, in 1904, gambling and prostitution houses in the city were forced to close. Mayor Speer was in the process of cleaning up. The Navarre continued to operate as a dining establishment. Upstairs, illicit traffic went on, old-timers report, well into the second decade of the twentieth century.

Chase and Chucovich prospered so well from the location that their philanthropies were of momentous nature. The Slavic area of Chucovich's origin, in particular, benefitted. The original treasury of the kingdom of Yugoslavia was largely funded by his gifts. He and his heirs helped finance hospitals, orphanages, and schools in that country. His Denver attorney, Miss Mary Lathrop (renowned for her representation of Quakers in the Rocky Mountain area), was commissioned to write the kingdom's constitution and statutes.

With some people, food does not rank that high after all!

# NORMANDY
## restaurant français

### Normandy French Restaurant ∾ Colfax and Eudora
### and Colfax and Madison

I could never write this book without giving full credit for the success of the Normandy Restaurant to my cousin, Heinz Gerstle, and his wife, Irmgard. Heinz immigrated to the United States in 1948 and began his culinary career at various pastry shops and restaurants in New York and Connecticut. In the meanwhile, I had established myself at the Patio Restaurant in Littleton. I asked Heinz repeatedly to join me here in Denver. The opportunities seemed very ripe for a partnership at another restaurant. Thus, in 1957, Heinz made his move to the West. Heinz found employment at the old Argonaut Hotel's Empire Dining Room, located at Grant and Colfax, operated by Vic Hawkins in conjunction with his popular Senate Lounge. Ironically, in 1960 this was to become the home of my Quorum Restaurant.

Heinz, in the meanwhile, had scouted the area for a restaurant that might have been for sale and thus discovered the Normandy at Colfax and Eudora. Andre Delbec and Lucien Braque, two Belgians, founded the restaurant in 1952 and found the going very rough without a liquor license. They then sold the Normandy to a Texan, who put a six-foot sign of a cowboy on the Colfax side of the building, heralding that one could buy a Texas-size t-bone steak for a mere $1.99. This insult to French cuisine spelled the doom of the restaurant, and thus Heinz and I were offered the place for $8,500. This deal was closed, and so began a thirty-two-year partnership between Heinz and myself.

My cousin, Heinz Gerstle. *Photo by Maureen Harrington; courtesy, Denver Post, 1988.*

Irmgard Gerstle. *Courtesy, Denver Post, 1988.*

The charming old house became one of the most beloved restaurants in town. We applied for a liquor license and were granted one. We then converted the porch into a bar area and began to build a very respectable wine list and customer base. Business boomed, and after Heinz's marriage to Irmgard, the restaurant had two great personalities. In 1960, I opened the Quorum Restaurant and continued my partnership with Heinz.

In the early 1970s, Heinz had outgrown the old Normandy—besides we were tired of paying rent. Heinz found a site and an old house at Madison and Colfax and converted it into a splendid plant with a magnificent kitchen and very romantic dining rooms. As our menu explained it,

We were frequently asked, "Was this a converted home?" Decidedly: "Yes." A major portion of our main dining

# Normandy Opens with New Owner

Denver now has a small, intimate-type restaurant designed to encourage deep discussions after dinner or over extra cups of coffee. The roaring fire makes lingering comfortable as well as fun. 4900 E. Colfax Ave. is having its grand reopening this week under the ownership of Heinz Gerstle. He likes to see his patrons come early and stay late.

"There is a great field in Denver for this kind of an operation," he said, "where good food is prepared in a proper setting."

Gerstle believes he has that setting and setup.

The Normandy is the realization of a dream which started years ago in Nurenberg, Germany, where Gerstle was born and raised.

"I had my early cooking and baking apprenticeship there," he said.

His later training included the School of Hotel and Restaurant Management of New York University and lots of on-the-job training.

"I've worked at Luchow's in New York," he said, "as well as the Ambassador and Waldorf-Astoria Hotels."

Before coming to the United States he spent time working in London.

"I've noticed a number of differences in European and American eating habits," he said. "Food means more to people over there. Europeans tend to spend a lot more time eating than Americans would ever think of."

Gerstle wants to change all of that.

The Normandy will specialize in Roast Squab Chicken with Wild Rice and also Veal Steak, Marie Antoinette, as prepared by Chef Hans Marti, formerly of the Profile Room and the Town Club.

—Excerpted from *Rocky Mountain News*, Jan. 23, 1958, with permission

room, private dining room, and wine cellar was the former residence of the late Edwin and Emma Knauss. Records show the home was built in 1904.

The private dining room (upstairs) contained draperies and wall coverings from the former Hughes mansion. The solid oak buffet was formerly in the Richthofen Castle of Denver. Two antique leaded glass windows in the main dining room were made in France. Beveled glass in the

Heinz Gerstle (left) and Pierre (right) with Mayor Bill McNichols in front of the original house that became the new Normandy, with plans for remodeling. *Wolfe collection.*

dining room dividers were antique, but their origin unknown.

The extensive collection of interiors, furnishings, and original woodwork were designed to complement the "country inn" ambience and old-world charm of our restaurant.

At the new location, the Normandy Restaurant flourished even more. I am hard pressed to recall all the prominent, loyal patrons of the Normandy, as well as important visitors from all parts of the world. (The original site of the Normandy was converted to Tante Louise, today operated by Corky Douglass.)

Aside from the romantic ambience, the Normandy featured one of the finest wine lists in the area. The legendary Chateau Lafite was a conversation piece, but the reputation of the Normandy rested on its food and service.

The next ten years were most enjoyable at the Normandy, serving old friends and making new ones. My involvement with the run-

View of the remodeled Normandy. *Wolfe collection.*

ning of the operation was minimal, mostly entertaining friends and stepping in when warranted. In April of 1990, the Quorum served its last meal, and at the same time, Heinz decided that thirty-two years of running a restaurant was quite enough, and thus the Wolfe family purchased the Gerstles' interest in the Normandy. My daughter, Karen Michelle Herrmann, became the general manager, and added her own personality to the restaurant.

Interior view of the Normandy dining room. *Wolfe collection.*

# lES gRillAdES

**Chauteaubriand Bouquetiere** (for two)
the gourmet's cut of tenderloin prepared to your taste and
surrounded by a colorful assortment of vegetables

Quotation
on
Request

**Carre D'Agneau** (for two)
**"Aux Fines Herbes"**
broiled rack of choice lamb seasoned with a mixture of fine herbs
and Dijon mustard; served with a bouquet of vegetables. mint
sauce served on the side. we recommend this item to be served
"medium" (pink).

Quotation
on
Request

**Tournedos Grille** "Monsieur Louis"................10.95
two broiled pieces of beef tenderloin set on artichoke bottom,
topped with mushroom caps, Bearnaise and a light Burgundy
sauce, we garnish the platter with a half tomato, au gratin.

> *"Monsieur Louis" was Louis Thomasi, the venerable sommelier
> at restaurant "La Pyramide" in Vienne, France. his love for
> a very good wine with tender broiled meat was legendary.
> this dish is a toast in his honor.*

**Filet de Boeuf** "Wellington" .......................11.95
**sauce bearnaise**
broiled tenderloin of beef in baked pastry, a la Wellington.
this item may be ordered as Filet Mignon without the pastry crust

**Steak au Poivre Grille**
**comme a notre creation**............................11.75
broiled pepper steak served with a bouquet of vegetables
and crushed spicy Java pepper.

> † this item may be ordered without pepper sauce.

In the year 2000, our family decided to accept an offer to sell the
building and grounds of the 1515 Madison location, retaining the
Normandy French Restaurant, Inc. This decision was predicated on
the fine offer we received, as well as consideration for Karen Michelle
and her family. Karen had given birth to adorable twins in 1998 and
already had a son, eight years of age at the time of this writing. It be-

Pierre and son, Ronald, cooking for the "goose festival." *Wolfe collection.*

came increasingly difficult to be a mother to her children or have a family life. The rest is restaurant history.

Especially for devoted fans of Normandy cooking, here are some classic recipes.

## Frog's Legs Sauté à la Provençale
*2 servings*

3 pairs frogs' legs, thawed
½ cup butter or oil
¼ cup consomme

2 cloves garlic, crushed
1 peeled tomato, fresh
salt, pepper, parsley

1. Sauté the frogs' legs in butter, as you would with chicken. When nicely browned, drain off part of the fat. Add the consommé and simmer until the liquid reduces by half.

2. Add chopped crushed garlic, chopped tomato, salt and pepper, and a sprinkling of parsley. Simmer about 5 minutes over low heat.

## Veal Scallopini Marsala

*2 servings*

| | |
|---|---|
| ½ tablespoon minced garlic | 4, 3-ounce slices of veal |
| ½ tablespoon minced shallots | ¼ cup consommé |
| ½ tablespoon chopped | 2 tablespoons Marsala wine |
|   green onions | salt & pepper to taste |

1. Heat some butter in a skillet. Add garlic, shallots, and green onions.

2. Sauté veal in the skillet; add consommé and wine. Simmer for 2 minutes. Sprinkle a little flour into the skillet to thicken the sauce.

## Potato Pancakes

*6–8 servings*

| | |
|---|---|
| 3 medium potatoes, grated | ¼ cup flour |
| ½ onion, grated | salt & pepper to taste |
| 1 tablespoon parsley, chopped | 1 egg |

1. Drain water off the potatoes and onion. Place in a convenient mixing bowl. Add all other ingredients and blend well.

2. Spoon into hot frying pan and fry until done on both sides.

## Zabaglione

*6 servings*

| | |
|---|---|
| 6–8 eggs, separated | ⅓ cup powdered sugar |
| 1 cup sweet Marsala wine | ½ lemon rind, grated |

1. Beat egg yolks in top of double-boiler. Beat in wine, sugar, and lemon rind. Continue beating over hot water until slightly thick.

2. Now beat egg whites until stiff. Fold egg yolk and wine mixture slowly into egg whites. Place some marinated strawberries at the bottom of goblets; top up with Zabaglione. Serve chilled or warm.

# Her Father's Daughter

I would not be Pierre Wolfe if I did not brag about my daughter, Karen Michelle Wolfe Herrmann. Karen's interest in the restaurant business began in her early teens. It was beyond me why my lovely daughter would seriously pursue a restaurant career. Long hours and work on holidays were hardly suitable to form a family and have a life. Karen worked just about every position at my Quorum Restaurant when her schooling permitted it. She began "bussing," cashiering, waiting tables, and hosting while Dad and Mom were traveling, and she trained in the Quorum kitchen. While attending Colorado State University, Karen Michelle pursued a food science degree, and upon graduation, we arranged for her to go to France to study French and get her first experience away from home—of all places in a three-star Michelin Guide restaurant, L'Ousteau de Baumaniere in Les Baux de Provence.

This marvelous background in the restaurant business made Karen Michelle a prime candidate to operate the Normandy French Restaurant. As general manager, Karen added her own personality to the restaurant and directed the food into the 1990s. Young chefs were hired, and the menu of the Normandy took on a decidedly contemporary French twist. In 1992, Chez Michelle opened in the front part of the Normandy. This bistro offered affordable French cuisine from the provinces. Karen maintained the superlative wine list of the Normandy, including the rarest and greatest of fine French wines—two bottles of Chateau Lafite 1870 Premier grand cru Pauillac, bottled by Cruse & Co. Bordeaux. Here's the write-up on this extraordinary wine:

> Original wooden case opened December 12, 1977. Case markings and tag read: "Purchased 1879." Straw sleeves,

white tissue wrapping, unusual deep punt special Bordeaux bottles with applied glass shoulder seals embossed, "Chateau Lafite Grand Vin," gold capsules, long corks, elegant calligraphic Cruse labels and wire mesh, wine color is brilliant deep garnet red. . . . These bottles were purchased by us at the Heublin rare wine auction on May 28, 1980. These bottles are mid-shoulder full and are believed to be in excellent condition. We do not guarantee the contents.

In 1995, Bill St. John wrote a feature on prominent women chefs in the Denver area for the *Rocky Mountain News* entitled, "Right Where They Belong." Here is his write-up on Karen Michelle:

> Fond memories of food often call to mind our mothers. It was their hands that first fed and nurtured most of us.
>
> But in restaurants it isn't women who feed us as much as men. Only one of five U.S. restaurant owners is a woman. Women executive chefs are even more scarce. . . .
>
> Karen Michelle Wolfe Herrmann operates Normandy French Restaurant, at East Colfax Avenue and Madison Street, and its smaller space, Chez Michelle, 1515 Madison St. She is the daughter of retired Denver restaurateur Pierre Wolfe, owner of the former Quorum restaurant. She has one son, Christopher, age 2.
>
> "I actually moved away to learn the business. I didn't want to work with Dad; I needed to learn from others. I've worked everywhere: in France at L'Ousteau de Baumaniere, and in Cincinnati, Hawaii, and Chicago, where I opened up a bunch of restaurants.
>
> "I took over the Normandy at the end of 1989. Running a restaurant is like being on stage every day. The curtain goes up when the dining room opens. The actors are the staff. People come in to eat, but they also come for entertainment.
>
> "It's difficult for me to tell people 'I'm Karen Wolfe and this is my restaurant.' When you go to the Tante Louise, you know who Corky (Douglass, owner) is. He is very definitely a figurehead in his restaurant. Everyone knew who Pierre (Wolfe) was in his restaurant.

Karen Michelle with one of her culinary creations. *Courtesy, Denver Post, 1985.*

"But I have not yet found a way to say, 'This is my restaurant; welcome to my place.' I wish I could do that.

"Still, it's fun to run a restaurant. You meet new people every day, you get to move around and talk to people and really enjoy them. Usually they're in a great mood when they're going out to dinner and, so, they're fun to be around.

"For me, it's a lot of fun to run a restaurant in my hometown. Friends come in and it's just wonderful to have that kind of rapport.

"My biggest challenge is being married, having a child and running the Normandy. It's three jobs in one. I remember, before Christopher was born, when an employee would call in with a sick child and not want to work. I didn't understand her. Now, I do."

Karen Michelle Wolfe Herrmann called me on Christmas Day 2000 and said, "Dad, thank you for selling the Normandy! I have never celebrated Christmas Day at home with our family on our busiest day of the year at the restaurant." Karen Michelle is now a very happy mother of three children.

# OHLE'S
## Deli-Restaurant

**Ohle's Deli-Restaurant**  **1520 East Colfax Avenue, Denver**

If any deli-restaurant deserves mentioning, it is Ohle's.

My family members—wife Jean, son Ronald, and daughter Karen Michelle—owe their exposure to Ohle's deli goods to my addiction to German cold cuts! Among my favorites: blood sausage, blood and tongue, headcheese, braunschweiger, and all kinds of salamis. Our Sunday brunch routinely consisted of the above-mentioned delicacies, as well as a variety of smelly cheeses such as Limburger and Harzer. Unsuspecting guests at this Sunday affair had their problems with my taste. What, no ham and eggs or pancakes? My friends loved the food at my restaurant but had their problems with my Sunday brunch offerings. Oh well—Americans!

I recently read a story entitled "Limburger Jinks." Some kids thought up this prank: open the hood of a car and place a hunk of Limburger on the engine block of an unsuspecting car owner. As the motor heats up, the cheese melts, releasing its pungent aroma as the driver motors down the highway. You could have done this to my car anytime. It depends on what you grow up with.

When Ohle's closed, the Ohle family sent the following letter to their faithful customers:

This is an open letter to all of our customers and friends who have helped make our business a success. In the past two months you have shared with our family in celebrating our 60th year in business.

It began in 1928 when Ernst and Esther Ohle opened their first store at 17th and Pearl (it was just a little hole in the wall), then to 828

# Sandwiches

*(Sandwiches are made to order — not readymade)*
Choice of dark or light rye, white or wheat bread, or hardroll
All sandwiches come with potato chips & pickle slices

|  | | reg. | jumbo |
|---|---|---|---|
| 1. | Beerwurst | 2.29 | 3.29 |
| 2. | Egg Salad (homemade) | 2.29 | 3.29 |
| 3. | Chicken Salad (homemade) | 2.29 | 3.29 |
| 4. | Tuna Salad (homemade) | 2.29 | 3.29 |
| 5. | Yachtwurst | 2.29 | 3.29 |
| 6. | Blood and Tongue | 2.29 | 3.29 |
| 7. | Salami | 2.29 | 3.29 |
| 8. | Braunshweiger | 2.29 | 3.29 |
| 9. | Roast Beef | 2.29 | 3.29 |
| 10. | Corned Beef | 2.29 | 3.29 |
| 11. | Pastrami | 2.29 | 3.29 |
| 12. | Ham and Swiss | 2.29 | 3.29 |
| 13. | Smoked Turkey | 2.29 | 3.29 |
| 14. | Reuben | 2.89 | 3.75 |
| 15. | Evergreen Sandwich | 2.79 | 4.05 |
| 16. | Westphalian Ham | 2.98 | 4.98 |

## EXTRAS

| | reg. | jumbo |
|---|---|---|
| Sprouts | 25¢ | 50¢ |
| Tomatoes | 25¢ | 50¢ |
| Domestic Cheese | 25¢ | 50¢ |
| *(Swiss, American, Cheddar, Muenster, Provalone)* | | |
| Imported Cheese | 50¢ extra | 1.00 |
| *(Tilset, Havarti, Bianco, Edam)* | | |
| Avocado | 50¢ extra | 1.00 |

East Colfax (which wasn't much bigger) then on to our present location for the past 25 years. Ernst and Esther were known for their compassion toward their customers. Immigrants came to them for help. They got them jobs; helped find them homes; or just were friendly faces who could speak their numerous languages. To this day, we still hear people tell us how much they helped them when they first came to this country.

Ernst died 25 years ago, but he would have been proud of what his family has done with his business. Esther (better known as

Grandma Ohle) is still working five days a week. She just celebrated her 92nd birthday on February 21st. Ohle's was the focal point of our family. We have always kept with Ernst's values of running a business; honesty and quality.

Ernie's family (second oldest son) took over the deli in 1983. His wife, Ila, and three of their children (Bob, Martye, and Debbie) are still running the business. Ernie passed away three years ago. After his death it was not the same around Ohle's. He was the backbone of the business. Everyone liked him. He was very personable and had time for everyone. It's great that everyone thought so highly of him. He taught us a lot about people and business the old fashioned way.

On April 15th, Ohle's will close the doors for good. Our lease is up and after 60 years it's time to say good-by to the deli business and hello to a new phase in our lives. We will all keep plenty busy with our other businesses, Colorado Soccer Camps, Ohle's Gifts, Trophies and Engraving and "The Little Angel Collection" children's clothing.

The closing of Ohle's will be an end of an era, a part of East Denver's history for 60 years. We've made many friends throughout the years. We've shared our customer's friendship, their joys and sorrows, their good times and their bad times. Ohle's has been a lot of fun and a lot of work but it's been an experience we will never forget.

To all of the deli owners out there, take care of our customers. Treat them well and they will be your customers for years to come. Listen to them and enjoy their friendships, from the very young to the very old. They all have precious memories to share. It only takes an extra minute or two.

So this is our farewell letter to all of you. Come in and say good-by. We will miss you.

From all of us at Ohle's

*Ila, Bob, Debbie, Martye, and Grandma Ohle*

**Patio Restaurant** ~
**Belleview and South Santa Fe**
**Drive, Littleton**

In 1952, Joe Sperte, then manager of Green Gables Country Club, recommended me for the chef position at the Patio Lamaze in Littleton, later renamed the Patio Restaurant. James Blankenship was the owner. The restaurant was not doing well, due to a number of changes in kitchen personnel. But Jim was a great promoter and knew how to get publicity for his newly arrived chef. In later years, I would adopt some of Jim's affinity for attracting the news media and famous people. But Blankenship had plans to move on to Las Vegas and tried to persuade me to come along, which I refused.

In 1954, Bob Allphin and brother-in-law, Vic Hawkins, took over the Patio. Poor business practices brought the Patio to its knees, and I was offered the opportunity by the landlord, Carroll Quelland, to become lessee of the operation. Carroll, however, cleverly kept the liquor operation for himself, which made it very hard for me to make a go of things on food alone. With hard work and determination, long hours in the kitchen, a fine staff of African American waiters, many of whom had formerly served on the railroads, and others from the Air Force Finance Center, part-timing at night, we succeeded. Joe Hamilton, an imposing six-footer, was our captain. To see him drop an egg into the Caesar salad bowl from his lofty height was a show worth watching. Ira Martin, from a poor family, would become everyone's darling. He cooked a mean Steak Diana tableside, a dish that in

**Christmas Treat for Starry Night**
Pierre Wolfe of Littleton cooked up a special "brown mash" for his thoroughbred race horse, Starry Night, Christmas morning. Wolfe, who owns the horse with Arkie McIntosh, Littleton businessman, were well pleased when Starry Night won four races in 1957 and earned $5,510. *Courtesy, Denver Post, 1957.*

later years at the Quorum would become our signature dish. We served tasty lobster, shrimp, and crabmeat canapés prepared tableside as well as Frog Legs and Lobster Sauté Cardinale. Crepes Suzette, Cherries Jubilee, individual Baked Alaskas, and Soufflé Grand Maniere were show stoppers!

The Patio was a unique restaurant. Its location opposite the Centennial Racetrack made it a popular meeting place for horse-racing enthusiasts, gamblers, and bookies, including prominent members of the Smaldone clan. They celebrated various "comings-out" and "goings-in" to the penitentiary. Francis Smaldone, son Eugene, Checkers, and other well-known Denver crime lords became good Patio customers. Later, at the opening of my Quorum Restaurant in 1960, a warm embrace by Francis and an enthusiastic greeting by a party of ten Smaldones caused consternation among my patrons. Who could blame them?

The Patio was also frequented by jockeys scheming to fix a race for "get-away money." I also owned a racehorse called Starry Night and had great fun racing my horse all over the country. Starry Night earned enough money to pay the hay bill and "Heavy Hulse," the trainer. Many customers of the Patio wanted to know when Starry

## ALL DINNERS ARE COMPLETE

### APPETIZERS

Chef Pierre presents

shrimp patio ... .90    marinated herring, sour cream --- .70    creamed vichysoisse-- .40
chicken livers, maison... .60    artichokes, a la greque ... .70    tomato or orange juice
shrimp or crabmeat cocktail --- .75    fruit cocktail, cottage cheese... .50    soup du jour
crepes neptune (delicate french pancakes, creamed seafood, hollandaise sauce) - 1.00
onion soup du chef    jellied consommé, madrilene ... .40

caesar salad
   serves two --- 2.00    |    tossed green salad or head lettuce
               thousand island --- roquefort --- oil and vinegar

### SEAFOOD ELEGANCIES
ENTREE INCLUDES SOUP, SALAD, DESSERT and BEVERAGE

fresh colorado mountain trout, sauteed in butter ------------------------ 2.75
curry of shrimp or lobster a l'indienne, chutney sauce ------------------ 3.50
frog legs, fine herbs, lemon butter ------------------------------------ 3.50
lobster sauté cardinale, cooked in white wine, chives and tomatoes -------- 3.50
south african lobster tail, maitre d'hotel ------------------------------ 3.50

### FOWL
chicken jerusalem, sauce suprême, rhine wine, artichokes, mushrooms -------- 3.25
le coq au vin ~ rooster in burgundy wine, baby onions, carrots, potatoes ---------- 3.25
breast of spring chicken gourmet, mushroom sauce, wild rice -------------- 3.75
long island duckling, bigarade orange sauce, cointreau, tangerine slices -------- 3.50

### BEEF DELICACIES
brochette of tenderloin (shishkebab)
     skewered filet, mushrooms, onions, tomatoes, green peppers ------------ 3.25
slices of tenderloin, sauteed in butter, fresh mushrooms, au jus ------------- 3.50
tournedos rossini
     two cuts of the heart of filet, red wine mushroom sauce, paté de foie gras ------- 3.75
filet of beef strogonoff, sour cream, mushroom sauce, sherry wine, brown rice ------- 3.50

### STEAKS
new york cut sirloin steak, charcoal broiled --- 4.00    |    special baked potato ---
filet mignon, charcoal broiled ---------------- 4.25    |    sour cream, chives | for two
chateaubriand, double filet steak, for two -- 8.50    |    parmesan cheese | 1.00

### PREPARED AT YOUR TABLE
chicken livers, au sherry --- 3.25        steak diana, sauce diablo -- 4.25
        parisian chicken -- 3.50

### DESSERTS
ice cream, sherbet, sundaes    pies --- .25    cheese pie --- .40    french pastry -- .25
crepes suzettes --- 1.50    baked alaska (for two) --- 2.50    fresh strawberries --- .25
souffle grand maniere (no less than two) ----- 3.00    cherries jubilee --- 1.25
camembert, liederkranz or roquefort --- .25

       coffee ~ tea ~ iced tea

Night was going to win. Heavy's answer was, "He's eatin' good."
Would you bet on the appetite of a horse? Go figure!

The Billy Wilson Trio, who had formerly performed at the Wolhurst Country Club for Eddie Jordan, along with Bill Bastien on bass

To The Chef —
Best wishes
D____ __ _____ ____

*Patio Lamaze*

Press Party

*Honoring*

# The Eisenhower Family

★
★ ★
★ ★

Colorado Celery Bowl

★★★★★

Shrimp Patio Lamaze

★★★★★

Onion Soup Ala Francaise

★★★★★

Denver Tossed Salad

★★★★★

Filet of Beef Poele Perigourdine
or
Boneless Roast Squab Chicken
Wild Rice Dressing

★★★★★

Pommes Chateau
Bouquetiere of Fresh Vegetables
Broccoli Au Gratin

★★★★★

Pineapple Mephisto

LITTLETON, COLORADO

Souvenir menu, printed on silk, from a special dinner for the Eisenhower family, held at the Patio. Note the president's signature at top. *Wolfe collection.*

and Mickey McGee on the guitar, brought dinner dancing to the Patio. From his vantage spot on the stage, Billy surveyed the crowd, winked at the ladies, and played the hell out of his accordion! For birthdays and anniversaries, Billy had a special song: "Stick out your can here comes the garbage man"! Billy repeatedly told me that he also closely observed my "working the room" as host, which would help him in later years at the Tally Ho Supper Club in Lakewood.

Ray Baker of KOA radio decided to pick up the Billy Wilson Trio music from 11:00 P.M. to midnight live from my Patio Restaurant. People driving toward Denver from other states and those cruising Colorado would follow the fine music right to our restaurant. Dinner dancing gave us a huge lift in business.

Among the celebrity visitors to the Patio was Anita Ekberg and her party, enjoying Pierre's tableside preparation. *Wolfe collection.*

The Patio became the place to see and be seen. Robert Six and Bill Daniels held private parties at my place. Ethel Merman and Audrey Meadows were seen frequently. Phil Harris and Alice Faye loved the Patio. President and Mamie Eisenhower along with family members frequented my restaurant. Jimmy Stewart and Audie Murphy became my friends. These were just a few well-known persons to visit us often. But the main corps of loyal customers came from Bowmar, Cherry Hills, and, of course, Denver.

But the most significant event took place in the summer of 1956. I met Jean Brown, who became my wife in 1960. Jean, throughout all my years in the restaurant business, gave me the utmost support and two fine children. (There's more about this remarkable lady in the story on the Quorum.)

The food at the Patio took on a form of a theatrical production, as many dishes were cooked in chafing dishes tableside. Morris Crawford along with Walter Clark, Bill Jackson, Don Thally, Vernon Baskerville, Ira Martin, and one-eyed Sammy followed me to the Quorum when I left the Patio on December 31, 1959. There was not one sober staff member on that New Year's Eve after we had finished serving. We joined a great crowd—some stayed well beyond normal closing time. My eight years at the Patio gave me a terrific start at what followed, the opening of the Quorum Restaurant on October 4, 1960.

For old time's sake, here's a recipe for my famous Steak Diane. Prepare it at your own risk!

## Pierre's Steak Diane
*2 servings*

4, $3\frac{1}{2}$-ounce trimmed sirloin strips, $\frac{1}{2}$-inch thick
$\frac{1}{2}$ teaspoon Poupon mustard
Worcestershire sauce
$\frac{1}{4}$ teaspoon fresh ground pepper
$\frac{1}{4}$ teaspoon fresh shallots and garlic mixture
$\frac{1}{2}$ cup sliced mushrooms
$\frac{1}{4}$ cup finely chopped green onions
1 ounce Cognac (for flaming)
1 cup basic brown sauce

1. Have your butcher cut strip sirloins into $\frac{1}{2}$-inch thick slices and remove all fat and sinew, resulting in small steaks weighing about $3\frac{1}{2}$ ounces each (2 steaks per person).

2. Prepare to sauté the steaks by slightly covering each steak with the Poupon mustard, a few drops of Worcestershire sauce, and the fresh ground pepper. Set aside.

3. Sauté garlic mixture, mushrooms, and onions lightly. Add the steaks to the ingredients already sautéed. Cook to desired doneness and flame with Cognac. Add the brown sauce and serve at once, spooning mushrooms, onions, and sauce over the steaks.

# The Restaurant Hall of Fame

To be inducted into the Restaurant Hall of Fame by your peers is indeed a great honor. My family and I were particularly elated that my good friend and fellow restaurateur, Ed Novak, gave my induction speech on April 10, 2000. Here is the text of that speech:

> One of the most exciting and significant events in your life is when you participate in honoring one of your friends— I am here tonight to honor my friend, Pierre Wolfe.
>
> Pierre was born in the Alsace region of France, trained at the Hotel School in Lausanne, Switzerland, and then worked aboard Cunard Cruise ships in the Mediterranean Sea.
>
> Pierre has been guest chef and lecturer on dozens of cruise ships since—as a matter of fact, I went on a cruise with Pierre last year—he was fantastic and a big hit.
>
> Pierre came to the United States in 1950 and attended the University of Denver, studying hotel and restaurant management. His first job in Denver was as a sous chef at the Brown Palace Hotel.
>
> Being an entrepreneur, he soon opened his own restaurant, the Patio, in Littleton. This is where he fell in love and married his wife, Jean.
>
> In 1958, Pierre and his cousin, Heinz Gerstle (who, by the way, is also a Hall of Fame recipient), purchased the old Normandy Restaurant, which then became Tante Louise. They moved to the location at Colfax and Madison in 1972.
>
> Pierre opened the Quorum Restaurant in 1960 and, being across the street from the State Capitol building, it

became a legend for legislative meetings and gourmet dining.

Pierre, Jean, and their daughter, Karen, for ten years ran the Normandy and Chez Michelle restaurants, where they won every culinary award known.

Many of us enjoy Pierre on his popular radio and television shows. Presently, his radio show called "America's Dining and Travel Guide" is broadcast on sixty-six stations across the United States. He also hosts a wonderful radio travel show locally called "The Good Life."

Pierre is on the advisory boards of the Culinary Program of the Art Institute of Colorado and the ACF Culinarians of Colorado.

Pierre is well known for his energy and enthusiasm, respected for his personal hospitality, and appreciated for his love of our industry.

As we induct him into this year's Colorado Restaurant Hall of Fame, please help me welcome my friend, Mr. Pierre Wolfe.

Pierre (left) receiving Hall of Fame plaque from friend and fellow restaurateur, Ed Novak. *Wolfe collection.*

# QUORUM
## RESTAURANT
### DENVER

**Quorum Restaurant, a.k.a. Pierre's Quorum** ⌖ **Colfax Avenue and Grant Street, Denver**

Not in my wildest dreams could I imagine that I would spend thirty years in the Argonaut Hotel at Grant and Colfax, running an upscale restaurant. This once highly regarded residential hotel was a sorry sight. Owner–manager Henry Schwalbe and his flamboyant wife, Thelma, used all their persuasion to convince me to come by to look at the Empire dining room in the Argonaut, the selected site for my restaurant. But the Schwalbes were very convincing. They would remodel the lobby of the hotel, create a separate entrance, put a new front on the building, build a banquet facility, and hire an architect to accomplish what I deemed to be "Mission Impossible."

While considering the Schwalbes' offer, I drove by the Argonaut on a number of occasions and each time I had more doubts. Just looking at the place gave me the shivers! This all took place in early 1959. Enter Dick Crowther, respected Denver architect. Soft-spoken, knowledgeable, capable Dick created a rendering that only in my wildest dreams could I imagine this old dump could be converted to become one of Denver's finest restaurants. The color scheme of red and black was very "in." The regal booths in black, cherry wood walls, designer red carpet adorned with black octagonal shapes, beautiful light fixtures, velvet drapes with purple, orange, and gold stripes, and windows with a view of our State Capitol across the street. I was hooked! 1959 was the year of great decisions: to leave the Patio

# AN EPICUREAN REPAST

Pierre Wolfe
suggests
VINS

APPETIZER                                      PIESPORTER

SCOTCH EGGS

CONSOMME MADRILENE

HEART OF PALM SALAD RAVIGOTTE                  MEDOC


TOURNEDO, MONT BLANC

Center slice of beef tenderloin nested in
a pastry shell topped with bernaise sauce

POMMES DAUPHINE                                POMMARD

Potato mixed with eggs, fried to golden
puffs

BROCCOLI, AMANDINE


DESSERT                                        PORT

ORANGES, GRAND MARNIER

Sliced fresh oranges prepared with
slivered orange rind and liqueurs


FOUR DOLLARS PAR PARSONNE


Restaurant, to build the Quorum, and to marry Jean Brown, my loving and supportive wife, a school teacher from Connecticut.

Bar service at the Quorum would be provided by Vic Hawkins, then operator of the Senate Lounge across the lobby of the Argonaut, a watering hole for lobbyists and legislators. But the Senate Lounge was also a very popular jazz club, thus attracting a great evening crowd. Effie, the Blonde Tigress, played the piano in the Senate Lounge, showing off a diamond in her tooth and a pronounced cleavage. My sister, Suzanne Joshel, who along with her husband, Lloyd, was responsible for persuading me to come to Denver, and with whom I resided for ten years, were helping me make decisions.

Postcard rendering of the old Argonaut hotel, facing the northeast corner of the State Capitol grounds. *Wolfe collection.*

Suzanne came up with the name Quorum, and Lloyd gave me sound financial advice, as well as lots of mental support.

The Quorum opened in the fall of 1960, around the corner from the prominent Profile Room. The restaurant was an instant success. The menu comprised many tried-and-true dishes from the Patio Restaurant in Littleton, including Casserole Neptune, chunks of lobster, crabmeat, and shrimp in a mild Mornay sauce; Duckling Bigarade, duck in orange liqueur sauce; Tournedos Rossini with foie gras; and our Steak au Poivre, pepper steak. My loyal waiters, now veterans from nine years at the Patio, were very adept at tableside preparation. Caesar Salad prepared tableside, the outrageous Steak Diane that for years dazzled the diners, and Crepes Suzette were some of the Quorum's specialties.

The wine list for those days could be considered one of the finest in the city. Along with fine wine came the cream of the crop of clientele. Pat Hanna, then *Rocky Mountain News* writer, spotted on one evening Richard Kaye of Lloyd's Furs, Attorney and Mrs. Gail Ireland, State Senator and Mrs. Sonny Mapelli, Mr. and Mrs. John (Luke) Hayden, Mr. and Mrs. Myron Neusteter, and King Schwayder. The Quorum served Denver's elite and many foreign dignitaries. Presidents and their entourages, movie stars, governors, mayors, and

# No Evidence McCartney's Ex Lived in Denver

**Question:** While reading a book about Linda McCartney, they mentioned that Paul and his then-girlfriend Jane Asher rented a home in Denver while Jane was acting somewhere here or in the surrounding area. Could you find out more on this home? —*Littleton fan*

**Answer:** No amount of prowling through dusty, 35-year-old stories in the newspaper's library could unearth any references to Jane Asher ever actually living in Denver while dating Paul McCartney. However, she did celebrate her 21st birthday here, and Paul showed up for the party. It was April 5, 1967, and Asher was about to start a three-day performance with the Bristol Old Vic Shakespearean troupe. The private party for about 30 people was in a room at the old Quorum Restaurant, across the street from the state Capitol.

—Reprinted from "Wacky Questions" column by Rebecca Jones, *Rocky Mountain News*, Mar. 25, 2001, with permission

Paul McCartney (white jacket) attends a birthday party for girlfriend Jane Asher and friends at the Quorum Restaurant. (Pierre, center, standing). *Courtesy, Denver Post, 1967.*

## LES GRILLADES

"For The Trusting"      *17.50*
The Chef de Cuisine And Pierre Combine To Bring You A
Fine Dinner Of 5 Courses, Sometimes New Creations

Pepper Steak "Mon Cousin"      *14.25*
Broiled Selected Sirloin Topped By A Spirited
Onion And Pepper Sauce

Le Biftek Tartare      *13.00*
The Finest Of Raw Colorado Beef, Prepared In The
Traditional European Manner

Pierre's Steak Diana      *14.75*
Cooked Tableside

Chateaubriand Bouquetiere
An Historic Dish Of The French Haute Cuisine      *Serves Two*
Sauce Au Cognac      *Nightly Quote*

Rack Of Lamb Persille "Troisgros"
     *Serves One*
"Spring Lamb," Baked With      *or Two Persons*
Our Special Crust      *Nightly Quote*

members of Colorado's press and media. And all along I enjoyed great press, supplemented by my own television and radio shows. My wife, Jean, bore us two great children, Ronald Pierre and Karen Michelle. Jean, whom I had met at the Patio, not only raised our children but worked and supported me through thirty years at the Quorum. I could not have done it without her. Thanks, Jean! And to enjoy our waning years, we have five adorable grandchildren, all right here in Denver.

A story by the late Greg Lopez of the *Rocky Mountain News* put the Quorum to rest after thirty years of operation. No one could have written "Last Course" better (see page 128). In conclusion, my sincere thanks to all the great customers and staff of the Quorum not mentioned here, but forever locked in my heart. To my wife, Jean, my children, as well as their spouses, and our grandchildren, my love and affection and thanks for their unswaying support.

Here are some recipes for those who miss the Quorum's cooking!

## Noisettes of Lamb à la Quorum

*2 servings*

4, 3-ounce medallions of lamb (or deboned loin chops)
1 tablespoon olive oil
½ teaspoon chopped garlic
½ teaspoon chopped shallots
¼ teaspoon dry mustard
½ cup chopped scallions
½ cup chopped mushrooms
½ cup chopped chanterelle mushrooms (optional)
pan juices reserved from lamb preparation
fresh ground pepper to taste
fresh or dried mint to taste
kiwifruit for garnish

1. Sauté medallions in a bit of olive oil until brown on both sides. Keep medallions very rare. Set aside. Reserve pan juice for sauce.

2. Sauté garlic and shallots lightly; add all other ingredients (except kiwifruit) and cook until done.

3. Before serving, put rare medallions into sauce. Cook for a few moments until medium or medium rare. Correct seasonings to taste.

4. Pour sauce over lamb medallions and serve garnished with peeled and sliced kiwifruit.

# Paupiettes de Boeuf

*4 servings*

2½ pounds of untrimmed tenderloin of beef
¾ cup finely diced American cheese
¾ cup cooked, diced mushrooms
¾ cup cooked, diced ham
1 jigger dry sherry
juice of ½ lemon

1. Cut tenderloin into 5-ounce portions. Flatten with cleaver until ¼-inch thick.

2. Place equal amount of ham, mushrooms, and cheese on each slice. Roll and tuck in sides and secure with toothpicks. Sauté in butter until brown.

3. Transfer to other skillet and add preheated mushroom sauce. Add sherry and lemon juice and simmer paupiettes in mushroom sauce for 10 minutes.

# Lobster Newburg

*2 to 4 servings*

1 large lobster tail
3 tablespoons butter
½ cup sherry
pinch of paprika

¼ cup mushrooms, diced
pinch of dry mustard
salt & pepper
2 cups light cream sauce

1. Remove lobster meat from shell. (Either raw or boiled lobster may be used.) Cut into cubes.

2. Sauté lightly in butter and drain excess. Add the sherry. Cook until reduced to half its volume.

3. Add the paprika, mushrooms, dry mustard, salt and pepper.

4. Add the cream sauce and blend well. Simmer for about 5 minutes.

# Last Course

An era comes to an end as Pierre's Quorum closes its doors after three decades of serving equal portions of food and class.

The arriving has not begun, and Pierre Wolfe is telling the story about the time he wouldn't let Marlon Brando in because he wasn't wearing a jacket.

He is getting ready for Tuesday evening and talking about the fact that everybody who is anybody, and even some who aren't, have eaten at Pierre's Quorum. He catches his reflection in the glass on one of the Chagall lithographs—he says one is worth $34,000—and adjusts the scarf in his breast pocket. It will be a good Tuesday night, because he has announced the Quorum will close April 28.

"So here is this man in a T-shirt that is not even tucked in," he says. "This was the 1960s, remember, when I kept jackets and ties for people who forgot their own, but he just goes back to his hotel and . . . Excuse me."

Wolfe is 5-foot-3, wearing a British wool suit tailor-made in Hong Kong, and the scarf in his breast pocket is red. The words have a French lilt you could pour over the Steak Diane à la Pierre. Guy Lombardo is playing a song that isn't *Auld Lang Syne,* and Wolfe interrupts himself to go and ask a waiter to turn it down.

He comes back and smoothes a wrinkle out of the linen tablecloth on Table 27, which is where the Simics and Al Davis always sat. Al Davis hasn't been back since the Broncos beat the Raiders in the 1960s, but the Simics have reservations for tonight. The Simics, Dolph and Thirza, have come to the Quorum for 30 years.

And for 30 years, Pierre Wolfe has remembered everybody's name and used it as often as possible, including his own.

"Pierre Wolfe served Marlon Brando after he went back to his hotel and got a jacket, and Karl Malden, Anthony Quinn, Maurice Chevalier, Dwight Eisenhower, Van Johnson, Anita Ekberg, Peter Ustinov, that fellow who was the mayor in California . . . Clint Eastwood," he says. "The famous Robert Taylor asked my wife and I to eat with him right there at table 24, and I have a photograph of Robert Taylor with me. You must ask my wife exactly why Robert Taylor was so famous, but you should see how he is smiling next to me.

"Now, there are thousands of people who are not famous and I also have had a love affair with them, so what would the Quorum be without Pierre Wolfe?"

So now he will find out what Pierre Wolfe will be without the Quorum.

First of all, Wolfe says business isn't the only reason he decided to close the Quorum.

Over the past 30 years, the Quorum was one of Denver's best-known restaurants, and Wolfe was the most famous restaurant owner. During the 1970s and early '80s, it had 300 customers on Friday and Saturday nights, and grossed as much as $1.2 million a year. For the past couple of years, a big night was 150 customers, and the annual grosses were $600,000–$700,000.

Wolfe also is 64, wants to travel, and the purple chairs need to be reupholstered.

"Now I will do things when other people do things, instead of working because everybody else wants to go out to the Quorum," he says. "Maybe some of our friends will invite us to dinner. Maybe I will even cook sometimes for my wife."

Wolfe will continue to do *The World of Food and Fine Dining* (9:01–11 A.M. Saturday, KDEN-1240) and the nationally syndicated *America's Dining & Travel Guide* on Business Radio Network (4:05–6 P.M. Sundays, KDEN).

He hasn't decided what to do with the vanity license plates on his Mercedes that say "Quorum," or the ones on the other cars that say "Qvorum," "Quorvm" and "Qvorvm."

Wolfe also owns Normandy French Restaurant, but says his daughter, Karen, will run it. He and his cousin, Heinz Gerstle, opened the Normandy in 1957 and Gerstle ran it until Wolfe bought him out last year. Karen, 28, studied at the three-star Oustau de Baumaniere in France and managed restaurants in Cincinnati, Maui and Chicago before her father brought her back.

"I have decided I will stay seated when somebody says hello just because they recognize Pierre," Wolfe says. "But if they were my friends at the Quorum and want to talk to me . . . Who is Pierre Wolfe to just say no?"

Wolfe was born in Alsace-Lorraine, where his father was director of a welding factory, and was raised Jewish. His mother and father sent his sister and him to London when the Nazis invaded. His parents died in concentration camps.

Wolfe joined the Free French Army in London, and was a lieutenant while they chased Rommel around North Africa. After the war, he got a job as a steward and assistant chef on Cunard luxury liners, then studied four years at École Hotelier de Lausanne in Switzerland. In 1950 he came to Denver to visit his sister, Suzanne Joshel.

He got a job as a night chef in the Brown Palace and in the next year was promoted to sous chef, then chef at the Palace Arms. He was hired to be chef at The Patio, at 5110 S. Santa Fe Drive in Littleton, in 1951. The owner defaulted on the lease three years later, and the landlord gave Wolfe the restaurant.

In 1960, Wolfe rented the coffee shop in the Argonaut Hotel at 233 E. Colfax Ave. and made it Pierre's Quorum.

The Simics met Wolfe at the Patio and followed when he opened the Quorum.

"He'd always remember where we sat, what you'd been doing, what you'd had the last time, your dog's name—anything," Thirza Simic says.

"Even when we got older and couldn't remember some of those things ourselves, Pierre would remember," Dolph Simic says.

The restaurant won national recognition in travel and dining magazines. Wolfe had cooking shows at different times on every channel. He made the front page of the *Beirut* (Lebanon) *Star* in 1967, standing behind Paul McCartney.

Heinz Schaeffer, co-owner of Figaro's European Coiffures, 5494 E. Evans, always took his receptionist to the Quorum, to learn how to treat people.

"I also brought my dates there and now I am getting married, so I guess you could say it is the end of two eras for me," says Schaeffer. "For all those years I had to kick Pierre under the table because it was a new girl, and when I finally find the one I will marry, the Quorum closes. I guess I am fortunate I no longer hope to impress a date, because Pierre always insisted everything was perfect."

For the same reasons, chefs walked out or Wolfe fired them at least 15 times during dinner, Wolfe says.

Selmon Fletcher was hired away from the Hilton Hotel in 1961, and over the next 21 years lost count of how many times he was fired or quit. He started as a waiter and retired as Wolfe's personal assistant. Now he eats at the Quorum once a month.

"He's the most difficult person to work for in some ways, and in others he's the easiest person in the world to work for," says Fletcher, 64, who owns the Ex-Servicemen's Club, 2627 Welton St., in Five Points. "You do it his way, and when we ran into trouble it was because I knew my way was just as good. The point is, I always went back.

"You just have to realize, the way he looks at that restaurant is the way some men look at their wife."

Her name is Jean, and her job is whatever Pierre's isn't. They met when Wolfe was the chef at the Patio and she was a third-grade teacher who worked summers across Santa Fe Drive at Centennial race track. She was impressed that Wolfe always remembered her name and everything about her.

Later, she learned Wolfe is that way with everybody, but by that time they were dating. They got married after he left the Patio and before the Quorum opened. She started to work at the Quorum because she didn't like the flower arrangements and now is in charge of remembering why the people in the photographs with Pierre are famous.

Sundays and slow nights, they go out to other people's restaurants.

"We'll be sitting there eating when somebody gets up to leave, and Pierre will jump up and say, 'Thank you for coming,'" she says. "It used to embarrass me, but now I understand that's just the way Pierre is. He is glad they came."

Wolfe has figured the Quorum has served 60,000 Steak Diana à la Pierres. It is two pieces of the eye of a New York strip steak with a light coat of Grey Poupon mustard, mushrooms, butter, garlic, shallots, parsley, green onions, Worcestershire sauce and fresh ground pepper, cooked in corn oil, flamed with cognac and served with brown sauce. Wolfe cooks it himself at the tableside.

It is a classic, but like all classics in this work, people ask if he could cook it in olive oil because it has less cholesterol.

"This is not a Healthmark menu," Wolfe says. "This is a restaurant where we serve the food so it is wonderful for your mouth, not your arteries and veins, and my guests must trust Pierre. I did make an exception for Mr. Javits, and that still bothers me."

Former U.S. Sen. Jacob Javits of New York ordered a New York strip steak, well-done. Then he wanted A-1, Heinz 57 and Worcestershire sauces. Wolfe let the waiters take it to him only because he was a well-respected man outside The Quorum, and because he had ordered the steak well-done.

There are more regrets.

Crepes suzette, for example.

"One night, I let a new waiter make the flame, because it was for his mother," Wolfe says. "I had to pull off the tablecloth at another table, right out from under the dishes at somebody else's table, to put out the flames."

There also are things that were beyond his control.

Al Davis, who owns the L.A. (formerly Oakland) Raiders, sat at Table 27 during the 1960s on the Saturday nights before his team beat the Denver Broncos, Wolfe says. Davis said the Quorum brought him good luck. When he finished his meal he would push aside the dishes and diagram plays with magic marker on the tablecloth.

After a couple of seasons of giving the Raiders good luck, Wolfe waited until Davis was finished with a play and started to gather up the tablecloth.

"It was all Xs and Os and line on my tablecloth," he says. "I said, 'Thank you very much. Mr. Davis, I shall forward this to the Denver Broncos.'

"For whatever reason, the Broncos won, and Mr. Davis never has been back."

Wolfe made the food lighter in the 1980s. In 1987, he opened the drapes on the windows so guests could see the gold dome on the capital. In the late 1960s, he went to Goodwill and dropped off the jackets and ties he kept for guests who forgot their own.

Some things Wolfe wouldn't change.

The restaurant was named the Quorum because it is across Colfax Avenue from the Capitol, and because it is named the Quorum he wouldn't move it to Cherry Creek or the Denver Tech Center when business got slow. The carpet is burgundy, the curtains are red, the chairs are purple. The decor was ahead of its time when the Quorum opened in 1960, but somewhere between then and now time got lost.

Some of the employees will go to the Normandy, and most of the rest have been offered jobs at other restaurants. The furnishings will stay. The owners of the buildings have not found a new tenant.

"Somebody else could do something different, something . . . casual," he says. "That might work, but Pierre could never do that with the Quorum. I don't like to talk like this, you know, but there were a lot of good things about the old days."

The old days were when Marlon Brando came back wearing a jacket and Dick Enberg had NBC add "Gourmet food by Pierre" to the credits at the end of a Broncos game. They were when a chef could use cholesterols like a painter uses oils. The old days are why Robert Taylor is smiling.

Saturday, April 28, 1990, will be the busiest night at the Quorum in several years.

"Every night, the curtain goes up, and Pierre has been on stage," he says. "Now, how many people have a chance to orchestrate their own ending?"

Now he will find out what Pierre will be without the Quorum.

Wolfe wants to travel. He wants to guide tours. He hopes he will be able to figure out a way to move the plot forward in his novel about an Aryan Nazi and a Free French Jew.

If that doesn't work, he has a plan.

"It would be a small place. There would be five appetizers, two soups, three salads and five main courses and a lovely array of desserts. I already have a name for this place.

"I will call it Encore!"

—By Greg Lopez, reprinted from *Rocky Mountain News*, Apr. 22, 1990, pp. 15M–16M, with permission

132 ∽ *Quorum Restaurant*

# My Media Career

For a guy in the restaurant business all his life, I did not do so badly in the media. How does one move from cooking to yakking? Or do the two go together? In any case, I must have been born with the gift of gab.

My avocation was, and still is, radio and television. Thus it all began with my first appearance on Pete Smythe's "Tin Cup Colorado" show, in black and white, on KOA-TV in the late 1950s. Pete invited me to cook on his potbellied stove in the studio, and I chose to prepare soufflé potatoes. No one who performs today on various cooking shows is crazy enough to undertake such a complex preparation.

My first try at radio had a different beginning. I was serving my highly acclaimed buffet luncheon ($.99) at my Patio Restaurant in Littleton when Frank Wade, an advertising guru, approached me to try my gab on radio. My reply: "Go back to the bar for another martini, Frank! Pierre doing radio? You must be nuts!" Frank, however, was very persistent. He had a sponsor, the Greeley Gas Co. (whatever that meant). "You can tell them why professionals cook with gas rather than electricity!"

Frank dragged me over to the studios at KFML Radio, owned by the late Bill Daniels, to let me try out for a fifteen-minute segment. After two minutes, I was out of words. The only thing I did right that day was say, "And I am Pierre Wolfe on KFML Radio"!

The rest is history.

It took some research to remember all of my appearances on television. KRMA-TV Channel 6 asked Heinz Gerstle (my cousin and partner in the Normandy French Restaurant) and me to "star" in our own series *For Gourmets Only,* Mondays at 8:30 P.M., prime time for half an hour, and Tuesdays at 2:30 P.M. The show was highly success-

# The Gallic Touch

A funny thing happened to Pierre Wolfe on his way to becoming a successful restaurateur. He stepped in the way of a radio program—and he hasn't been the same chef since. That was nearly two years, 200 radio shows, and 30 TV programs ago. In the meantime, he managed to develop a profitable sideline—running the Quorum Restaurant, a place not unfamiliar to habitues of the State Capitol, and other people of good taste.

While his radio-TV career didn't become a major avocation until he went on KFML 24 months ago, Pierre was not a stranger to video studios. One of his first appearances was on Pete Smythe's old TV show on which he cooked a soufflé on a pot bellied stove. At that time, he was just an unknown French chef turning out all sorts of foreign dishes whose names only he could pronounce.

Today, thanks to his unique way of spieling cooking information over the air and his customer relations savvy, Pierre is something of a personality who is on a first-name basis with more people than you can shake a ladle at.

When he first began his show, "Gourmet Cooking," on KFML, he ran out of things to say after 2½ minutes. To talk for a quarter-hour seemed like a nightmare, especially when he didn't have a prepared script. "Now," he states proudly, "they can't shut me up!"

He later did two seasons of a 30-minute cooking program on KRMA, Channel 6, and has appeared numerous times as a guest on various TV shows. . . .

As a critic who believes that if you've heard one cooking show you've heard them all, I was curious about the ingredients in Pierre's program. What was his success, did he give the housewife exotic and secret European recipes or what?

"Recipes, schmesipes," he replied disgustedly in a slight Gallic accent. "There are thousands, maybe a million, recipes in magazines, on sale in bookstores, on labels of canned food, and on the boxes of instant mashed potatoes. A housewife needs another

ful, with requests for recipes numbering upward of five thousand per month. Heinz and I were keenly aware of competition from Vince Edwards, star of a medical show (the name escapes me) that appeared opposite our show. And so one night we dressed as doctors and performed a "delicate" beef heart operation. Ratings soared!

recipe like she needs another husband."

"What our show (the 'our' referring to cousin Heinz Gerstle who participates in the activities) tries to do is stimulate her thinking about gourmet cooking and to develop her interest in food preparation. We don't want her to write anything down on paper. We just want her to listen and think."

Pierre and Heinz not only talk about various dishes, but they discuss menu planning, give some historical background on the how and why of certain preparations, what to look for when buying meat in a supermarket, herbs and spices, etc.

"And we devote some time to the husband, too," Pierre said.

The who?

"The husband. We try to instill in the man an appreciation for his wife's cooking (a device which won't lose him many feminine listeners). And we offer a few hints on how he can impress guests with his cooking ability. But primarily, the show is for women, women who want to prepare something other than pork chops, mashed potatoes, and green beans every night."

The results indicate he has had a modicum of success thus far.

—By Del Carnes, reprinted from *Denver Post,* Mar. 6, 1963, p. 79, with permission

Heinz Gerstle (left) and Pierre at work on KRMA's *For Gourmets Only* program. *Courtesy, Rocky Mountain News TV Dial,* Dec. 10, 1961, p. 29.

In the second season, Heinz and I hosted *Gourmet Cooking* on KRMA with guest chefs such as Joseph Sperte representing the Scotch 'n' Sirloin and William Dumas representing Saltwater Dumas. On September 11, 1961, Max Hummel was the host with special guests Gene Amole, Terry Obrey, and Donna McEncroe. KRMA was in its infancy, but Louise Wilson our producer made it happen.

Then I hosted a television series on ABC Channel 9, *A World of Foods,* for about a year, sponsored by Tappan Ranges. But no doubt, my most successful television show was the *Friday Feast* on KOA-TV Channel 4 with Jim Hawthorne and news anchor Morris Jones. The fun part of the show was Jim Hawthorne's refusal to eat anything unusual. I made up for it, munching on caviar with my wife, Jean, during a Bronco football game, live from Mile High Stadium. Jim Hawthorne, an old-time comedian radio host on many major networks, added a great deal of humor and fun to my show. This segment ran for four-and-a-half years, thanks to General Manager Jim Schafbuch of KOA-TV.

Jim Hawthorne and Pierre contemplating an egg (with knife at the ready) for a segment of their show *Friday Feast. Wolfe collection.*

# Denver Chef Pierre Wolfe Cooking as Talk-Show Host

Restaurateur, raconteur and wine connoisseur Pierre Wolfe has assumed additional duties as national radio schmoozeur.

In addition to running Denver's Quorum, he is also Maitre d'Airwaves.

For nearly 40 years, Wolfe has had a local media presence as well as being a certified chef and world traveler who's not shy about promoting himself.

"I call local food critics in Cleveland, Sacramento, Baton Rouge," Wolfe said recently over cream of asparagus soup at the Quorum. "I ask, for instance, 'What's the worst meal you ever had in Portland?'" He got a laugh and a candid answer out of *New York Times* food critic Mimi Sheraton when he asked, "Who hates you the most?"

"We think of him as our version of Robin Leach," said BRN program director Mark Murray. Murray holds his breath during Wolfe's show because "he may not follow the rules when it comes to being a talk-show host. There are a dozen things he's invented on the air. He doesn't think of the implications."

Most recently, Wolfe spontaneously promised free meals at restaurants around the county without clearing the idea first. Luckily, all 13 restaurants mentioned on the show complied.

But while Wolfe is "a restaurateur first and a radio person second," Murray said, "he's never gotten us in serious trouble." He has provided "a few headaches, nothing illegal."

—By Joanne Ostrow, reprinted from *Denver Post*, Apr. 11, 1989, p. D1, with permission

According to Gene Amole of the *Rocky Mountain News*, Jim Hawthorne had many careers. Jim partnered with Pete Smythe on KMYR with their *Meet the Boys in the Band*. Jim also pioneered wacky West Coast commercial television. All in all, he was a terrific fun guy to work with on the *Friday Feast*. He often rolled his eyes behind those horn-rimmed glasses and never gained a pound because most often he would not touch my more exotic concoctions.

Pierre as man of the airwaves. *Wolfe collection.*

When *Friday Feast* ended, I had to find a new home and KMGH TV Channel 7 offered me a great opportunity. We took the cameras on location to restaurants, bakeries, specialty meat markets, and picnic grounds.

Also on KMGH, we took a camera operator with us to the Napa Valley and filmed *Colorado Connection,* at wineries such as Joseph Phelps of Hensel-Phelps, Tom Jordan's Jordan Winery at his beautiful French chateau. Great fun that turned out very productive. In a two-year run on television Channel 53, *The Restaurant Show* offered live cooking segments with chefs from Denver restaurants.

My most successful radio show, by some lights, was called *Pack Your Bags,* with Jim Conder on the "old" KVOD. For seven years prior to the sale of KVOD to Colorado Public Radio, Jim, program director for KVOD, cohosted our Saturday broadcast and added classical music to the subject of discussion. This pacified the classical radio devotees and made this a very popular show. Not a day went by while I was at the Normandy that patrons would not mention *Pack Your Bags,* most often saying, "We love your show."

I had a long stretch of broadcasting on All News Radio KDEN with Doug Stevens—thirteen years of food vignettes while cousin Heinz waxed his "Grapevine" program. It was during that time that I

# KNUS Courting Cuban Top Banana

Pierre Wolfe, the loquacious restaurateur and talk-show yapper, may finally met his match. Someone who talks more than Wolfe and Rush Limbaugh and Tom Martino, all on speed. Try Fidel Castro.

Wolfe is going to Cuba in late April with KNUS radio for five days of live, interactive broadcasts to Denver. And maybe, just maybe, he'll get to ask El Presidente what's with the bad food in Havana.

Wolfe just returned from a three-day visit to Cuba, during which he arranged the KNUS visit with the help of Denver art dealer Dean Knox (Knox Galleries), who has an ongoing cultural relationship with the alienated island.

According to KNUS general manager Ron Crider, morning host Ken Hamblin will spearhead the April 24–29 call-in-to-Cuba shows, along with Wolfe and a high-profile personality who is soon to join the station. KNUS will use a pop-up satellite, like the ones CNN used during the Gulf War. The five days of Cuban call-in shows will mark the first live radio broadcasts form Cuba to the U.S. since 1953, claims Crider.

"We are not going to Cuba as journalists," Crider says. "We will be talking about what is right in Cuba. We already know what's wrong. We'll look at the art, the history, the food, the travel and tourist potential. This is part of a cultural exchange." . . .

—By Bill Husted, reprinted from *Rocky Mountain News*, Mar. 2, 1993, p. 86, with permission

got invited to try out for a national radio show called *America's Dining and Travel Guide.* Since 1988, I have hosted this national, live call-in show, heard on sixty to eighty stations all across America. Many of our country's most prominent "foodies" have been guests, including Jaques Pepin, Julia Child, Paul Prudhomme, Martin Yan, Emeril Lagasse, as well as Arthur Frommer for travel, Tom Parsons of Best Fares, and a host more. The initial show commenced in October 1988 with the Business Radio Network. Name changes occurred as often as ownership of the network. Business News Network, Business Talk Radio, and currently Business Talk Radio.net. Was I lucky to survive all these ownership and management changes or was I simply "most talented"?

Since the inception of my national show, I have broadcast from many lands around the globe as well as from cruise ships at sea, by satellite telephone or ISDN line. I must tell you, this is exciting stuff!! A long stretch on KNUS, under the management of Ron Crider, afforded me the opportunity to broadcast live from Havana, Cuba.

At the time of this writing, I am doing a live show called *The Good Life* on KLMO 1060 AM Longmont–Denver on Saturday mornings, and my national show keeps rolling along. From Alaska to Honolulu from New York to Texas coast to coast Sundays over the Business Talk Radio Network.

Perhaps that makes me the oldest continuous broadcaster in Colorado! I still was restaurateur first and having fun as a media member second.

Just for kicks, I've included a few of the very popular recipes from my early television shows:

~

## Duckling Bigarrade

*2 servings*

| | |
|---|---|
| 3–4-pound duckling | 1 tablespoon currant jelly |
| 4 cubes sugar (white or brown) | $\frac{1}{2}$ jigger Cointreau |
| juice of 6 oranges | kumquats and orange rind |
| juice of 1 lemon | and sections for garnish |

1. Roast and braise duckling to tenderness, approximately 2 hours at 350 degrees. Save braising stock and strain until clear. Remove grease.

2. In a separate sauce pan, caramelize sugar. Add juice of oranges, lemon, the jelly, and duckling stock. Reduce to half its volume.

3. Before serving, add Cointreau, kumquats, orange rind and sections.

# Parisian Turkey

*4 servings*

1 pound leftover cooked turkey,
  dark or white meat
prepared mushroom sauce

1 ounce sherry
½ teaspoon ground pepper
pimiento strips

1. Brown turkey meat lightly. Add wine, mushroom sauce, fresh ground pepper; garnish with pimentos.

2. Serve in a ring of wild rice or brown rice.

# Eggplant Stuffed with Clams

*4 servings*

1 large eggplant, halved lengthwise
½ cup butter
½ onion, minced
½ garlic clove, minced
2 tablespoons minced celery

2 small cans chopped clams,
  drained
1 cup bread crumbs
little chopped parsley
½ teaspoon thyme
salt & pepper to taste

1. Scoop out center of eggplant leaving a wall ½-inch thick all around, chop the pulp of the eggplant and sauté in butter with onion, garlic, and celery, until onion is golden brown.

2. Add all the other ingredients, blend well.

3. Fill this mixture back into eggplant and bake in a moderate oven for about 30 minutes.

# Bleu Cheese Dressing

1 pint mayonnaise
6 ounces Bleu cheese, crumbled
1 tablespoon sour cream
  garlic powder, salt & pepper to taste

½ cup buttermilk
1 teaspoon Worcestershire
  sauce

1. Blend all ingredients in a convenient bowl. Chill.

# Seafood Curry Bengal

*1 serving*

2 tablespoons butter
⅓ cup mushrooms
  (stems & pieces)
⅓ banana, sliced
¼ apple, peeled and sliced
1 teaspoon shallots
1 teaspoon chopped onions
⅓ cup sliced pimientos

1 ounce heavy cream
4–5 ounces white wine sauce
1 teaspoon Madras curry
2 shrimp cut in half
4 pieces crabmeat
⅓ cup scallops
salt & pepper to taste
1 teaspoon coconut flakes,
  roasted

1. Melt butter in pan until very hot. Pour in mushrooms, banana, apples, shallots, onions, and pimientos. Sauté briefly.

2. Add heavy cream, white wine sauce, and curry; stir slowly until all ingredients blend evenly.

3. Add seafood and cook for about 3 minutes. Add salt and pepper according to taste. Just before serving, sprinkle on coconut flakes.

⌒

# Almond Crepes

*4 servings*

½ cup unsalted butter
½ teaspoon almond extract
¼ cup slivered almonds
½ cup granulated sugar
½ cup melba sauce (or fresh raspberry sauce)
1 jigger almond liqueur

4 crepes (bought or prepared)
½ jigger Cognac
raspberries, blackberries,
  or strawberries as garnish

1. Almond butter: put unsalted butter, almond extract, slivered almonds, and sugar into mixing bowl. Mix with a wire wisk until smooth (or use food processor). Check flavor and add almond liqueur as desired.

2. 10 minutes before serving: in a copper skillet, melt the almond butter, but do not brown. Add melba sauce and mix well. Reduce heat. Fold in crepes (one per person). Flame with Cognac.

3. Garnish plates with fruit, ample sauce, and a few almonds on top.

# THE RATTLESNAKE CLUB

## Rattlesnake Club and Adirondacks
### ∽ Tivoli Center, Denver

They rode into town in the mid-1980s on their high horses, looking down on the lowly dining scene in Denver. Michael McCarty and Jimmy Schmidt settled comfortably into their allotted space in the re-developed Tivoli Brewery and then decided on a name, the Rattle-snake Club. They lured gullible investors to foot their bills, and quickly became the talk of the town. The Rattlesnake Club, with Jimmy Schmidt as chef, had potsfull of good food and a large helping of arrogance. Prices rivaled the peaks of the Rockies and, for good measure, they added an eighteen percent service charge.

Haughtiness soon melted into concern, so McCarty and Schmidt covered their anxiety with a name change to Adirondacks. In an interview with *Rocky Mountain News'* Karen McPherson, Schmidt and McCarty said, "The name Adirondacks was selected because it suggests the 'casual elegance' of the cabins built by the wealthy in the eastern mountains." Hmmm. . . . And your point is . . . ? In any case, it did not save the restaurant from its demise. Perhaps the place was snake-bit!

As for the investors, they were just waiting for their favorite snake to bite them one more time. Jimmy Schmidt obliged them by opening a Rattlesnake restaurant in the Cherry Creek Shopping Center and relieved the "believers" of some more cash with this ill-fated reincarnation.

**BREAST OF CHICKEN** . . . . . . . . . . . . . . . . . . . . . . . . . . . . . . . . . . . . . . . . *13.95*
  *Grilled With Chanterelle & Apple Compote **(9)*
**STERLING SALMON** . . . . . . . . . . . . . . . . . . . . . . . . . . . . . . . . . . . . . . . . *16.95*
  *Grilled with Barbeque Glaze and Roast Sweet Pepper Salsa, Corn Fritter*
**YELLOWFIN TUNA** . . . . . . . . . . . . . . . . . . . . . . . . . . . . . . . . . . . . . . . . *16.95*
  *Grilled with Chanterelles, Carmelized Onions and Red Wine Sauce*
**PORK LOIN CHOP** . . . . . . . . . . . . . . . . . . . . . . . . . . . . . . . . . . . . . . . . *16.95*
  *Broiled with Dried Cherries, Tequila and Crispy Sage*
**ATLANTIC SWORDFISH** . . . . . . . . . . . . . . . . . . . . . . . . . . . . . . . . . . . . *17.95*
  *Grilled with Grapefruit, Pinenuts and Ginger*
**LOBSTER, SCALLOP AND SHRIMP CAKES** . . . . . . . . . . . . . . . . . . . . . . *17.95*
  *Sauteed with Cracked Mustard, Dill and Baby Greens*
**FILET OF BEEF** . . . . . . . . . . . . . . . . . . . . . . . . . . . . . . . . . . . . . . . . . . *18.95*
  *Grilled with Hazelnut-Pepper Crust, Pearl Onions and Pomegranate Seeds*
**RACK OF VEAL** . . . . . . . . . . . . . . . . . . . . . . . . . . . . . . . . . . . . . . . . . . *21.95*
  *Roasted with Wild Mushrooms, Shallots and Tarragon*
**COLORADO RACK OF LAMB** . . . . . . . . . . . . . . . . . . . . . . . . . . . . . . . *22.95*
  *Grilled with Rosemary and Persillade Crust, Red Wine and Olive Sauce*

If you feel that I am a bit harsh on those boys, Michael and Jimmy, you should read what my friend, Bill Husted of the *Denver Post,* wrote in his article of March 2001—and I quote, "McCarty tried Denver once at the Rattlesnake, Schmidt tried Denver three times at Adirondacks and two Rattlesnakes. Denver just never cottoned to the boys. They arrived in town with a certain bravado, bragging that they would show us cowpokes what food was all about. That went over like a case of foot-in-mouth disease." Amen.

> *If food is an art, I think we're in our Dada phase.*
>
> —David Sedaris

# Why Do Restaurants Fail
# and Disappear?

*In memory of a cast of thousands of hardworking restaurateurs, who have faded into the annals of Denver restaurant history . . .*

The answer to why restaurants fail or disappear lies in the nature of the restaurant business itself. To cite some of the more common causes, let's begin with: underfinancing, ill-conceived concepts, trying to be everything to everybody, poor food and service, inconsistency, poor business practices, changing times and economic conditions, poor choice of location, urban renewal, deteriorating neighborhoods, lack of personal attention, poor management, divorce, breakups of partnerships, and not being able to compete with chain operations.

Other factors involve foolish investors who, having suffered significant losses, pull their support out from under the restaurant, or perhaps there is death or retirement of key figures around whom the business was built. With so many variables, one can easily understand the demise of thousand of restaurants, many not mentioned in this book. To quote Ed Novak, owner of the Broker Restaurants, why restaurants fail: "Lack of customers"—a true and profound statement.

Take my advice: Despite the allure of the restaurant business, not everyone is cut out for it. Failure breaks your pocketbook and your heart.

*Never trust the food in a restaurant that spends a lot of time folding napkins.*

*—Andy Rooney*

### Restaurant Edelweiss  ~
### 1644 Glenarm Place

Personally, I know very little about this restaurant; however, I discovered a menu from the Edelweiss at the Denver Public Library, which appears to be from 1947. I chatted with my good friend, Bob Weil, founder and former owner of the Westman Commission Company, who remembers the owner of the Edelweiss as a Charles Suhatsky. (I hope this is the correct spelling!) Bob remembers the place as big, seating about 150 patrons. According to Bob, the restaurant was very popular with business people and the after-theater crowd. Because of the Edelweiss' fine reputation in the late 1940s and early 1950s, the menu is featured here.

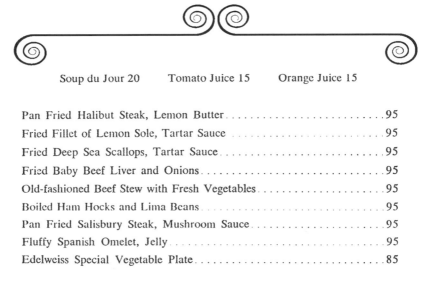

Soup du Jour 20     Tomato Juice 15     Orange Juice 15

Pan Fried Halibut Steak, Lemon Butter . . . . . . . . . . . . . . . . . . . . . . . .95

Fried Fillet of Lemon Sole, Tartar Sauce . . . . . . . . . . . . . . . . . . . . . . .95

Fried Deep Sea Scallops, Tartar Sauce . . . . . . . . . . . . . . . . . . . . . . . .95

Fried Baby Beef Liver and Onions . . . . . . . . . . . . . . . . . . . . . . . . . . . .95

Old-fashioned Beef Stew with Fresh Vegetables . . . . . . . . . . . . . . . . .95

Boiled Ham Hocks and Lima Beans . . . . . . . . . . . . . . . . . . . . . . . . . .95

Pan Fried Salisbury Steak, Mushroom Sauce . . . . . . . . . . . . . . . . . . .95

Fluffy Spanish Omelet, Jelly . . . . . . . . . . . . . . . . . . . . . . . . . . . . . . . .95

Edelweiss Special Vegetable Plate . . . . . . . . . . . . . . . . . . . . . . . . . . .85

**(The Original) Sam's No. 3 ～ 1527 Curtis Street, Denver**

Spiro Sam Armatas, son of the proprietor of the original Sam's No. 3, graciously offered to tell the tale of this amazing eatery himself:

Sam's No. 3 had a very straightforward mission statement: Cleanliness—Quality—Service, and this is what the customers got. Circa 1954, and Curtis Street was hoppin'! It was the street to be on. Sam's No. 3 was located at 1527 Curtis Street (Est. 1927). No. 3 was one of the most famous "Coney Island" operations in downtown Denver. Curtis Street Chili became famous because of all the Greek-owned chili parlors and Coney Islands such as the Hi-Spot, the Old Mexico, the Boston Lunch, and Pig on a Bun. However, Sam's Coney Island Greek Chili soon became the best "Greek Chili" in town. This is where my Dad became a living legend. His menu was limited, but customers loved it. I constantly met people who recall Denver as it was in the 1920s, 1930s, 1940s, 1950s, and 1960s, who reminisce fondly about the old downtown. A highlight would have been eating at Sam's No. 3.

This incredible little diner was only fifteen feet wide and forty-six feet long with a sixteen-foot ceiling that had decorative tin tiles and three large rotating fans. The walls running the length of the back bar and counter had mirrors so that it felt bigger inside. The grill and steam table were in the front window with bright red and

Sam Armatas, founder and proprietor, peeling homefries.
*Courtesy of S. Armatas.*

green neon, which emphasized exhibition cooking on the street. A monster two-sided neon sign with sparkling lights made the front look like a theater marquee. There were only nineteen stools to sit on and they were constantly occupied.

The unique thing about Sam's No. 3, through the years, is that it has been real. Always full with people from all walks of life. On any given day in Sam's history the nineteen stools were filled with . . .

- Judge from the Denver courthouse
- Gene Amole
- Bill Clemens, White Spot founder (in for his favorite Tomato Burger)
- Railroad switchmen
- The Schwayders, founders of Samsonite
- The Levys, Fashion Bar founders
- A drunk
- Phone company workers from across the street
- A guy proposing over a bowl of chili, to cheers from those around him
- Tabor Theatre patrons
- Rich Gazetta, Italians from the northside
- Miller Stockman workers

- Smaldone gang (of course we cleared out when they arrived)
- Daniels and Fisher saleswomen
- Soldiers
- Cops on the beat
- University Building jewelers
- Denver Dry Co. and Gart's workers
- Traveling salesmen, downtown businessmen

Sam's was a place with honest food at honest pricing. It was not about who you were when you were at Sam's. . . . You were always there for Denver's finest and famous bowl of red chili, burgers, and Coney dogs.

Sam's No. 3 was in the heart of theater row. On our block was the Tabor Grand and across the street there were the Victory and Rialto theaters. In addition to the theaters, our block also had Joslins, Fashion Bar, the old Baurs, Zotazar, Allison candy companies, the Tabor barber shop, the Blue Front shoe repair, the Black Orchid bar, Lloyd's upstairs pool hall, Pacific and Herman's pawn shops, Brooks Brothers clothing, and A Pig on a Bun. We were a three-minute walk to the Loop Market.

Long counter of Sam's No. 3, circa 1930s. *Courtesy of S. Armatas.*

Federal Judge J. Foster Symes was [...] ad's favorite customer. He sponsored Dad to bec[...] Mr. Max
Brooks, the founder of Central Bank, [...]lar. Gene
Amole, when he was growing up, wo[...]asible to
frequent Sam's. The Smaldone brot[...]id-after-
noon—we always knew when they w[...]ce man
would walk in and secure four count[...]d stand
by the front door, and another wo[...]of their
double-parked Caddy and wave traf[...]biggest
tippers we ever had. It did not matte[...]would
always pay and leave a $10 tip. In tho[...]s to a
40-cent-an-hour waiter.

Power brokers from 17th Stre[...]orkers, service
men, judges, police, young and old all came to Sam's. During the
lunch hour, customers would stand three deep behind each stool and
wait in lines to get in. Sam's No. 3 was a virtual gold mine. On a daily
basis, we would serve an average of 250 pieces of Puritan pie at 15
cents each, over 500 bowls of chili at 20 cents each, gallons and gallons of Millar's coffee at 10 cents a cup, or 14 different kinds of soda
pop at 10 cents each. My dad only bought quality products so we
used Dolly Madison ice cream, Star bread, and Mapelli meats to
name a few. Everything was fresh, I mean daily—the only day we did
not get deliveries was Sunday.

Some of the other popular menu items were the half-pound
hamburger steak dinners at 30 cents. This included hash browns fried
in butter, a tomato, roll, and coffee. The steak was smothered in chili.
Bacon, ham, or sausage and eggs with toast and coffee were 30 cents a
plate. A two-egg breakfast was 20 cents, a stack of hot cakes was 25
cents.

The front window displayed a pyramid of steaming hot dogs
waiting to be put on a bun. One of my Dad's tricks was to constantly
grill fresh onions and have a little fan above the grill to push the
aroma onto the street. I can only wonder how many customers were
enticed to eat a burger or hot dog because of the smell of the grilling
onions.

Fortunately, there was never any down time. We were open at
5 A.M. till 2 A.M. daily. If you had nothing to do, you could find something to clean.

Exterior of Sam's, 1950s. *Courtesy of S. Armatas.*

There was no time to write guest checks. All the orders were called in. A typical order called in would be, "One of each on one with a bowl easy." This meant a hamburger and a hot dog on the same plate with all the works and a bowl of chili, easy on the beans. Another order could be, "Two hot without a bowl straight." This meant two Coney dogs, no onion, and a bowl of chili, no beans. There were many combinations of orders. It was fun and varied and everyone had a part to play. Only a team effort could handle the volume.

Sam's had a great system for identifying what the customers ate. There were different colored plates with different shapes. Each menu item went onto its specific plate; therefore, anyone would know what to charge.

Many of Sam's employees had worked for him for many years. Jack Flaherty worked at No. 3 for over forty years as the number-one grill man. People would stand on the sidewalk and watch Jack flip pancakes in the air or flip a hamburger patty onto a bun. He could also line Coney dogs up his arm and then flip them onto a plate. This was daily showmanship. When you worked the grill you had to perform. The hamburgers and Coneys were served on a steamed bun smothered with mustard, chili sauce, diced onion, and pickle chips. One bite and you were hooked.

Everyone who worked had to wear white shirts, a starched overseas hat, a tie, and long white apron. Only the dishwasher was exempt from wearing a tie.

Another long-tem employee was Pete Lambetis. Pete was a gentleman who came in 1930 dressed as a hobo. My dad gave him five dollars and told him to clean up and come to work. In the mid-Sixties Pete Lambetis finally retired. In 1944, a homeless fourteen-year-old by the name of Joe Archuleta became my Dad's ward. Dad made Joe go to school while he worked. In addition, my Uncle Pete Fotinos came to Denver in 1940 from a farm in Nebraska and worked with Dad into the late 1950s.

In 1954, my older brother, Andy, was already working the counter. I was the rookie. On a typical hot summer night we would see lots and lots of servicemen, local Jezebels, the theater crowd, and the locals living downtown walk by, and they would be walkin' and gawkin'. We had eight countertop jukeboxes that were played so much they had to be emptied three times a week.

No. 3 was spotless. I know because my Dad would buy TSP in thirty-pound barrels. He made us wash the marlite walls daily, mop the floor after each rush, and then shine the windows and mirrors.

I would not have traded this street education for anything; a young kid had to grow up.

In closing, I would like to express my gratitude to Pierre Wolfe for this opportunity to write about my father.

*Contributed by Spiro Sam Armatas*

# Restaurant Critics

Restaurateurs and restaurant critics nurture a love–hate relationship. Those reviewers and critics of days gone by include Marjorie Barrett, Pat Hanna, Robin Cruise, Michael Carlton, John Kessler, and some that were like Duncan Hines. And then there was Barry "Never-Had-a-Bad-Meal" Morrison and his charming wife, Pinky. Barry wrote for the *Denver Post* in the 1960s and 1970s. Both Morrisons were much loved by us restaurateurs and chefs because his writings and critiques were nearly always favorable, and he positively promoted dining out. Barry was a swell guy!

By contrast, Michael Carlton, also with the *Denver Post,* following Morrison, had his own unique style of writing. He shredded and tore apart those restaurants he deemed inferior, and, in so doing, wrote in an amusing, entertaining way. Those restaurateurs and restaurants on the short end of Carlton's sarcastic and vicious attempts to defame those places that offended his educated taste buds did not smile. Oddly enough though, after a very negative review, those victimized restaurants were packed on the evening of the published critique. People wanted to see first-hand how awful a place can really be, or simply to show support to their favorite restaurant owner and chef.

And then there is Casa Bonita: critics can say and write anything they want to, but the place remains indestructible! So, in some cases where the food and service is not the best, the restaurant survives because of the entertainment value people perceive to be more important than the basic performance of the establishment.

Sadly enough, Denver has never ranked among the top ten dining cities of America. And for that reason, our fair city has never attracted national restaurant critics or writers of the caliber of Mimi Sheraton, Bryan Miller, Ruth Reichl, Phyllis Richman, or Arthur

Portrait of Barry Morrison, by Joe Barros, *Empire Magazine*,
October 3, 1976, with permission.

Schwartz. Of course, local papers and magazines would not pay them enough either.

At one time or another all of us wanted to be a restaurant reviewer. After all, we are born critics. But the job of a restaurant reviewer or critic is by no means easy or always enjoyable. It takes endurance and a strong stomach and direct acquaintanceship with the proper taste of food and wine and the ability to evaluate service and ambience.

It also helps if one has a unique style of writing—entertaining and at times amusing, but above all factual!

I am certain that newspaper and magazine editors often direct their charges to seek out the "in" places, the "hot spots" to satisfy the lust of the "trendetties." By the same token, Denver's critics and reviewers alike love to discover the hidden jewels, often small storefront restaurants that would never see the light of print in other major cities of the United States.

Recently, one of our critics sent many of us to a Middle Eastern eatery, having described the place as the second coming of Muhammed. Our visit proved be a dismal disappointment. Nonexistent service and OK food. Lead and mislead!

Finally, there are radio restaurant gurus, who shower lavish praise on their favorite places, often proclaiming personal biases and expressing subjective opinions. And they get paid well for doing so! Well, I should know—I have had my own restaurant radio and television shows over the years. Mostly just for the fun of it!

In conclusion, I will name my favorite current restaurant critic, strictly a personal opinion: *Westword* restaurant reviewer Kyle Wagner has all the ingredients to spice up her writing. She writes with humor and fun, while demonstrating her own culinary prowess and knowledge. A stylish writer, who has been given a large ladle to stir any soup by her employer, Patricia Calhoun, Kyle remains mostly undiscovered by restaurant owners.

Of a recent experience of an Asian restaurant, she wrote, "Even the fortune cookies were a bummer because only half of them contained fortunes." Kyle, keep it up!

# THE TIFFIN
## Gracious Dining

### The Tiffin ～ 1600 Ogden Street, Denver

Just a short walk from the venerable Brown Palace Hotel in Denver stood a greystone mansion built in 1889, which became home to the Tiffin Restaurant. This mansion was formerly a doctor's office and had caught the eye of the former dishwasher and baseball fan, Paul Shank. The Tiffin opened in 1945 and became an instant success. Post–World War II "hungries" and prominent visitors to Denver wore out the front porch of the Tiffin. Among the visiting celebrities, the Tiffin hosted Leopold Stokowski, Helen Traubel, gourmet Lucius Beebe, and even John D. Rockefeller.

One of Paul Shank's "gastronomic offerings" was a thick cut of beef tenderloin, served on a plank, surrounded by an assembly of colorful vegetables, perhaps like a Chateaubriand presentation of yesteryear. In the 1960s, Paul Shank moved his operation to Writers' Manor on South Colorado Boulevard, which became known as the Tiffin Inn at Writers' Manor. Later the Tiffin Inn became part of John R. Thompson Co. of Chicago, where Paul Shank remained as president and consultant. To the best of my knowledge, Paul retired to Arizona where he died.

According to Helen Messenger, writing about Shank for *Colorado Wonderland,* he was known as "the architect of appetite." As he said to Messenger, "Where else but in America, could a former dishwasher do so well?"

The only menu available to me was Shank's Easter menu, which is reproduced on the next page, and an article from the *Denver Post* gives a sense of the ambience of the South Colorado Boulevard location.

# Easter Sunday Dinner

### Soups and Appetizers — choice of one

"Tiffin-Maid" Chicken Soup with Egg Noodles

Cold Creme Vichyssoise    Fruit Cocktail    Seafood Cocktail

Tomato or Orange Juice    Chilled Half Grapefruit

Marinated Herring 40    Fresh Crab Louie 65    Shrimp Cocktail 50

Chilled Watermelon    Chilled Cantaloupe

---

Rose Radishes    Pascal Celery    Mixed Olives

Pickled Watermelon    Sweet Pickles

### Entrees

BAKED HICKORY SMOKED HAM, Sauce Cumberland ......................3.75

BAKED ONE-HALF SPRING CHICKEN, Sauce Supreme, Spiced Peach .........3.75

★ **TIFFIN CHOICE CLUB STEAK, Char-Broiled, Mushroom Sauce** ...............4.95

BONED INDIVIDUAL COLORADO RAINBOW MOUNTAIN TROUT,
Saute Amandine .....................................................3.95

ROAST PRIME RIBS OF FINEST STEER BEEF (Roasted in Rock Salt) ..........4.50

ROAST LEG OF HI-CLIMATE SPRING LAMB, Mint Jelly ....................3.75

---

Frosted Fruit Salad, Princess Dressing  or  Tiffin Crisp Garden Salad, Bleu Cheese Dressing
Assorted "Tiffin-Maid" Rolls

### Potatoes and Vegetables — choice of two

Buttered New Peas with Mushrooms    Fresh Rhubarb Sauce    New Cauliflower au Gratin

Little New Potatoes, Parsley Butter    French Fried Potatoes    Cream Whipped Potatoes

Spiced Beets    Creamed Slaw    Apple Sauce    Cottage Cheese with Chives

Golden Fried Onion Rings 75c. additional

### Desserts

Peach Shortcake, Whipped Cream    Old-fashioned Gooseberry Pie

Coconut Cream Pie    Devil's Food a la Mode

Hot Apple Pie, Honey Rum Sauce    Coffee Ice Cream    Chilled Half Grapefruit

Peppermint Stick Ice Cream    Fruit Gelatin, Whipped Cream    Chocolate-Mint Parfait

Roquefort or Camembert Cheese    Cheese Cake, Pineapple Topping

Choice of Sundaes    Chilled Watermelon    Chilled Cantaloupe

# Tiffin to Offer Entertainers

The Tiffin Inn at Writers' Manor, 1730 S. Colorado Blvd., has opened the Denver area's newest live entertainment lounge—the Bon Vivant with singer Joann Henderson, veteran of such night clubs as the Thunderbird in Las Vegas and Henrici's Golden Barrel Supper Club in Chicago, as the first attraction.

More than $26,000 was spent to decorate the former Tiffin cocktail lounge and add a stage and sound system for the conversion.

Remodeling by Aiello, Inc., of Denver took two months.

The new theme is French and the colors are burgundy and gold with accents of black and antique mirrors.

David Sterling, who manages the Tiffin Inn for the John R. Thompson Co., said entertainers will be changed frequently to provide variety.

Creation of the Bon Vivant is the latest in a series of remodeling and other changes at the Tiffin in the two years Sterling has been manager.

"Business is up 10 per cent this year and we expect the Bon Vivant to raise that even higher," Sterling said. "We now serve up to 2,500 meals daily in the main dining room alone, not counting the coffee shop."

Sterling says the Tiffin's facilities now are keyed to his philosophy that the eating, traveling and entertainment-seeking public has become more sophisticated in its demands.

—Reprinted from *Denver Post*, Aug. 17, 1966, p. 37, with permission

*It is not greedy to enjoy a good dinner, any more than it is greedy to enjoy a good concert. But I do think there is something greedy about trying to enjoy the concert and dinner at the same time.*

*—G. K. Chesterton*

# Top of the Rockies
## A restaurant above it all

**Top of the Rockies**  **1616 Glenarm Place, Denver**

Over the years, my wife and I enjoyed some lovely dinners at the Top. Let's let Tom Cygnar tell his own story:

I was general manager at the Top of the Rockies from 1977 through 1983. Top of the Rockies was part of the Stouffer Food Corporation. I worked for them before college, and after graduating I went into the manager training program in Cleveland. I worked a short time in their hotel division in Oakbrook, Illinois, and was transferred to Top of the Sixes in New York City—from there it was Top of the Hub in Boston to Columbus, Ohio, and I was offered the general manager job in Denver.

My first vision of the Denver skyline—a friend told me that I would be working in the tallest building downtown. It didn't take long for that to change. I met my wife, Claudia, at the Top; we have been married almost twenty years. As most of us who ran restaurants in the 1970s and 1980s in Denver know, it was an incredible ride. From the small-town days of kids cruising 16th Street to the amazing oil boom to the bust. The Top of the Rockies enjoyed a wonderful twenty-year career in Denver. The Stouffer Corp. had just made a long-term commitment to remodel the space to keep the restaurant going, only to be chased away by building owners who got too greedy. That space sat empty for almost the next twelve years.

The Top always had a wonderful variety of customers, all begging for the golden ring, a table by the window. Business people jammed the restaurant during the week and couples on the weekend,

# Specialties

## Steak Diane Flambé
Medallions of Filet Mignon sauteed in butter
with Mushrooms and Green Onions.
Flamed tableside with Cognac.    18.95

## Roast Duck with Ginger Brandy Sauce
Crisp semi-boneless Duck highlighted
with a sauce of fresh Ginger.    14.95

## Roast Prime Ribs of Beef
The ultimate in roasts cut to your preference
and served with a Horseradish Sauce.
Heavy Cut:    17.95    Lesser Cut:    14.95

## Filet de Boeuf Wellington
Filet Mignon covered with Duxelle of Mushrooms wrapped in
puff pastry and served with Sauce Béarnaise.    17.95

## Poulet aux Artichaut
Sauteed boneless Chicken Breast enhanced with
rich Cream Sauce, Artichokes and Mushrooms.    11.50

## Veal Homard
Cutlets of Veal sauteed in Butter and
crowned with Asparagus Spears and an
elegant Lobster Sauce.    14.95

## Veal Cordon Bleu
Delicate Veal filled with Cheese and Ham,
lightly breaded and sauteed in Butter.    14.50

## Filet Mignon Béarnaise
The tenderest of all steaks enhanced with Mushroom Caps
filled with Béarnaise Sauce.    17.50

## New York Strip Steak
A well-marbled Sirloin Steak, specially trimmed and
crowned with Tarragon Butter.    16.95

and then there was prom time. I talk to people all the time who spent their prom night at the Top.

The worst time up there was during a storm—especially the tornadoes that made the windows creak and bend almost to implosion. The night a man found his lover in the restaurant with someone else and threw his chair through a window was also exciting. And then there was the Easter Sunday brunch with over four hundred reservations, only to all of downtown closed due to poisonous gas leaking from an overturned tanker train.

The great times and the great people you meet in this business remain with you forever. I stay in contact with many of my old employees.

When it came time not to renew the lease, I was offered a transfer back to the Midwest: however my wife and I had come to love Colorado, and I started my second career in the wine business. I became marketing director for Bodegas Olarra, a Rioja winery, and worked for them for three years. In 1986, I opened my own business—The Wine Company, located in Littleton. I continue to be amazed about how restaurants come and go now.

*A restaurant is a fantasy—a kind of living fantasy in which diners are the most important members of the cast.*

—*Warner LeRoy*

# A Smorgasbord of Eateries

While my memory is still pretty good, for my age, there are no doubt lapses when it comes to remembering details about some restaurants that deserve to be mentioned.

I had great help from many kind persons who contributed with their collection, menus, publications such as *Denver Epicure, Colorado Gourmet Gold, Dining in Denver* by Jaydee Boat, and many more!!

Thank you one and all.

Now here are a few words about those restaurants where either my memory faded or I never visited them in the first place. I did some poking around in old Denver phone books of years prior to my arrival. The Summer 1925 Denver Telephone Directory listed about two hundred restaurants, designated as lunchrooms, cafés, coffee shops, food and doughnut shops, parlors, dairy cafés, sandwich shops, cafeterias, a grill or two, a fountain lunch room, a buffet, and the Parisienne Rotisserie Inn. Eating places featured in display ads were:

> Joe's Place, 1451 California (phone Champa 1827), "Chile and First-class Lunch"
>
> M. & K. Restaurant, 1435–37 Stout Street (phone Champa 2721), Roy Miller, Manager, "Good Place to Eat"
>
> The Moonlight Ranch, Morrison Road, "Chicken Dinners our Specialty," "Ravioli-Spaghetti," "Dancing every Night"

Dominating the page with a large ad was the Edelweiss Café, 1625 California St., "Meals are Relished," "Never Closed." The luncheon special ran a hefty $1.00 to $1.50, whereas other luncheons were available at $.95. Steaks and chops were very expensive for the day, from $1.25 to $3.75.

# Banquet
## Commemorating the
# Forty-fourth Anniversary
# of the Founding of Denver
## Monday Evening, November
## Seventeenth, Nineteen
## Hundred and Two
## Adams Hotel

1858  1902

| | |
|---|---|
| *Blue Points* | |
| *Celery* | |
| | |
| *Consomme, en Tasse* | *Haut Sauterne* |
| *Olives*    *Salted Almonds* | |
| | |
| *Fillet of Sole, Sauce Remoulade* | |
| *Julienne Potatoes* | |
| | |
| *Tenderloin of Beef, with Mushrooms* | *Pontet Canet* |
| *Browned Sweet Potatoes*   *French Peas, en Cases* | |
| | |
| *Punch Romaine* | *Cigarettes* |
| | |
| *Broiled Quail on Toast, with Bacon* | |
| | |
| *Fresh Shrimp Salad* | |
| | |
| *Tortoni Bisque* | |
| | |
| *Fancy Assorted Cake* | |
| | |
| *Fruit* | |
| | |
| *Cheese*    *Toasted Crackers* | |
| | |
| *Demi Tasse* | *Perfectos* |

An 1885 menu cover from the Windsor Hotel's Tabor Bonanza Room. The prix fixe, 7-course menu included boiled codfish, corned beef and cabbage, maraschino sherbet, roast spring lamb, baked cracker pudding with champagne sauce, port wine jelly, edam and cream cheese, coffee.

In the directory for "Denver and Adjoining Towns, Winter 1935–36," about three hundred restaurants are listed—despite the Depression. Among those I recognize by name are:

Bennett Coffee Shop, 308 17th Street

Buckhorn Exchange Restaurant, 1000 Osage (still operating)

Edelweiss Restaurant, 1644 Glenarm Place

Manhattan Restaurant, 1635 Larimer Street

Moon Drive Inn, 3503 East Colfax Avenue

Old Heidelberg, 741 East Colfax Avenue

The Blue Parrot Inn on 1716–30 Broadway in Denver was quite well known in its heyday. For good reason! Their menu had so many items that I like. I wish they were still around, particularly with those prices!

On Monday, October 31, 1938, the following menu items were offered:

Roast Prime Rib of Beef au jus with Cream, Whipped Potatoes and Pepper Relish (60 cents)

Veal Birds with Celery Dressing, Fresh Mushroom Sauce and Creamed Whipped Potatoes (60 cents)

Broiled Young Lamb Chops (3) on Toast Points and Cream (85 cents)

Broiled Tenderloin Steak, Fresh Mushroom Sauce, French Fried Potatoes (70 cents)

Broiled Sixteen-ounce T-Bone Steak with French Fries (1 dollar)

Now catch this one: Seafood Grill of Fried Fresh Scallops on Toast Points, Filet of Sole with Tartar Sauce, Fresh Shrimp on Tomato Slices, French Fried Potatoes and Crabmeat Cocktail center (all for only 80 cents). What a deal!

By May 1945, there were Yellow Pages! That year's pages were certainly a lot livelier, and restaurant listings exceeded seven hundred! Featured in the ads were:

Edelweiss Café, "Best Dinner in the State, 60¢"

Lande's of Denver, East Colfax at Steele, "Excellent cuisine," "A Place for the Discriminating," "Fine Liqueurs"

Boggio's Rotisserie, Tremont at Broadway, "Distinctive for Fine Foods," "Cocktail Lounge"

Golden Lantern, "Denver's Most Beautiful Restaurant," "The Steak House of the West," "Air Conditioned, 350 Seats," "Recommended by Duncan Hines." The Golden Lantern featured Blue Ribbon steaks, fried chicken, mountain trout, roast turkey, fresh seafood, and homemade pastries.

From more recent years, I can certainly pick a few more restaurants to comment on, but I lack details. Take Boccalino's and Chez Thoa, with Thoa Fink and Bill Husted as waiter. Café Franco where

# BLUE PARROT INN

**DENVER**
1718 BROADWAY

*Dining Places of Distinction*

IN HOLLYWOOD
**GOURMET HOLLYWOOD**

IN CHICAGO
**LE PETIT GOURMET**

IN OAK PARK
**BLUE PARROT PATIO**

**ALL DINNERS INCLUDE:** Appetizer, Salad, Entree, Beverage, Vegetable and Dessert

|  | Complete Dinner |
|---|---|
| **Filet Mignon Wrapped in Bacon** | **1.85** |
| With Fresh Mushroom Sauce and French Fried Potatoes | |
| **Baked Tender Swiss Steak** | **1.65** |
| With Fresh Mushroom Sauce and Creamed Whipped Potatoes | |
| **Blue Parrot Seafood Grill** | **1.65** |
| Fried Fresh Shrimp, Eastern Scallops, Fillet of Sole with Tartar Sauce, Marinated Herring on Tomato Slice, Seafood Cocktail Center and Potato | |
| **Fresh Mountain Trout** | **1.75** |
| Rolled in Cornmeal, Fried Golden Brown with Lemon Slice and Potato | |
| **Shortcut Steak** | **3.25** |
| With French Fried Potatoes | |
| **Sliced Breast of Chicken and Ham** | **1.75** |
| On Toast Points with Fricassee Gravy, Fresh Mushrooms and Creamed Whipped Potatoes | |
| **Broiled T-Bone Steak** | **3.75** |
| With Fresh Mushroom Sauce and French Fried Potatoes | |

**DANIELS and FISHER**

## Appetizers and Soup

| | | |
|---|---|---|
| Marinated Herring . . . . . . . . . . . . . . . . . . . . . . . . . . . . . . . . . . . . . . | | 25 |
| Vegetable Soup . . . . . . . . . . . . . . . . . cup 15 bowl . . . . . . | | 25 |
| Chicken Broth with Rice . . . . . . . . . . . cup 15 bowl . . . . . . | | 25 |
| Grapefruit Half . . . . . . . . . . . . . . . . . . . . . . . . . . . . . . . . . . . . . . | | 20 |
| Fruit Cup . . . . . . . . . . . . 25 Frosted . . . . . . . . . . . . . . | | 35 |
| Fresh Orange Juice . . . . . . . . . . . . . . . . . . . . . . . . . . . . . . . . . . . | | 25 |
| Tomato or Grapefruit Juice . . . . . . . . . . . . . . . . . . . . . . . . . | | 15 |
| Toasted English Muffin with Whipped Butter & Marmalade . . . | | 20 |

## Salads

| | |
|---|---|
| A Salad Plate of Moulded Perfection Salad, Cottage Cheese | 65 |
| Chicken Salad & Peach Half . . . . . . . . . . . . . . . . . . . . | 95 |
| Fresh Combination Salad with D & F Dressing . . . . . . . . . . . . | 65 |
| Fruit Plate with Cottage Cheese & Paradise Dressing . . . . . . | 95 |

**With Thousand Island Dressing 10c extra**

## Sandwiches

| | |
|---|---|
| Peanut Butter & Pickle Sandwich . . . . . . . . . . . . . . . . . . . . | 45 |
| Turkey Salad Sandwich . . . . . . . . . . . . . . . . . . . . . . . . . . . . . | 75 |
| American or Swiss Cheese Sandwich . . . . . . . . . . . . . . . . . . . . | 50 |
| Open-face Tower Sandwich- Sliced Chicken, Ham, | |
| American Cheese, Tomato and Egg Slices | 1.10 |
| Ham Salad . . . . . . . . . . . . . . . . . . . . . . . . . . . . . . . . . . . . . . . | 45 |
| Bacon and Tomato . . . . . . . . . . . . . . . . . . . . . . . . . . . . . . . . | 55 |
| Baked Virginia Ham Sandwich . . . . . . . . . . . . . . . . . . . . . . | 65 |
| D. & F. Club Sandwich . . . . . . . . . . . . . . . . . . . . . . . . . . . . | 95 |
| Sliced Chicken or Turkey with Lettuce and Mayonnaise . . . . . . | 80 |

**With Thousand Island Dressing 10c extra**

Daniels and Fisher was the prime department store of downtown Denver; its distinctive tower still stands on 16th Street. Having lunch or a light snack did much to revive energies for more shopping, and in addition to the restaurant (featuring, among other items, a Peanut Butter and Pickle sandwich!), the Gourmet Shop offered imported delicacies such as chutney from India, Russian caviar, marrons with vanilla or brandy from France, Dutch tangy cheeses, and herbs and exotic seasonings from the Spice Islands.

Bridge Director Marvel Heinsohn and his wife, Sally, enjoyed many good meals. Andy's Smorgasbord, which much later became Shotgun Willie's.

And talking about strip joints, I must mention the Tropics on Morrison Road. In those days, during the late 1950s, this was a pretty classy place. Most patrons wore coat and tie, and my wife, Jean, could not get enough of Tempest Storm performing tassle twisting—where one went to the left and the other in the opposite direction. Mesmerizing stuff!

Footers and Emerson Street East were quite popular, and Mon Petit on the west side of town did very well, operated by the late Frank Pourdard. Roncetti's was the forerunner of Strings and Al Stromberg strutted his stuff on top of Neusteter's and in the location of Soapy Smith downtown. Shaner's and Hummel's were everyone's favorite delicatessens. Many fine memories of the Top of the Park with Mike de Salles's orchestra playing for dancing and dining, and many top stars performing, including George Gobel.

Victoria Station should be mentioned for their fine prime rib, and the Peacock Tavern were Bill Husted worked his first job as a waiter. The Chat and Chew, the China Café, and the Fuji Inn were frequented. The Library was great for prime rib, owned at one time by the late activist, Bud Hawkins. Corky Douglass bought the Library from Bud and rued the day.

I could go on forever but my publisher really wants this book to be ready for printing before I die. Who can blame her?

*Once learnt, this business of cooking*
*was to prove an ever growing burden.*
*It scarcely bears thinking about, the*
*time and labour that man and woman-*
*kind has devoted to the preparation of*
*dishes that are to melt and vanish in a*
*moment like smoke or a dream, like a*
*shadow, and as a post that hastes by,*
*and the air closes behind them, after-*
*wards no sign where they went is to*
*be found.*

*—Rose Macaulay*

## Wilscam's ~ 17th and Arapahoe Streets, Denver (also, Hungry Farmer ~ Dutchman ~ Original Broker ~ pti)

What ever happened to the former gridiron star, also known as the other guard? A man who spent three years in the Marine Corps and graduated from the University of Southern California, but got a lot of press playing the left guard on the University of Colorado's team next to an All-American, Joe Romig. We should remember Tom Wilscam for a lot of things. It would take a whole chapter to recall his entrepreneurial endeavors. But for now, let's call Tom the Father of Theme Restaurants in Colorado. Early on, Tom Wilscam was certainly not destined to run restaurants. But somehow this major in business and advertising/marketing created fun theme eateries. All but one are memories.

Gimmicks were a useful tool for Tom, beginning with the Terrace Restaurant in Golden. "The food was terrible," said Tom. Business was bad, so his fertile mind thought up a come-on. Wilscam was well acquainted with prominent athletes at the University of Colorado, so he persuaded stars Charlie Gardner, Joe Romig, Gail Wagner, Teddy Woods, and others to wait tables at the Terrace. Each table at the restaurant had the name of one of the athletes on it, proudly proclaiming "Joe Romig is your Waiter." Despite the so-so food, people lined up outside the restaurant to be served by a sport celebrity.

Now Tom was bitten by the restaurant bug. He had his eye on the Alpine Village Inn on South Colorado Boulevard, which greatly appealed to him. With no job openings, he persuaded owner Ray Dambach to take him on for free, and Ray obliged him. Stuck into the kitchen, Tom washed potatoes and did other menial jobs. But Ray also taught Tom food and labor costs and became his mentor.

Ray Dambach purchased the Country Kitchen from Colonel Hudson, renamed it the Northwoods Inn, and appointed Wilscam the manager. After two years, Tom was rewarded 20 percent for his efforts.

But Tom still wanted his own place. With money in his pocket from the Northwoods, Wilscam attracted investors, those eager people who love to "own" a restaurant! Thus, the first Hungry Farmer (menu selections below) was born in May 1964. Business was good

# FARM SPECIALTIES

### Cherry Duck
Roasted crisp and juicy, topped with black bing cherry sauce and served up on a bed of homemade cornbread dressing
$11.95

### Beef Steak Pot Pie
Braised choice beef tips simmered with mushrooms, carrots, onions and peas in a delicate wine sauce and topped with a latice of puff pastry
$9.50

### Country Fried Steak
A tenderized top sirloin steak breaded with cornmeal and pan fried, topped with a hearty country gravy
$10.25

### Country Style BBQ Ribs
Granny slow cooks fresh pork loin then bastes them in her own special sauce
$10.50

### Liver & Onions
Sautéed and smothered with onions, a special treat for special tastes!
$8.50

### Country Fried Chicken
No ordinary fare! Specially breaded and deep fried to a golden brown
$8.50

### Country Style Pork Chops
Two center-cut pork chops dipped in egg wash and flour then pan fried
$10.50

# COLD ENTREES

**1** CHICKEN SALAD IN CANTALOUPE
*One-half ice cold California cantaloupe crowned with a generous helping of "Chef Luigi's" famous chicken salad.*
TODAY'S QUOTE   2.10

**2** STUFFED AVOCADO OR STUFFED TOMATO   *Your choice of avocado or tomato stuffed with King Crabmeat from Alaskan waters.*
TODAY'S QUOTE   2.50

**3** BROKER'S FRUIT PLATE   *A refreshing platter of succulent fruits highlighted by a center of sherbet or cottage cheese.*
TODAY'S QUOTE   2.00

**4** LUIGI'S CHEF SALAD   *Our Chef's own creation of an old favorite with his special Frank-furt dressing.*
TODAY'S QUOTE . 1.95

and the investors did well. Then came the Dutchman in July 1966. The Boulder Farmer in 1969 was followed by the surviving Farmer in Colorado Springs in October 1972.

Going back a bit, Tom had his eye on downtown Denver. The Broker Restaurant opened February 1969 (menu selections above). People had warned Wilscam against this location, 17th and Champa, because the renewal of downtown Denver had not begun, and Larimer Street was still a haven for Denver's drunks and homeless.

While lunch business flourished, the nights were simply bad. Enter Ed Novak, who had previously managed the Boulder Hungry Farmer for Wilscam, and, with a partner, Fred Borra, Ed bought the Broker in 1972.

Whenever I mention the "pti" restaurants to anyone, I get a blank stare. Yet, in October 1972, a futuristic restaurant designed by architect Fred Mikawa, who had joined Wilscam Enterprises early on, was built on Hampden Avenue right by I-25. The pti (these letters had no meaning) was to become the fulfillment of Tom's dream for

# Specialties

### Steak Diane Flambé
*Medallions of Filet Mignon sauteed in butter
with Mushrooms and Green Onions.
Flamed tableside with Cognac.*    18.95

### Roast Duck with Ginger Brandy Sauce
*Crisp semi-boneless Duck highlighted
with a sauce of fresh Ginger.*    14.95

### Roast Prime Ribs of Beef
*The ultimate in roasts cut to your preference
and served with a Horseradish Sauce.*
Heavy Cut:    17.95      Lesser Cut:    14.95

### Filet de Boeuf Wellington
*Filet Mignon covered with Duxelle of Mushrooms wrapped in
puff pastry and served with Sauce Béarnaise.*    17.95

### Poulet aux Artichaut
*Sauteed boneless Chicken Breast enhanced with
rich Cream Sauce, Artichokes and Mushrooms.*    11.50

### Veal Homard
*Cutlets of Veal sauteed in Butter and
crowned with Asparagus Spears and an
elegant Lobster Sauce.*    14.95

### Veal Cordon Bleu
*Delicate Veal filled with Cheese and Ham,
lightly breaded and sauteed in Butter.*    14.50

### Filet Mignon Béarnaise
*The tenderest of all steaks enhanced with Mushroom Caps
filled with Béarnaise Sauce.*    17.50

### New York Strip Steak
*A well-marbled Sirloin Steak, specially trimmed and
crowned with Tarragon Butter.*    16.95

national expansion. The luncheon menu was solid aluminum, weighed four pounds, and cost twenty-five dollars.

pti's in Dallas, Austin, Cleveland, and Atlanta followed. Later, Wilscam Enterprises overextended and was sold piecemeal, but kept the Dutchman, which was later sold to the Peterson Brothers.

The first and last attempt by Tom Wilscam to operate an up-scale, white-tablecloth restaurant came in 1980: Wilscam's, located between 17th and 18th on Arapahoe Street. A number of investors lined up to shell out $100,000 apiece (menu selections on previous page). The first year the restaurant grossed $6.7 million. Three hundred patrons for breakfast was the norm, with oilman Marvin Davis booking a table three times a week for lunch. The restaurant was well designed, appointed with beautiful china and glassware. The food was normally great, depending on who officiated in the kitchen. Here Tom discovered the pleasures of dealing with prima donna chefs! With the oil bust in the 1980s, revenues declined, and it was all over for Wilscam's in 1983. Tom was not alone with suffering the loss of his restaurant.

The wheels in the mind of Tom Wilscam never stopped turning. He and his partner, Gary McGill, have consulted in franchising fifteen bagel operations as far away as Dublin, Ireland. Knowing Tom, he will soon explore space for opening theme restaurants ("Heaven 'n' Earth"?) and hire famous ex-astronauts as waiters. Line up now!

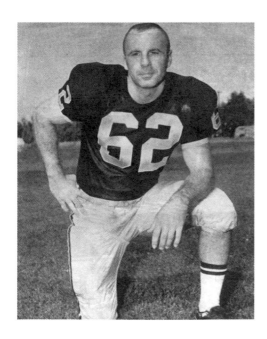

Tom Wilscam as left guard for Colorado University's winning football team of 1960. *Courtesy, Empire Magazine, January 19, 1975.*

# Looking Back,
# It Wasn't about the Food

## By Nancy Clark

My memories about the dining out aren't about ambient lighting, food prepared and designed with genius, or even the art of service. No. As a kid growing up in Denver, I found every dining experience flush with new adventure. Our family didn't dine out much, which wasn't so different from most of the families we knew and grew up with. Dining out as a family was a rare experience in the 1950s and 1960s for most of young America. Even a hot school lunch, rather than a sack lunch carried from home, was a treat. Schools then still served fish sticks on Fridays. Milk was 2 cents a carton and the best school lunches in Littleton District 6 were the days the cafeteria marms baked oversized caramel rolls served with, well, who even remembers what they were served with.

Dining out in those years was more about the distance we had to travel to get to a restaurant. (Are we there yet?) And it was about being together as a family. Some bits and pieces of those grand events—grand because we dressed in our Sunday best to go out to eat, unlike today's shorts-and-t-shirt diners—left indelible impressions.

We rolled over hill after hill like a roller coaster along County Line Road to get to the Hungry Dutchman. The windmill fascinated every kid lucky enough to get on site and gaze up at it. It was the mounds of peanut shells on the floor of the Northwoods Inn that impressed children most. This was a place that actually wanted you to throw your shell remains on the floor—unwelcome behavior anyplace else. The oversized, aluminum foil-wrapped baked potatoes at

Georgia Boys Bar-B-Que on South Broadway overwhelmed every plate served to the table. (The aluminum foil was tightly secured to those potatoes with a resin, so that even bored little fingers couldn't peel away the foil during the course of the evening.)

Our longer treks to Denver included a dinner at the Apple Tree Shanty on East Colfax Avenue, where waitresses dressed in Dutch costume wore full white caps, reminiscent of nuns. On a warm Easter Sunday, we waited for what seemed to be hours outside Baur's for our brunch. At one point, my little sister, Julie, grew so tired she sat down on an exposed floodlight—which happened to be turned on—and burned her bottom. I really don't recall if we stayed to eat or went home to have more hard-boiled eggs and chocolate when the crying stopped.

Dining out in those years isn't what it is for kids today, or for that matter, what it was like for my own children growing up in the 1980s and 1990s. They became so accustomed to fast-food stops, pizza deliveries, and casual dining at chain after chain that eating out was more the rule than was a sit-down family dinner at home. Just prior to my son's return home from college for Thanksgiving vacation, I detailed the menu I had planned—turkey and all the trimmings. He countered with, "I was kind of thinking about Chipotle." He missed his daily dose of Mexican food while in the East.

And yet when it comes to our family recalling special times spent together, some of those memories do, in fact, center around dining out. Curiously, though, it still comes back to the minute details of the adventure: the time my son ate so much at Cordillera's Picasso Room that he had to leave the table to unbutton his slacks so that he could continue to eat even more. Or the day my daughter got to hold a pet rabbit in her arms after brunch at the Arizona Biltmore.

Even for modern-day kids, it's almost never about the food.

*What is patriotism but the love of good things we ate in our childhood.*

—*Lin Yutang*

# Gene Amole:
# The Frustrated Chef

For all his talents as a radio personality and newspaper columnist, Gene Amole also loves to cook. His regular column for the *Rocky Mountain News* often contained recipes along with musings on life and current events. A number of his columns-cum-recipes were published in his 1978 book, *Morning,* which is no longer in print, but folks keep asking him for more. When I asked him for permission to reprint some of his columns and material from his book, he was delighted—"Now maybe folks will quit bugging me to write a new book," he said. With many thanks to Gene, for his permission to include his work here, and for the many years of great writing about food and life and all the rest! One caveat: any failure as a result of using Gene's recipes should be directed to the originator! —*Pierre Wolfe*

## Take This Bird and Stuff It!

Stuffing is important. As Gertrude Stein might have said, "A turkey is a turkey is a turkey." But what goes inside gives the old bird character. It is a part of the Thanksgiving feast we all remember. Mine is unforgettable.

First, open a bottle of Harvey's Bristol Cream Sherry. Actually, any brand will do, but Harvey's is the best. Have yourself a little nip and then pour exactly 8 ounces into a measuring cup. Put it aside while you prepare the other ingredients.

Take 17 slices of dry white bread and 3 slices of dry pumpernickel. Cut into crouton-size cubes and place in a large mixing bowl. Sprinkle with 1 teaspoon pepper, 1 tablespoon salt, and 1 tablespoon sage, thyme, or poultry seasoning. Marjoram works OK, too.

Brown and crumble in a skillet $\frac{1}{2}$ pound of bulk breakfast sausage and $\frac{1}{4}$ pound of Italian bulk sausage. After thoroughly mixing the sausage, remove with slotted spoon and put in the big bowl.

Add 1 cup each of chopped celery, onion, and chopped walnuts. Throw in 3 tablespoons of parsley and 2 cups of sliced fresh mushrooms. Add 1 tart crisp apple, peeled, cored, and chopped. Granny Smiths are nice. So are Jonathans and Newtons.

I know what you are thinking. You are concerned about the pumpernickel and the Italian sausage. Just seems out of character, doesn't it? Trust me. And you probably want to sauté the onions and celery. Don't.

Everytime I make this stuffing, I am reminded of Chinese philosopher Lao-tse's observation about bean sprouts. "They should be firm but yielding," he wrote. So should the celery and onions in this dressing. The nuts and apple will retain a nice crispness, too.

Heat 1 cube of unsalted butter in 2 cups of chicken broth until the butter melts. Campbell's works fine. Pour the liquid into the bowl. Do not mix yet. There is one more important ingredient.

Right you are! It is the sherry. Never forget the sherry. Very carefully pour 3 tablespoons of sherry into the bowl. Sip away at the sherry you have reserved in the measuring cup. Good old Harvey's. Here's to you, Harvey!

Carefully toss the stuffing with two wooden spoons until all ingredients are evenly mixed. Do not bruise the sausage! If mixture is too dry, add warm water.

*Voila!* It is done. Lightly stuff the bird fore and aft. You'll have dressing left over. Place it in a casserole dish, cover with foil, place in oven for the last hour of roasting time.

Drizzle on the giblet gravy.

# Chicken Recipe

There you are in your kitchen. You are carefully following a recipe for "Chicken with Apricots." The sauce calls for 2 cups of apricot brandy.

But shortly after you put the bird in a 350-degree oven, BAM! The oven door blows open, and there is what is left of tonight's dinner. A drumstick here. What's left of the wishbone over there. And look at that pathetic little wing!

Now you are thinking I am going to make sport of this. To the contrary, being a person of sensitivity, I extend my heartfelt sympathy to all who have been touched by this tragic chicken mutilation incident.

And because of my generous nature, I have decided to lend a helping hand. I am going to donate one of my favorite chicken recipes. What are friends for?

I call my recipe "Chicken and Dumplings." It is not actually mine. It has been handed down for generations in our family. My Great-grandma Fiedler gave it to my Grandma Amole, who in turn, bequeathed it to my mother.

Mine also calls for apricot brandy. We'll get to that later.

Get a nice plump hen at the butcher shop. Second-best is a 5- or 6-pound roasting chicken. The fatter, the better. Cut up the chicken, put it in a pot and cover with water. Add salt, pepper, 1 onion, 1 carrot, and a celery stalk with leaves. Cover and simmer for at least 2 hours.

You are thinking that is just stewed chicken, and you are right. Nothing complicated. It is absolutely the simplest way to cook chicken. Nothing to it. The aroma is marvelous. When I was a boy, it wasn't Sunday unless we had stewed chicken.

So what's so special? The dumplings! Yes, those wonderful, light, fluffy dumplings. Your old Uncle Geno is going to reveal Grandma Fiedler's dumpling secret right here and now.

Combine $1\frac{1}{2}$ cups of sifted flour with 2 teaspoons of baking powder, $\frac{3}{4}$ teaspoon of salt, $\frac{1}{2}$ cup of milk, and 1 egg. Mix with old wooden spoon. And the shortening? No shortening. Not one bit. That's the first half of the secret. Grandma used to say, "It's just like making biscuits, except you don't use fat."

Uncover the pot and reduce the pot likker until it is just below the level of the chicken. Leave it as stock for the gravy. Spoon the dumpling dough on top of the chicken. Don't let it get in the liquid that's left in the pot. That's the second half of the secret.

Most recipes say to float the dough right in the soup. Not this one. We don't want soggy dumplings, now do we? We want those dumplings to draw up the steam of that rich pot likker.

Simmer uncovered for exactly 10 minutes. Cover the pot and simmer for another 10 minutes. DO NOT PEEK! Never peek. Don't mess up the dumplings by peeking. Ever. Trust me.

While the dumplings are steaming, make gravy with reserved pot likker. Usual way, milk, flour, salt, and pepper. Uncover pot. Lift out those lovely dumplings and serve with chicken and gravy.

The apricot brandy? You drink that. Whatever you do, don't put it in the pot. You don't want to blow up the chicken, do you?

## Pot Roast

Pot roast is easy. I've always said any fool can cook it if he knows how to read. You start with a 3- or 4-pound chuck roast or bone-in roast. Flour, season, and brown it in bacon grease or cooking oil on the stove in a pot. An electric skillet is OK.

Drain off the grease and return the roast to the pot and pour a couple of cups of cheap red jug wine around it. Does Gallo still bottle Hearty Burgundy?

Let me take a little pit stop here. Do you remember when the Gallos sneaked in some of their jug Hearty Burgundy into one of those classy French wine competitions and won? Wow, was that ever fun!

But back to the pot roast. Next you want to slather the top with regular store-bought chili sauce and top it with sliced fresh onion. Cover the pot and return it to the stove, or cover the electric fry pan with a high-dome lid.

It's true that "cheap meat ain't good, and good meat ain't cheap." If you simmer the pot roast for about an hour per pound, however, it will be tender as young love.

During the last hour of cooking, add quartered potatoes and diagonally sliced carrots, and parsnips, if you like them. Add more wine if necessary. Take a little nip for yourself.

When the vegetables are fork-tender, remove and brown them in the oven while, on the stove, you make the most magnificent gravy you've ever tasted. Thicken the liquid with Wondra flour or cornstarch.

Slice the roast against the grain, arrange the vegetables around the slices, and drizzle some of the gravy on top.

Anybody hungry?

## Cheap Cuts of Meat Aren't Always Tough

I wish I could tell you the recipe was handed down in our family from Aunt Gladys, but it wasn't. I adapted it from one that appeared last year in a *Gourmet* magazine article on braising, a method of slow-cooking meat with liquid in a tightly covered container.

Brisket, I'm sure you know, is that tough, grainy meat from the lower chest or breast of the animal. It is the cut of beef most frequently used for corned beef.

You're going to love this recipe because it is so easy, and it makes one of the incredibly delicious gravies of our time. I mean that.

Chop and brown $\frac{1}{4}$ pound of generic bacon in your Dutch oven (heavy flameproof casserole). Remove bacon bits with a slotted spoon and keep for further use. Dredge 3-pound brisket in seasoned flour, shake on generous amount of paprika, and brown that baby on both sides in the pot.

While the brisket is sizzling, peel and cut 4 carrots into 1-inch pieces. Cut up similar amount of celery into 1-inch pieces. Process 3 onions with steel blade, or chop onions as fine as possible.

Remove browned brisket from the pot and place on a plate. Toss the onions, carrots, celery, and bacon bits back into the pot and stir and sauté until onions become transparent. Return the brisket to the pot, placing it fat side up on top of the vegetables.

Mix 1 tablespoon of brown sugar in 1 pint of dark ale and pour over meat. Actually, that's about a bottle and a half. What do you do with the remaining ale? Throw it out. Whatever you do, don't drink it. Makes you gassy and tastes terrible.

Sprinkle a couple of pinches of dill seed on top of the brisket. Bring it to a simmer on top of the range. Cover and put pot in 300-degree oven for $2\frac{1}{2}$ hours. You'll know it's done when it's fork-tender.

It's a good idea to turn the brisket every half-hour or so. You'll like that part because you liberate more beautiful aroma into the kitchen. This part will drive your family crazy, crazy, crazy.

When the brisket is tender, remove to a cutting board and cover with foil. Scoop out the carrots and celery with a slotted spoon. Strain the remaining liquid and thicken with Wondra flour for gravy. You will not need to add any seasoning at all. It will be perfect.

Thin-slice the brisket across the grain and arrange slices on a platter, surrounding them with carrots and celery. Drizzle a little gravy on top and serve with Kluski noodles.

Good snappin'.

## Spicy Meatballs

I became addicted to the meatballs served at Ernie Capillupo's Restaurant and Lounge back in 1946. You remember the place. It's at 2915 W. 44th Ave., just a block east of Federal Boulevard. Lordy, how I loved those meatball sandwiches!

I was never able to get Ernie's recipe, so I have evolved my own. Like Edward Elgar's "Enigma" musical composition, Uncle Geno's North Side Spicy Meatballs recipe is a variation on an original theme.

Certainly you will require $\frac{3}{4}$ of a pound of ground beef and $\frac{1}{2}$ pound of ground pork. Do not hesitate to throw in a modest amount of Italian bulk sausage, if available.

Combine 2 eggs in a large bowl with $\frac{1}{2}$ cup of milk, $1\frac{1}{2}$ teaspoons of salt, 3 tablespoons of Mexican picante sauce, 1 tablespoon of parsley, and a pinch each of black pepper, oregano, marjoram, thyme, basil, rosemary, and sage.

Fine chop 1 medium-size onion, either by hand or by using the steel blade in your processor. Add the onion and 1 minced clove of garlic to the other ingredients and beat them mercilessly.

Put the meat in the bowl and stir with an old wooden spoon. Take care that the ground beef and pork are properly blended. We don't want a lump of pork here, and another lump of beef there, do we?

Now you are ready to add 1 cup of seasoned bread crumbs and ½ cup of Parmesan cheese. The mixture will become thick and difficult to manage, but manage it you will. And after that is done, form meatballs of 1⅜-inches diameter by rolling the meat between your palms. This is sticky work but wonderful stress-reduction therapy.

The meatballs should be fried in oil until brown all over and done clear through. You should be alone during this part of the process, as family members will be drawn to the kitchen by the aroma and will eat the meatballs as rapidly as you cook them.

Simmer them in your favorite tomato sauce for at least 45 minutes. Serve those little beauties on firm-but-yielding homemade pasta. The flavor of egg pasta, by the way, is enhanced by the addition of a bit of Parmesan cheese and a shake or so of cayenne pepper to the dough. That, I suppose, is another story.

Don't forget the Chianti.

## Meat Loaf

Now that there is a little chill in the evening air, and there are yellow leaves at the top of the cottonwoods, there is nothing nicer to come home to than meat loaf and oven-browned potatoes.

There are certain rewards to the actual making of meat loaf. I find it relaxing to squish the ingredients by hand. I suppose it is a form of regression, resembling in some ways the making of mud pies. Some kids sucked their thumbs—I was more of a mud pie man. You can read into that any kind of psychological meaning you wish.

Get a great big mixing bowl. Begin with 1 egg and 1 cup of milk. In no particular order, add 1½ teaspoons of salt, 1 tablespoon of Worcestershire sauce, and a teaspoon of A-1.

You'll need some garlic salt, sage, celery salt, pepper, and dry mustard. Add about a quarter-teaspoon each. If you like a peppy meat loaf, drizzle in a teaspoon of Mexican salsa. Mix like crazy with an egg beater.

Add 1 chopped white onion. Do not use yellow onions; they are too stout. Combine with 1 pound of lean ground beef and ½ pound of ground pork. Fairly ordinary so far, huh?

Here's the big difference. Instead of using bread crumbs, tear up 3 medium slices of Jewish pumpernickel bread and mix with the rest of the ingredients.

Wow, does that ever make it special! The meat loaf has a robust, down-home flavor. The aroma when it is baking is even more enticing.

As I pointed out, it wasn't my idea. Trish was making meat loaf one night and found we were out of bread crumbs. We had nothing but the pumpernickel we keep around for hot corned beef and pastrami sandwiches. So, she improvised.

After you have completely mixed all the ingredients, place into ungreased loaf pan. Be sure to punch it down well to eliminate all air pockets.

Now you would just know to slather the top with a generous lay of chili sauce, wouldn't you? Ketchup is OK, but chili sauce is better. Sprinkle on some chopped parsley. Pop into a preheated 350-degree oven and bake 2 hours.

The loaf will shrink somewhat, making it easy to remove from the pan with a couple of spatulas. Let it sit a spell on a trencher cutting board before slicing. Gravy made from the drippings is mighty tasty with the spuds.

A good vegetable with this pumpernickel loaf is backyard green beans. They should be simmered with fatback or bacon until all the vitamins are cooked out. Serve with chopped raw onion on top.

Collard or turnip greens are also nice. Steam them with more fatback, chopped green onions, and a little Tabasco. This gives the meat loaf a sort of soulful touch.

*Voila!*

## Slumgullion or Boeuf Bourguignon

We'll need a couple of pounds of stew meat—chuck, or round, if you want to be fancy. Cube, trim off the fat, and throw the whole works into a Dutch oven. Do not brown. Instead, toss the meat with 1 tablespoon of Kitchen Bouquet. Next, sprinkle with ¼ cup of uncooked cream of rice cereal. Mix.

Isn't that slick? No grease. No flour.

You'll need 1 cup of thinly sliced celery. You can do this with your processor, or as has been pointed out here before, slicing by hand builds character and gives one a sense of accomplishment. Add the celery and 1 minced clove of fresh garlic.

You now are ready for the spices. Use 2 teaspoons of salt and a generous pinch each of pepper, marjoram, and thyme. For Pete's sake, don't forget the wine. That's where the bourguignon comes in. Use el cheapo red burgundy. You'll need $2\frac{1}{2}$ cups. One cup for you to nip at, and the rest goes into the stew. *A votre sante.*

Peel 4 good-sized carrots. Either quarter them or cut them in 1-inch pieces. I like the pieces better. They'll be about the size of the meat cubes. Looks nicer. Add the carrots and mix lightly with the rest of the ingredients.

Cover and put in a preheated 325-degree oven. It will take about $2\frac{1}{2}$ hours before it is ready. Figure on stirring with a wooden spoon about every 30 minutes. This will keep the ingredients from sticking and will flood your kitchen with a beautiful aroma.

You are not finished. After you put the pot in the oven, peel 12 of those little onions that start turning up in early spring—the ones that come in string bags. Next, thick-slice about a half-pound of fresh mushrooms. If the mushrooms are small, no need to slice. The onions and mushrooms are added for the last hour of cooking time.

You will know your boeuf bourguignon is ready when the vegetables are tender. Not too tender, mind you. As Lao-tse, the Chinese philosopher once wrote of bean sprouts, "They should resist, but not too much." Come to think of it, that's true of many of life's pleasures.

This boeuf bourguignon should be served on noodles—big flat ones. It can be prepared a day in advance. Matter of fact, it sometimes tastes even better if you do. Just refrigerate and reheat. Needless to say, the leftovers are superb.

You may find you want to Americanize this French classic by eliminating the noodles and putting spuds in with the carrots, and maybe adding a pack of frozen peas that last half hour in the oven. That makes it more like slum.

I kind of like it the French way. You know, tossed green salad, fresh Brussels sprouts, more el cheapo wine, candlelight, maybe a little TV after dinner.

*Ooh la-la!*

# Super Bowl Soup

There is an old saying that "cheap meat ain't good and good meat ain't cheap." That's generally true. It doesn't apply to beef shank, however. The shank is from the front leg of the animal.

Use 1 or 2 pounds, depending on the size of your brood. Cover with about $3\frac{1}{2}$ quarts of salted water in a large pot. Add a pound of peeled and cored fresh tomatoes, or use a can of generic tomatoes. Whack up 1 medium white onion and throw it in.

Bring to a boil and then back off to a simmer and let cook for a couple of hours or so. You'll know when to put the rest of the stuff in when the meat starts to get tender.

Keep breaking up the tomatoes with a wooden spoon. This will give you an excuse to keep going to the pot and enjoying the aroma. The next thing that goes in is $\frac{1}{2}$ cup of medium-pearled barley.

Peel and cube 1 good-sized red potato and coarse-chop some celery. Stir it in with the meat, barley, onion, and tomatoes. Cook another half hour and start to taste.

The final ingredients are corn, green peas, carrots, green beans, and baby limas. The easiest and cheapest way of doing this is to simply use a 10-ounce package of mixed frozen vegetables.

You can add other vegetables if you like. I would advise against using cabbage, however, as it will make you gassy. Once these last vegetables have been added, your Super Bowl Soup will begin to assume its real character. You can adjust the taste by adding salt and pepper.

Put a bottle of Tabasco on the table for those who like their soup zingy. Have ketchup available for the shank, which may be eaten separately.

This is family soup. It will bring you all closer together. Serve it with mixed green salad, hard crust bread, and Monterey Jack cheese. Super Bowl Soup is even better the next day.

# Sweet 'n' Sauer Holiday Relish

The nice thing about it is that the results suggest long hours have been spent in the kitchen. Not so. It takes only a few minutes. If your guests choose to be deceived, let them.

The basis for this crispy relish is sauerkraut. It doesn't even have to be the good stuff grandma stomped in the bathtub. Any kind will do. Get a 16-ounce can, the cheaper the better.

Open it and put the contents into a mixing bowl. Don't drain. Throw in the whole works. Break the kraut apart with a fork, nibbling some of it as you go.

Kraut is such honest food. It is wonderful as the basis for a Choucroute Alsacienne, into which kassler ripchen, pig's knuckles, Polish sausage, bacon, frankfurters, and other smoked meats are baked. It is a delight when served with boiled and buttered potatoes, garnished with parsley and washed down with a good spatlese. But that is another story.

Getting back to the relish, chop up 1 white onion and add to the kraut. Don't use a yellow onion. Unless cooked, I find yellow onions a bit stout for my taste. Good, firm white ones are the best.

One cup of chopped celery is next. No leaves. For the sake of appearance, try to keep the ingredients chopped to the same size. Pretty food tastes better.

The original recipe for this relish didn't call for green bell pepper. I impulsively added some and have found the results pleasing. A half-cup of chopped pepper is just enough for color and taste.

Beginning to look pretty nice? You bet. But wait until you add the pimiento. Yes. Get one of those little 4-ounce jars of chopped pimiento, drain off the juice and add to the bowl.

You are almost there. Combine $\frac{3}{4}$ cup of sugar and a like amount of white vinegar in a sauce pan. Heat until the sugar has dissolved. Don't boil, just stir.

Pour liquid over other ingredients. Mix again. Carefully spoon everything into a 1-quart glass jar. Screw on the top and refrigerate 24 hours.

After you have made your first batch, you may want to change the sugar-to-vinegar ratio. Try adding a tablespoon of either caraway or celery seeds. For a little more authority to the relish, splash a little Tabasco into the liquid.

"Sweet 'n' Sauer Holiday Relish" is a name I made up. The green pepper and red pimiento give it a nice holiday appearance. It goes well with meat and cheeses.

Be sure to get up in the night several times and go to the refrigerator to keep sampling the relish. Take note of how it improves with each tasting.

## Chili Sauce

Messy business. Worth it, though. It has been a great year for backyard gardeners and making chili sauce is the best way to make use of surplus tomatoes.

Chili sauce fits right in. It is marvelous slathered over pork loin on a cold Sunday afternoon. It dresses up rump roast and is perfect with pumpernickel meat loaf.

You will need a jug of burgundy wine, a peck of tomatoes, 6 green peppers, 6 big white onions, and some spices. A peck, by the way, is about a quarter of a bushel.

Wash, peel, core, and quarter the tomatoes. You probably know the easy way to peel tomatoes. For the few who do not, just lower each tomato with a slotted spoon into boiling water. Hold it there for about a minute. Take it out and run some cold water over it. The skin will slip right off.

Put the tomatoes in a large stainless steel or porcelain-lined kettle. Remove stems, seeds, and membranes from the peppers. Either grind or chop the onions and the peppers and add to the tomatoes.

Use a food processor if you have one. Some find it good therapy to do the chopping by hand. Sense of personal accomplishment. Back to the fundamentals.

You'll need about a tablespoon of crushed red pepper pods. For Pete's sake, don't put in the seeds. They would make the sauce hotter than a depot stove. Too hot.

Add 2 level cups of brown sugar. I like a couple of tablespoons of dry mustard. Some prefer mustard seed. Put in 3 tablespoons of salt, coarse if you have it. Then comes the fresh ground black pepper. About a tablespoon. Maybe a tad more.

Now the good stuff. You will need a tablespoon of allspice. Put in a teaspoon each of ginger, cinnamon, nutmeg, celery seed, and ground cloves.

Don't forget the vinegar. Get cider vinegar, the brown kind. Look on the label. Be sure it has 5 percent to 6 percent acetic acid. Use 3 cups. That's it.

Some people like their chili sauce more exotic, using crushed garlic, cumin, and curry powder. I don't. Chili sauce is good because it is simple, honest, without guile.

Back to the kettle. Stir the ingredients with a long-handled wooded spoon, preferably an old one. Simmer over low heat for at least 3 hours.

Now don't go running down to the shopping center or go to sleep on the patio. Stay near the kitchen and stir the sauce frequently. Don't scorch the sauce! Keep the heat low.

By the time the sauce cooks down to the right consistency, there should be about a gallon. While this is taking place, your house will be flooded with exquisite aroma.

Crack the window so that it wafts out into the neighborhood. Lovely children will come to your door. A great peace will descend. That aroma is so American. You'll want to run up Old Glory.

Ladle the chili sauce into small sterilized jars and seal tightly according to the instructions on the box in which the jars came. Be sure the jars are sterilized, otherwise your family could get the trots.

The wine? Don't put it in the chili sauce. It's for you. Take a little nip every now and then while you are doing all the stirring.

## Zucchini Nut loaf

Using a steel blade in your food processor, chop 2 cups of zucchini. If you don't have a processor, you can shred by hand, or better yet throw out the zucchini and forget the whole thing.

Combine the zucchini with 2 cups of sugar, 2 eggs, and 1 cup of cooking oil. Mix well by hand until it is a bile-colored glop. In another bowl, mix 3 cups of flour with 1 teaspoon of baking soda, $\frac{1}{2}$ teaspoon of baking powder, 1 teaspoon of nutmeg, 2 teaspoons of cinnamon, and 1 teaspoon of grated lemon peel.

Gradually mix the dry ingredients with the glop. Then add 4 to 6 ounces of chopped walnuts. Pour into two greased and floured loaf pans. Bake for a little more than an hour at 325 degrees. The loaves are done when a toothpick inserted in the center comes out clean.

The most rewarding part of this culinary adventure comes while they are baking. The aroma is not half bad, not because of zucchini, mind you, but because of the nutmeg and cinnamon.

Cool pans on a rack. Remove loaves and wrap with foil and refrigerate for 24 hours. Don't try to slice until the next day, otherwise those suckers will fall apart on you.

The reason you make two loaves is so you can throw one of them away and freeze the other and give it to some unsuspecting soul at Christmas. Ho, ho!

## Baur's Chocolate Torte

Soften $\frac{1}{4}$ cup of shortening, gradually adding 1 cup of sugar, creaming thoroughly. Add 2 egg yolks, one at a time, beating well each time. Stir in 2, 1-ounce squares of melted unsweetened chocolate.

Sift together $1\frac{1}{4}$ cups of all-purpose flour and $\frac{1}{4}$ teaspoon each of salt, baking powder, and baking soda. Add to creamed mixture, alternating $\frac{3}{4}$ cup of milk and 1 teaspoon of vanilla, beating well after each addition. Fold in 2 stiffly beaten egg whites until well blended.

Spread into two 9×1$\frac{1}{2}$-inch round pans and bake 18 to 20 minutes in a 350-degree oven and cool. Next comes the truffle filling.

Melt 8, 1-ounce squares of semi-sweet chocolate over hot water, stirring constantly, and cool. Whip 1 cup of whipping cream until soft peaks form. Fold in chocolate and $\frac{1}{2}$ cup of slivered, blanched almonds. Mixture should be smooth and dark.

Spread the truffle filling between the two layers and top with this chocolate glaze: Melt $1\frac{1}{2}$, 1-ounce squares of unsweetened chocolate and 2 tablespoons of butter over low heat, stirring constantly. Remove from heat and stir in $1\frac{1}{2}$ cups of confectioners' sugar and 1 teaspoon of vanilla. Blend in 3 teaspoons of boiling water or enough to form medium glaze.

Pour over torte and spread over top and sides. There! If that doesn't clog your arteries, nothing will.

# Recipes from Current Restaurants

## Barolo Grill
### 3030 East Sixth Avenue, Denver, 303-393-1040

### Lamb Shank "Osso Buco Style"
*4 servings*

4 lamb foreshanks
1 yellow onion, diced
1 carrot, diced
3 celery stalks, diced
1 leek, diced
1 tablespoon paprika
1 tablespoon thyme, dried
1 tablespoon fennel seed
1 tablespoon coriander seed
2 teaspoon crushed red pepper

2 bay leaves
$\frac{1}{2}$ cup fresh rosemary, chopped
zest of a lemon
16 ounces diced tomatoes
1 quart white wine
1 cup brandy
2 anchovies
$\frac{1}{2}$ gallon chicken stock
2 cups marsala wine

1. In a roasting pan, brown the shanks until they reach a dark caramel brown, take out and set aside.

2. Add the vegetables, spices, and lemon zest to the roasting pan and sauté for about five minutes or until the vegetables start to soften.

3. Add the tomatoes, wine, brandy, and anchovies.

4. Place the lamb shanks back into the liquid and cover with chicken stock. Bring the mixture to a boil and place into the oven at 275 degrees for about 3$\frac{1}{2}$ hours, depending on how tender they are.

5. Take out the shanks and set aside.

6. Skim the sauce of fat and add the marsala. Reduce by $\frac{1}{2}$ to $\frac{2}{3}$.

7. Place a lamb shank on the plate and ladle the sauce over it.

## Braised Duckling with Black Olives

*4 servings*

| | |
|---|---|
| 2, 5-pound fresh ducks | 1$\frac{1}{2}$ cups kalamata olives with brine |
| 4 ounces butter | 1 tablespoon fresh sage leaves |
| 2 yellow onions (large), julienned | 1 tablespoon fresh rosemary |
| 1 quart Barolo wine | 1 pinch fresh rosemary |
| (or other full-bodied red wine) | |
| 1 quart homemade chicken broth | |
| $\frac{1}{2}$ cup plus 1 tablespoon balsamic vinegar | |

1. Remove backbone and quarter ducks. Splitting down the breast bone, separate breast and wing from thigh and leg.

2. Brown pieces skin side down in melted butter and onions until skin is dark and fat is rendering out.

3. Turn duck skin side up and add remaining ingredients except 1 tablespoon balsamic vinegar, $\frac{1}{2}$ cup olives, and pinch of fresh rosemary; continue cooking until the broth starts to simmer.

4. Cover and braise in a 400-degree oven for one hour.

5. Remove duck from broth and store in a warm spot.

6. Skim fat from remaining broth, strain broth, and bring to a boil until reduced by half.

7. Add remaining $\frac{1}{2}$ cup olives, 1 tablespoon balsamic vinegar, and rosemary.

8. Place duck on serving plates and spoon sauce over top, making sure everyone receives several olives.

## Semifreddo di Limone (Lemon Semifreddo)

*10 servings*

| | |
|---|---|
| 1$\frac{1}{2}$ cups heavy cream | 4 large egg yolks |
| $\frac{1}{4}$ cup lemon juice | $\frac{1}{2}$ cup sugar |
| 2 large whole eggs | |

1. Whip cream and lemon juice with electric mixer until soft peaks form. Reserve in refrigerator.

2. Whisk whole eggs, yolks, and sugar in double boiler until the mixture is hot and thickened. It should be a pale yellow color.

3. Remove from heat and whip with electric mixer until the mixture is cooled.

4. Fold whipped cream into cooled egg mixture just until combined and uniformly colored.

5. Pour into 2-quart mold or individual soufflé cups, cover with plastic, and freeze until solid.

6. Dip mold in hot water to unmold; serve with fresh berry sauce.

# Bruno's Italian Bistro
## 2223 South Monaco Parkway, Denver, 303-757-4500

### Tuscan Lamb Shank

*4 servings*

| | |
|---|---|
| about 2 cups flour for dredging | 2 medium onions, roughly cut |
| salt, black pepper, granulated garlic | 4 stalks celery, roughly cut |
| 1½ cups olive oil | 1 bulb fennel, roughly cut |
| 4 lamb foreshanks | 1 large tomato, fresh, chopped |
| (1 to 1½ pounds each) | 3 tablespoons tomato paste |
| ¼ pound butter | 1½ cups Chianti |
| 5 garlic cloves, whole | 4 cups demi-glace |
| 2 carrots, roughly cut | large bay leaf |

**To finish the sauce:**

2 tablespoons shallots
1 cup Chianti
1¼ cups kalamata olives, sliced in half
1 cup red peppers, roasted, peeled, cut in strips
1½ cups diced fresh tomatoes

1. Season the flour with the salt, pepper, and granulated garlic.

2. Heat the oil in a heavy-bottomed Dutch oven. Dredge the lamb shanks in the flour and brown on all sides in the hot oil. Remove the shanks from the casserole.

3. Add the butter to the remaining oil and using the same seasoned flour to make a roux.

4. Cook the roux, stirring for 8 to 10 minutes over a moderate flame until a dark chestnut brown color is achieved.

5. Remove the roux from the pan. Add another tablespoon of oil and vegetables, and sauté for five minutes.

6. Stir in the tomato paste; increase the flame to high and pour on the Chianti. Allow the wine to reduce to half.

7. Add the demi-glace and bring to a simmer. With a wire whisk add the brown roux and simmer for five minutes.

8. Return the shanks to the casserole and add the bay leaf. Cover tightly and braise in a preheated oven at 350 degrees for approximately 3 hours or until the meat is very tender and easily falls off the bone.

9. Remove the shank from the cooking liquid and press the sauce through a sieve.

10. In a large saucepot, reduce one cup of Chianti with the shallots to almost dry. Add the strained sauce, olives, tomatoes, and peppers.

11. Adjust the seasoning with salt and pepper and serve this sauce over the shanks.

## Gangster Chicken

*2 servings*

| | |
|---|---|
| 1 fryer chicken | $\frac{1}{2}$ cup white wine |
| $\frac{1}{2}$ cup olive oil | $\frac{1}{3}$ cup vinegar (from pepper jar) |
| $\frac{1}{4}$ cup minced garlic | 2 cups demi-glace |
| 9 pepperoncini peppers, sliced | |
| 6 ounces Italian sausage, cooked & sliced | |

1. Cut the chicken into eight pieces and season with salt and black pepper.

2. Heat the oil in a heavy casserole and brown the chicken on all sides. Add the garlic and allow to brown.

3. Stir in the peppers and sausage. Deglaze with the white wine; then add the remaining ingredients.

4. Bring to a simmer and cover tightly.

5. Braise in a preheated 350-degree oven for 45 minutes or until the chicken is quite tender and removes easily from the bone.

# Buckhorn Exchange
## 1000 Osage Street, Denver, 303-534-9505

## Famous Bean Soup
*8 servings*

1 pound Great Northern beans
$\frac{1}{2}$ cup diced onion
3 ounces diced ham
1 ounce chicken base
$\frac{1}{2}$ teaspoon seasoned salt
1 teaspoon Liquid Smoke

1 teaspoon granulated garlic
1 teaspoon white pepper
$\frac{1}{2}$ gallon water
1 ounce cornstarch
$\frac{1}{2}$ cup water

1. Place all ingredients except cornstarch and $\frac{1}{2}$ cup water in a large pot, cover and place in 200 degree oven for 8 hours.

2. When beans are tender, remove from oven, place on stove-top and bring to boil.

3. Dissolve cornstartch in $\frac{1}{2}$ cup water and add to soup to thicken; let simmer for 15 minutes.

## Lavender Pepper Duck Breast with Raspberry/Red Zinfandel Sauce
*6 servings*

### Raspberry/Red Zinfandel Sauce

2 cups cold water
12 ounces raspberries
$1\frac{1}{2}$ teaspoons chicken base
$\frac{2}{3}$ cup sugar
2 cups Zinfandel

$\frac{1}{3}$ cup dark rum
2 tablespoons cornstarch
$\frac{1}{2}$ cup cold water
2 tablespoons crème de cassis
6 boneless duck breasts

1. Combine raspberries and water in heavy sauce pan and bring to boil. Reduce heat, simmer for 5 minutes; add chicken base and sugar; stir until sugar dissolves and continue to simmer.

2. Add Zinfandel and rum and continue to simmer until reduced by $\frac{1}{4}$.

3. Combine cornstarch with $\frac{1}{2}$ cup cold water and add to sauce.

4. Bring sauce back to a boil, simmer for 5 minutes and remove from heat.

5. Stir in crème de cassis.

6. Force sauce through double-mesh strainer.

### Lavender Pepper Rub

2 tablespoons black peppercorns
2 tablespoons sea salt
2 tablespoons fennel seeds
2 tablespoons lavender
1 tablespoon white pepper

Combine all ingredients in a blender and process until all seeds are reduced to a coarse grind.

### Assembly

1. Skin duck breasts and rub with lavender mixture 1 hour prior to cooking.

2. Grill duck breasts over hot fire until medium rare. Allow to stand for 5 minutes and slice.

3. Serve each breast with 2 ounces of sauce.

# Chez Walter

### 5969 South University Boulevard, Littleton, 303-794-4026

## Sliced Veal Zurich Style

*4 servings*

1 pound lean veal,
  sliced thin by hand
3 ounces butter or canola oil
2 tablespoons chopped shallots
½ cup chopped onions
½ tablespoon chopped garlic
5 ounces mushrooms, sliced
1½ cups white wine
1½ cups clear brown stock or beef bouillon
2 tablespoons flour
1 cup fresh cream
juice from ½ lemon
1 teaspoon white pepper
1 teaspoon salt
1 teaspoon dry basil
½ teaspoon Hungarian paprika
2 teaspoons chopped parsley

1. Sauté veal in hot pan quickly to brown on all sides.

2. Remove from pan and set aside in dish.

3. Sweat shallots, garlic, onions, and sliced mushrooms in butter. Cook until beads of moisture appear on the surface of vegetables and season.

4. Deglaze pan with wine and the brown stock. Reduce 2 to 3 minutes.

5. Strain the stock.

6. Return the sauce to the pan and whisk in the flour to the sauce while it is cooking. Bring the sauce to a light consistency.

7. Add the cream and the veal. Stir gently for 3 to 4 minutes.

8. Add the lemon juice and season with white pepper, salt, basil, and paprika to taste.

9. Sprinkle with chopped parsley.

10. Serve with Roesti (recipe below).

### Roesti (Potatoes Swiss Syle)

| | |
|---|---|
| 2 pounds potatoes | $\frac{1}{2}$ teaspoon salt |
| 1 ounce butter or canola oil | $\frac{1}{2}$ teaspoon white pepper |
| 1 medium onion, chopped | 1 teaspoon chopped parsley |

1. Partially cook potatoes in their skins and cool (preferably overnight in the refrigerator).

2. Peel and grate potatoes by hand (peel potatoes lengthwise).

3. In a frying pan, add butter or oil and heat.

4. Add the onion and the potatoes. Season to taste with salt and white pepper.

5. Cook over low heat, pressing the potatoes down with a spatula. Turn frequently until potatoes are crusty and golden brown.

6. Place potatoes on a hot serving dish, crusty side up. Sprinkle with parsley and serve immediately.

## Crème Caramels

*24 caramels*

| | |
|---|---|
| $1\frac{3}{4}$ quarts milk | 9 egg yolks |
| 14 ounces sugar | pinch of salt |
| 17 whole eggs | 1 teaspoon vanilla |

1. Heat caramel (see recipe below) to liquid form.

2. Place 24 timbale molds in a 2-inch hotel pan.

3. Divide caramel among timbales. Place enough caramel to cover the bottom of timbale (about 1 tablespoon).

4. Set hotel pan aside.

5. In sauce pan, combine milk and sugar. Place on high heat, stirring occasionally. Bring to boil and set aside.

6. In mixing bowl, combine whole eggs, yolks, and salt. Stir well to combine.

7. Temper together milk and eggs. Add vanilla now if you are using extract. (If you use a vanilla bean, add when heating milk.)

8. Strain through china cap into mixing bowl, about 2 to 3 times. This will help combine mix and collect any shells that might be in the mix.

9. Using ladle, fill timbales with mix.

10. Fill hotel pan $\frac{1}{2}$ full of water; place hotel pan in oven at 425 degrees for 45 minutes.

11. When caramels are finished, place on cooling tray for 30 minutes, then place in cooler.

### Caramel

$2\frac{1}{2}$ pounds sugar      $\frac{1}{2}$ quart hot water

1. Place in sugar saucepan.

2. Cook on medium heat stirring often. Cook until all sugar is dissolved. Texture should be smooth, and caramel a dark brown color.

3. Turn off heat. Hold water 1 foot above saucepan and pour a slow stream of water into the sugar. (When adding water to sugar cover your stirring hand to avoid burns from the sugar.) Stir constantly till all water is gone. Immediately plunge into cold water and remove quickly.

# Chinook Tavern
## 265 Detroit Street, Denver, 303-394-0044

## Stuffed Pork Chops with Red Onion Marmalade
*6 servings*

| | |
|---|---|
| 12 ounces peeled red onions, diced fine | $\frac{1}{2}$ cup red wine |
| 1 ounce unsalted butter | $\frac{1}{4}$ cup port wine |
| 2 tablespoons canola oil | 3 tablespoons balsamic vinegar |
| 1 bay leaf | kosher salt & pepper to taste |
| 3 tablespoons sugar | 2 tablespoons honey |
| 2 lemons, juiced | 6, 6-ounce pork chops, Frenched |

## Breading
4 eggs, mixed well to form an egg wash
3 cups Japanese bread crumbs
1 cup flour

1. Peel the red onions and dice fine.

2. Heat the butter and canola oil in a pan and add the onions along with the bay leaf.

3. Sauté the onions until translucent; mix in the sugar.

4. Add the lemon juice and cook for about 1 minute and then add both wines.

5. Cook this mixture until the wine has completely reduced.

6. Add the balsamic vinegar and again reduce completely. The mixture should be thick and have a dark burgundy color.

7. Season to taste with kosher salt and black ground pepper.

8. Set aside. When cool, mix in the honey.

9. Take the pork chops and cut a slit into them from the outside edge towards the bone. Make sure that it is long and wide enough to stuff the chops with the red onion marmalade. Fill with $1\frac{1}{2}$ tablespoons of the red onion marmalade and press down on the outside edges to seal.

10. Breading the pork chop: Take the chop and dip into the flour (shake off any excess), dip into the egg wash, turn the pork chop to coat it evenly. Take the pork chop and transfer it to the bread crumbs. Press the bread crumbs evenly over the surface and remove to a holding plate. Prepare Port Wine sauce.

## Port Wine Sauce
| | |
|---|---|
| 1 cup red wine | 1 tablespoon sugar |
| 3 cups port wine | $\frac{1}{2}$ teaspoon kosher salt |
| 1 lemon, juiced | 3 ounces butter |

11. Mix everything together and reduce down to 1 cup and set aside.

12. Heat up two sauté pans with 1 ounce butter and 1 tablespoon of canola oil in each pan. Sauté the pork chops until golden brown on each side, and place the pans in the oven to finish cooking (about 6 minutes at 375 degrees). Gently heat up the sauce mixture and finish with the butter.

13. Serve with new potatoes and spinach.

## Chinook Brule

*8 servings*

1 each vanilla beans spice  
¼ gallon heavy cream

6 ounces granulated sugar  
5 eggs, yolks only

1. Preheat oven to 320 degrees.

2. Split the vanilla beans and add to sauce pot with cream and sugar.

3. Bring to 120 degrees slowly.

4. Whisk the yolks and slowly add the hot cream mixture to the yolks. This is called tempering. Keep whisking and make sure that you do not curdle.

5. Scrape out vanilla beans with the back of a knife and add this to the egg mixture; strain everything through a fine-mesh sieve.

6. Fill shallow ramekins with the custard; place in water bath and bake for about 40 minutes or until set. Cool completely.

# Flagstaff House Restaurant
### 1138 Flagstaff Road, Boulder, 303-442-4640

## Kalamata Olive–Crusted Rack of Colorado Lamb with White Polenta and Ratatouille Vegetables

*4 servings*

### Lamb

2, 8-chop lamb racks,  
   all skin removed  
salt & pepper  
½ cup Dijon mustard

½ cup chopped kalamata olives  
1 teaspoon chopped rosemary  
½ cup bread crumbs

1. Salt and pepper lamb racks; sear in hot pan until brown.

2. Remove and let rest.

3. Brush lamb with mustard and mixture of olives and rosemary; roll in bread crumbs.

4. Roast in 400-degree oven for 20 minutes and slice.

### Ratatouille

1 onion  
garlic, chopped fine

1 yellow bell pepper  
1 red bell pepper

| 1 eggplant | 2 tablespoons tomato paste |
| 1 zucchini | thyme, basil, salt & pepper |
| 1 yellow squash | |

1. Sauté onions and garlic on low heat until translucent.

2. Chop remaining vegetables and add to pan.

3. Stir on stove and add tomato paste, herbs, and seasoning.

4. Place in oven and bake at 350 degrees for 1 hour.

### Polenta

| 1 cup heavy cream | salt & pepper |
| 1 cup whole milk | 1 tablespoon butter |
| $\frac{1}{2}$ cup white polenta | 1 teaspoon truffle oil |

1. Bring cream and whole milk to a boil, and then add the polenta.

2. Stir slowly over low heat for 45 minutes.

3. Season with salt and pepper; add butter and truffle oil.

### Rosemary Jus

| 10-pounds lamb bones | 1 garlic clove |
| $\frac{1}{2}$ quart white wine | 2 leeks |
| 2 carrots | 1 cup tomato paste |
| 2 onions | rosemary, bay leaf, and thyme |
| 1 stalk celery | salt & pepper |

1. Roast lamb bones in oven until brown.

2. Remove from pan and place in stockpot.

3. Add white wine and let it reduce to a glaze.

4. Add vegetables, tomato paste, herbs, and cover with water.

5. Let simmer for 4 hours.

6. Strain through strainer and finish with salt and pepper and 1 table-spoon butter.

## Hot Valrohna Strudle with Cocoa Sorbet

*4 servings*

| 250 grams Valrohna | melted butter |
| extra bitter chocolate | 3 sheets filo dough |
| 1 cup heavy cream | |

White Genoise or sponge cake, sliced approximately $\frac{1}{8}$-inch thick

1. Melt chocolate and cream over double boiler until liquid. Pour into 1½-inch thick pan. Chill.

2. When chocolate is firm, cut into pieces 1½×1½×3½ inches. Roll cake around chocolate.

3. Brush butter on the sheets of filo dough. Place one on top of the other. Roll the filo dough around cake and seal.

4. Chill.

5. Bake at 400 degrees for 5 to 8 minutes or until brown. Serve.

### White Genoise Cake

| | |
|---|---|
| 110 grams sugar | 150 grams flour, sifted |
| 6 eggs | 1, 10-inch pan, buttered |
| 150 grams butter, melted | and floured |

1. Whip eggs, sugar, and butter rapidly over flame until pale in color.

2. Fold into flour slowly, and then pour into cake pan.

3. Bake at 350 degrees for 30 to 40 minutes depending on the oven used, checking for doneness with toothpick.

# The Fort
## 19192 Highway 8, Morrison, 303-697-4771

## Gonzales Steak
*Per person*

| | |
|---|---|
| 3 green Anaheim chiles, roasted and peeled (fresh are best) | 10 to 12 ounce thick-cut New York strip, top sirloin, or tenderloin of beef or buffalo steak |
| salt & fresh ground pepper | ½ teaspoon salad oil |
| 1 clove garlic, chopped | 1 teaspoon butter (optional) |
| pinch of Mexican leaf oregano | |

1. Slit the chiles to remove the seeds, and chop 2 into fine dice and mix with the salt, garlic, and oregano.

2. With a very sharp knife, cut a horizontal pocket into the steak. Stuff the chopped chiles into the pocket. Brush the meat and the remaining chile with salad oil.

3. Grill the steak on both sides to the desired doneness. If using buffalo, watch carefully so as not to overcook! Because it contains less fat than chicken, bison cooks much faster than beef and is best medium-rare.

4. Salt and pepper the meat. Grill the remaining whole-roasted chile to get a nice patterning of grid burn on it. Lay it across the steak as a garnish.

*Note:* A teaspoon of brown butter on the steak as a special treat is heaven. To make brown butter, simply place the butter in a sauté pan over medium-high heat and allow it to melt and turn golden brown.

# Negrita
*10 servings*

1¼ pounds Ghirardelli sweet
   dark chocolate (see note)
6 eggs
1 tablespoon vanilla extract

¼ cup dark rum
½ pint heavy cream,
   whipped for topping

1. To melt the chocolate, place it in a double boiler over simmering water. Do not let the water touch the bottom of the bowl holding the chocolate. Stir the chocolate periodically.

2. When it is about half melted, turn off the heat and leave it over the warm water to finish melting and to keep it warm.

3. Separate the eggs. In a dry, clean bowl, beat the egg whites until stiff. In a separate bowl, beat the egg yolks until they're pale yellow.

4. Carefully add the chocolate, vanilla, and rum to the egg yolks, then fold in the beaten whites. Stir until thoroughly blended.

5. Ladle into 2½-ounce ramekins or wine glasses and chill. Serve topped with whipped cream.

*Note:* Don't use chocolate chips for this recipe. They don't contain as much cocoa butter as whole bars do, and they don't melt as well or taste as rich. It is important not to let the chocolate cool too much before blending with the other ingredients, or it will become grainy. If you think it has become too cool by the time you're ready to use it, turn on the heat to warm it slightly.

# Pumpkin Walnut Muffins
*Makes about 4 dozen*

5 cups flour
1 cup sugar
2½ cups dry powdered milk

1½ cups chopped walnuts
4 large eggs
1¼ cups vegetable oil

| 4 tablespoons baking powder | $1\frac{1}{4}$ cups water |
| 3 tablespoons cinnamon | 2, 29-ounce cans pumpkin |
| 1 tablespoon salt | (not pie filling) |
| $1\frac{1}{2}$ cups brown sugar | |

1. Preheat the oven to 325 degrees. Grease 3-inch muffin tins or line with paper.

2. Mix all the ingredients together. The batter should be easily scoopable. If it is too thick, add a little more water.

3. Fill the tins three-quarters full and bake for 40 to 45 minutes. Let the muffins cool before removing them from the pan.

# Fourth Story Restaurant
## 2955 East 1st Avenue, Denver, 303-322-1824

## Porcini Mushroom and Bacon-Infused Beef Consommé
*7 gallons*

| 6 julienned white onions | 1 bay leaf |
| 3 whole porcini mushrooms | 4 gallons chicken stock |
| 1 pound bacon | 2 gallons miso stock |
| 1 tablespoon garlic | 2 quarts demi-glace |
| 1 cup brown sugar | $\frac{1}{2}$ tablespoon salt |
| 1 bottle sherry wine | 25 egg whites |
| 2 bunches thyme | |

1. In a large stockpot, caramelize white onions with a little oil. Then add porcinis and bacon, caramelize for about 10 minutes or until a nice caramelized fond is present.

2. Add garlic, brown sugar, and cook for another 5 minutes. Deglaze with sherry and scrape with a wooden spoon.

3. Finally, add thyme, bay leaf, stocks, demi-glace, and salt. Cook for about 30 to 40 minutes to develop flavor.

4. Strain and cool consommé; whip in egg whites well.

5. Put back on stove on low heat. Allow raft to form. Use wooden spoon to check bottom of pot for sticking from time to time, being careful not to break raft.

6. Carefully lift raft with spider. Strain remaining consommé.

# Strawberry Soup

*5 gallons*

2 lemongrass, cut lengthwise
20 pounds strawberries
½ gallon apple cider
½ gallon lemonade

3 gallons miso
2 bay leaves
4 cups honey
4 cups chopped fresh mint

1. In a large pot, sweat lemongrass with a little oil (blended). Add 10 pounds of strawberries and remaining ingredients except for reserved strawberries, mint, and honey.

2. Bring to a boil and reduce heat to a simmer for about 30 minutes. Remove from heat.

3. Purée and strain through a fine chinois.

4. Finally, purée reserved strawberries, mint, and honey. Add to strained soup. Adjust to taste and chill.

# Institute of Culinary Arts/Art Institute of Colorado
### 303-837-0825

## Garlic and Rosemary Roasted Leg of Lamb

*6 servings*

3 pounds leg of lamb, boneless
2 cloves garlic, peeled and sliced
2 tablespoons olive oil
½ teaspoon kosher salt

¼ teaspoon ground black pepper
½ teaspoon dried rosemary
¼ teaspoon dried thyme

### Sauce

2 ounces onions, medium dice
1 ounce celery, medium dice
1 ounce carrot, medium dice
2 cloves garlic, crushed

½ ounce tomato paste
2 ounces all-purpose flour
8 fluid ounces red wine
1 quart beef stock

1. Trim the excess fat from the lamb leg. Cut slits about ½ inch deep into the lamb and insert garlic slices.

2. Rub the olive oil over the entire leg of lamb.

3. Combine salt, black pepper, rosemary, and thyme in a small bowl.

4. Rub the herb mixture over the lamb and let rest at room temperature for 20 minutes.

5. Tightly roll the lamb and truss with butcher's twine so it will retain its shape while roasting and assist in cooking evenly.

6. Preheat an oven to 450 degrees and roast the lamb on an elevated rack in a roasting pan for 15 minutes.

7. Turn the oven down to 350 degrees and continue to roast until the desired degree of doneness is reached. Baste the lamb with the pan juices once or twice during the roasting process. For medium-rare, the lamb will take approximately 1 hour. Use an instant-read thermometer to determine the exact internal temperature.

8. Add the onions, celery, carrots, crushed garlic, and tomato paste after the lamb has roasted 30 minutes.

9. Once the lamb has reached the desired internal temperature and has reached a minimum internal temperature of 145 degrees or higher for at least 3 minutes, remove the lamb from the pan and allow it to rest undisturbed for 15 to 20 minutes.

10. Clarify the fat from the pan drippings and stir in the flour to make a roux. Add additional oil if needed.

11. Cook the roux in the roasting pan over low heat for approximately 5 minutes while stirring frequently.

12. Stir in the red wine and reduce the volume of liquid by half over medium high heat.

13. Stir in the stock and continue to reduce until the desired consistency is attained.

14. Strain the gravy through a chinois and season to taste with salt and black pepper.

15. Slice the lamb and serve approximately 8 ounces on each hot plate. Carefully ladle the sauce over part of the slices. Keep warm until served.

*Note:* If desired, root vegetables such as carrots, parsnips, and onions along with small potatoes can be roasted in the pan with the lamb.

## Red Chard Casserole

*6 servings*

### Béchamel Sauce

2 ounces butter, clarified
2 ounces flour
1 quart milk

¼ teaspoon salt
⅛ teaspoon ground white pepper
nutmeg to taste

## Red Chard

| | |
|---|---|
| 2½ pounds red Swiss chard, washed, chopped | 20 fluid ounces béchamel sauce, prepared |
| 2 ounces scallions, chopped | 4 ounces butter |
| salt & ground white pepper to taste | 4 ounces fresh breadcrumbs |
| | 3½ ounces grated Parmesan cheese |

1. Prepare a béchamel sauce by melting the butter in a sauce pan and incorporating the flour to make a roux.

2. Cook the roux over low heat while stirring frequently for 5 minutes. Let stand at room temperature for 10 to 15 minutes.

3. Bring the milk to a boil and gently stir in the roux a little at a time until it is fully incorporated. Bring back to a boil while stirring frequently and reduce the heat to a simmer.

4. Simmer over low heat for 40 minutes. Do not allow the simmering sauce to fall below a temperature of 140 degrees. Use a wooden spoon to stir and make sure not to scrape the bottom of the pot while cooking.

5. Season the sauce to taste with salt, white pepper, and a pinch of nutmeg.

6. Strain and hold in a bain-marie at 140 degrees or higher until needed.

7. Blanch the chard in boiling, salted water. Drain thoroughly.

8. Mix the chard with chopped scallions and season to taste with salt and white pepper.

9. Place the chard mixture in an ovenproof casserole or baking dish and top with béchamel sauce. Set aside briefly.

10. Melt the butter in a saucepan over medium heat and add the breadcrumbs. Toss or stir until thoroughly coated.

11. Remove the breadcrumbs from the heat and stir in the Parmesan cheese.

12. Top the chard casserole with the breadcrumb and cheese mixture, evenly coating the surface and bake in a preheated 375 degree oven for approximately 35 minutes or until hot and golden brown.

13. Let the casserole rest for 10 minutes before serving.

*Note:* To prepare the fresh breadcrumbs, use only fresh white bread with the crust removed. Slice and tear into pieces and place in a clean, dry food processor. Process until the bread resembles a coarse meal.

# Huckleberry Pie

*6 servings*

## Filling

2 each pie crust (recipe follows)
1 cup granulated sugar
½ cup brown sugar
¼ cup quick cooking tapioca
½ teaspoon cinnamon, ground
6 cups huckleberries, picked
   and cleaned

1 tablespoon lemon juice
2 tablespoons butter, chilled,
   cut into medium dice
1 tablespoon granulated sugar

## Topping

1 cup whipping cream

2 ounces powdered sugar

1. Preheat oven to 450 degrees.

2. Place one piece of the pie dough in a 9-inch pan and press into the pan firmly.

3. Reserve the pie pan with the dough and the second piece of the pie dough under refrigeration until needed.

4. Combine the first quantity of sugar, brown sugar, tapioca, and cinnamon in a large bowl.

5. Fold in the huckleberries and lemon juice and let stand at room temperature for 10 to 15 minutes.

6. Place the huckleberry mixture into the center of the pie dish over the lower piece of dough, mounding the mixture in the center of the pie.

7. Dot the top of the filling with the pieces of chilled butter.

8. Place the second piece of pie dough on top of the pie and seal by crimping the dough together.

9. Cut vents in the top crust, brush the surface of the dough with water and sprinkle with the remaining granulated sugar.

10. Bake the pie in the center of the oven for approximately 15 minutes. Lower the heat to 350 degrees and continue to cook for 45 to 50 additional minutes, or until the juices are thick and bubbling and the crust is nicely browned.

11. While the pie is baking, prepare the sweetened whipped cream by whipping the cream with the powdered sugar in a small mixing machine on high speed. Be careful not to overmix the cream, as this small amount can quickly turn to butter. Reserve under refrigeration until needed.

12. Slice the huckleberry pie into wedges and serve chilled or at room temperature.

13. Garnish each slice with a dollop of the reserved whipped cream.

*Note:* Blueberries are the normal substitute for huckleberries, as fresh huckleberries can only be procured from Montana and Idaho during the late summer months. Frozen huckleberries can be purchased year round but are known to be rather expensive compared to other berries. When using blueberries as a substitute, add a little extra lemon juice to the recipe to simulate the unique astringent flavor of huckleberries.

### Pie Crust

*2 pie crusts*

| | |
|---|---|
| 12 ounces all-purpose flour | 4 ounces butter |
| ½ teaspoon salt | 4 fluid ounces cold water |

1. Combine the flour and salt.

2. Blend or cut the butter into the flour by rubbing the ingredients lightly between the fingers to incorporate the butter into the flour. Continue to rub until the dough resembles pea-sized balls.

3. Add the cold water a little at a time into the rubbed flour and butter.

4. Blend the mixture until the dough forms.

5. Let the dough rest in refrigerator for at least 1 hour or until needed.

6. Turn the dough onto a lightly floured surface and roll out the dough with a rolling pin into 2 round shapes approximately ¼ inch in thickness.

7. Firmly press one piece on the bottom of a pie pan. Reserve the second piece.

# Inverness Hotel & Golf Club
## 200 Inverness Drive West, Englewood, 303-799-5800

## Smoked Salmon with Quinoa Waffle

*Per person*

| | |
|---|---|
| 1 waffle cut into triangles | ¼ ounce American caviar |
| 3 ounces smoked salmon fillet | 1 ounce lemon dill vinaigrette |
| 2 ounces fresh horseradish cream | 3 ounces mixed greens |

1. Cut waffle into triangle, diamond, circle, or shape of choice.

2. Stake 1 ounce smoked salmon on top of waffle. Stack three layers high.

3. Top with horseradish cream and caviar. Vinaigrette goes around the outside of the tower; greens are used as a garnish. Use your creativity!

### Horseradish Cream

| | |
|---|---|
| 1 pound cream cheese | 1 bunch dill, chopped |
| 2 lemons juice and zest | $^3/_4$ cup grated fresh horseradish root |
| 2 cups sour cream | salt & pepper |

Mix all ingredients together in medium size bowl.

### Lemon Dill Vinaigrette

| | |
|---|---|
| $^1/_2$ cup walnut oil | 1 bunch dill, chopped |
| 2 cups extra virgin olive oil | $^1/_4$ cup rice wine vinegar |
| $^3/_4$ cup lemon juice | salt & pepper |

Mix all ingredients together in medium-size bowl; vinaigrette will be coarse in texture.

### Quinoa Waffles

| | |
|---|---|
| 6 cups all-purpose flour | 3 pints milk |
| 1 tablespoon salt | 6 whole eggs |
| $^1/_2$ teaspoon white pepper | 3 ounces walnut oil |
| 6 ounces sugar | $3^1/_2$ cups cooked quinoa |
| 1 tablespoon baking soda | (available at specialty markets) |
| 2 tablespoons baking powder | 1 cup bran |
| $^1/_2$ cup chopped chives | |

1. Place all dry ingredients except quinoa and bran through a sifter.

2. Mix all wet ingredients together and add the quinoa and bran.

3. Combine wet and dry ingredients and let the batter sit for at least 30 minutes before using.

4. Use a waffle iron to make waffles, or substitute as pancakes.

## Herb Crusted Fallow Venison Loin
## with Salsify Purée and Huckleberry Mint Sauce

*4 servings*

| | |
|---|---|
| 4, 4-ounce, cleaned venison loins (seasoned with chopped thyme, rosemary, black pepper) | 1 tablespoon unsalted butter |
| | 1 cup port wine |
| | 4 ounces fresh huckleberries |

1 pound salsify, peeled
  (available at specialty markets)
¼ cup milk

2 cups venison demi-glace or
  other beef demi-glace
1 tablespoon chopped fresh mint

1. Coat the venison loins with the herbs and pepper, then pan sear (on high heat) in a pan until brown on all sides.

2. Remove from pan and cook in 350 degree oven for 5 to 8 minutes; reserve until ready to plate.

3. Place the peeled salsify in a pot with milk and bring to a slow boil. Cook until tender, then remove from the pot and process in a food processor, adding the butter and some of the cooking milk.

4. Process salsify until smooth and season with salt and pepper to taste.

5. Reserve salsify until ready to plate.

6. Place port wine in a pot and reduce it by ⅔. Add huckleberries and venison demi-glace and bring to a slow simmer.

7. Add mint, 1 teaspoon butter, and season with salt and pepper.

8. Place a small 4-ounce portion of salsify purée in the middle of the plate. Ladle 3 ounces of huckleberry mint sauce around the purée. Slice each 4-ounce piece of venison and fan around the purée. Use whatever vegetable you desire to accompany this dish.

*Note:* If salsify is not available, substitute potatoes, parsnips, celery root, or sweet potatoes.

## Demi-glace

5 pounds venison, beef,
  or veal bones
  (cut into 2-inch pieces)
2 yellow onions
½ head celery, chopped
4 carrots, chopped
2 cloves garlic

¼ cup tomato paste
3 cups red wine
bouquet garni
  (thyme, bay leaves, black
  peppercorns)
water to cover

1. Place the bones into a roasting pan and cook in a 350-degree oven until golden brown. Remove from oven and allow to cool.

2. Place the vegetables in a large stock pot and slowly cook until vegetables have become soft and caramelized.

3. Add tomato paste and continue to cook for 10 minutes.

4. Add red wine and garni and reduce by ¼.

5. Add enough water to cover bones by 2 inches and allow to simmer for at least 8 hours.

6. After cooking the stock, strain the liquid through a china cap and pour stock back into a pot. Turn the flame onto low and slowly reduce the stock by ½. It should appear thick and at this point is ready for sauce production.

## Seared Prosciutto-Wrapped Ahi Tuna with Cucumber Red Onion Relish and Fennel Potato Cakes

*4 servings*

2 pounds fresh Ahi tuna (center cut only)
12 slices prosciutto (try to get Prosciutto di Parma if available)

1. Cut Ahi tuna steak into 4 equal pieces.

2. Next, take 3 slices of prosciutto per Ahi tuna steak, lay 2 pieces of prosciutto parallel to each other and spaced slightly apart with the third piece crossing perpendicular over the top.

3. Season Ahi tuna steak with salt and pepper, place in the center of the prosciutto and wrap the prosciutto around Ahi tuna steak.

4. Sear seam side down in a hot pan with a small amount of oil. Continue to sear on all sides.

5. Finish in a 350-degree oven for 5 minutes (medium to medium rare) or 8 to 10 minutes (well done).

### Cucumber Red Onion Relish

| | |
|---|---|
| 1 English cucumber | 2 tablespoons chopped fennel top |
| 1 red onion | 2 tablespoons rice wine vinegar |
| 1 yellow pepper | salt & pepper to taste |
| 2 tablespoons chopped chives | |

1. Using a mandoline, cut cucumbers to spaghetti-type consistency.

2. Julienne the red onion and yellow pepper. Chop chives and fennel.

3. In a medium-sized bowl, mix all ingredients together and set aside.

### Fennel Potato Cake

| | |
|---|---|
| 1 bulb fennel root, sliced | 2 tablespoons chopped fennel top |
| 1 tablespoon chopped garlic | 1 each red and yellow pepper, diced |
| 1 tablespoon chopped shallots | 2 green onions cut on bias |
| 2 cups potato purée | 2 egg yolks |
| ½ cup toasted panko bread crumbs | salt & pepper |
| (Japanese bread crumbs available in specialty grocery stores) | |

1. Place fennel bulb in pan and sauté for 3 minutes over medium heat.

2. Add garlic and shallots and cook for 2 minutes more. Remove from heat; cool.

3. Once cool, add all remaining ingredients.

4. Mix well and season with salt and pepper.

5. Form into pancakes and sear in a hot pan until brown.

6. Place on a cookie sheet and warm in the oven at 350 degrees for 3 to 5 minutes.

### Green Onion Buerre Blanc

1 cup white wine
$\frac{1}{8}$ cup rice wine vinegar
2 shallots, chopped
1 teaspoon coriander seeds,
  toasted

2 ounces heavy cream
1 pound unsalted butter
  (room temperature)
2 bunches green onions or
  $\frac{1}{2}$ bunch chives, chopped

1. Place wine, vinegar, shallots, and coriander seeds in a pot and bring to a boil.

2. Reduce the liquid by $\frac{2}{3}$ and add cream. Reduce again at medium heat by $\frac{2}{3}$.

3. Turn the heat to low and begin whisking in the butter, a small amount at a time. Whisk regularly to prevent the sauce from breaking.

4. Once all butter has been added, season with salt and pepper to taste, and strain through a fine-mesh strainer.

5. Place sauce in a blender and add chopped green onions or chives. Pulse in blender until sauce turns green. Beware: over processing will also break the sauce.

6. Strain again and reserve on the stove in a warm area for dinner.

### Plating

Cut Ahi steaks and prosciutto on a bias cut like sushi rolls. Place Ahi steak offset on Potato Fennel Cake, then add Cucumber Relish between portions of Ahi steak and on top of Potato Fennel Cakes. Finish with a drizzling of Green Onion Buerre Blanc sauce around plate.

# Loews Giorgio Hotel
### 4150 East Mississippi Avenue, Glendale, 303-782-9300

## Tuscan Warm Summer Salad
*6 servings*

4 large garlic cloves, roasted
¼ pound pancetta, diced
  (see note)
¼ cup crumbled Gorgonzola
  cheese
¼ cup olive oil

12 cups romaine lettuce,
  torn into bite-size pieces
4 cups radicchio,
  torn into bite-size pieces
1 cup focaccia croutons
18 large spears Belgian endive

1. Place a large wok over a gas or electric burner and let it warm over medium heat 1 minute.

2. Add garlic, pancetta, Gorgonzola, and oil simultaneously. With a spoon or fork, toss mixture until the cheese is melting and the mixture starts to sizzle.

3. Immediately add romaine and radicchio, tossing together swiftly.

4. Once lettuces start to warm up, but just before they start to wilt, remove from heat, and add croutons; toss to combine.

5. To serve, place 3 endive spears each in large shallow bowls. Divide salad mixture evenly over endive spears. Serve at once.

### Roasted Garlic

Remove papery outer covering of whole garlic head, but do not separate or peel the cloves. Place in a piece of heavy-duty foil, drizzle with a bit of olive oil and crumple foil around garlic to enclose. Bake in an oven, preheated to 375 degrees, for 1 to 1¼ hours. Separate the cloves. Holding each clove, squeeze to remove the garlic purée. This is delicious spread over buttered toast or used as an ingredient in other recipes.

### Focaccia Croutons

Cut focaccia or country-style bread into ¾-inch cubes. Add 1 tablespoon olive oil and some minced garlic for every cup of croutons. Spread in a single layer in a jelly-roll pan and bake in a preheated 375-degree oven for 15–18 minutes until golden.

*Note:* Pancetta is Italian bacon and can be found in Italian delicatessens and specialty stores. If it is not available, lean slab bacon of excellent quality is an acceptable substitute.

# Porcini Mushroom Risotto

*6 servings*

1 1/2 ounces dried Porcini
  mushrooms
1 1/2 cups hot water
4 1/2 to 5 cups chicken stock or
  canned low-sodium broth
6 tablespoons unsalted butter

1/2 cup finely chopped onion
1 1/2 cups Arborio rice
3 tablespoons chopped parsley
1 cup freshly grated
  Parmigiano-Reggiano cheese
freshly ground black pepper

1. In a medium bowl, combine Porcini with hot water. Let stand until softened, about 30 minutes. Drain through a paper towel-lined strainer set over a small bowl.

2. Coarsely chop mushrooms and pour soaking liquid into a measuring cup, discarding any sediment in bowl; reserve soaking liquid. There should be 1 cup.

3. In a medium sauce pan, bring the reserved Porcini liquid and the chicken stock to a boil; adjust heat to maintain a slow, steady simmer.

4. In a large, heavy skillet over medium heat, melt 1/4 cup (4 tablespoons) butter. Add the onion and sauté until tender. Add the rice and stir to coat with butter. Add 1 cup hot broth to just cover the rice.

5. Adjust heat to maintain a slow simmer and cook, stirring constantly, until all the broth has been absorbed, about 3 to 4 minutes.

6. Repeat process of adding hot broth about a 1/2 cup at a time, until the rice is tender, the mixture is creamy and the rice begins to pull away from the sides of the pan, about 25 minutes.

7. Add remaining 2 tablespoons butter, chopped Porcini, parsley, and 1/4 cup Parmigiano-Reggiano.

8. Cover and let stand off heat for 2 minutes.

9. Spoon into a shallow bowls and serve at once with additional cheese and a few grindings of black pepper.

# Espresso Chocolate Torte

*16 servings*

1 cup water
2 tablespoons instant
  espresso coffee powder
1 cup granulated sugar

8 large eggs, at room temperature
1/4 teaspoon salt
raspberry coulis
fresh raspberries

16 ounces semi-sweet chocolate,     confectioners sugar
   cut into chunks
2 cups (4 sticks) unsalted butter, softened and cut into pats

1. Preheat oven to 350 degrees. Butter a 9×3-inch spring-form pan. Line with parchment paper; butter paper.

2. In a 3-quart, heavy saucepan, combine water with espresso coffee powder. Bring to a boil, stirring to dissolve the espresso; lower heat.

3. Add sugar and chocolate and cook over low heat, stirring constantly, until sugar is dissolved and chocolate has melted.

4. Add butter, stir until melted and mixture is smooth; remove from heat and cool slightly.

5. In a medium bowl, beat eggs lightly with the salt, using a wire whisk, until just combined. Stir into cooled chocolate mixture. Pour into prepared pan.

6. Bake 1 hour or until cake tester inserted near center comes out clean.

7. Cool completely on wire rack. Cake will rise to top of pan and will sink slightly during cooling.

8. Cover and refrigerate until cold, several hours or overnight.

9. To serve, pool some Raspberry Coulis onto dessert plates. Cut cake into thin wedges using a knife dipped into warm water and wiped dry. Place wedge of cake on coulis, garnish with raspberries and dust lightly with confectioners sugar. Store cake in refrigerator.

# Mel's Restaurant and Bar
### 235 Fillmore Street, Denver, 303-333-3979

## Mussels "La Cagouille"
*1–2 servings*

1 pound black mussels         1 ounce parsley, chopped
3 ounces butter, melted       salt (kosher or sea)

1. Place iron skillet over medium high heat. When skillet is hot arrange mussels evenly in the skillet. Cook for 5 to 7 minutes.

2. Once mussels are open, pour 1 ounce of butter over them, as well as the parsley and a generous pinch of salt.

3. Pour remaining butter into a ramekin and serve immediately.

*Note:* Don't burn your table with the iron skillet; put a trivet or a heat-proof pad below the iron skillet.

## Grilled Chilean Sea Bass with Red Wine Lentils, Grilled Figs, and Grilled Red Onion

*4 servings*

olive oil
1 small yellow onion, chopped fine
1 tablespoon minced garlic
6 ounces dried black lentils
2 quarts red wine
salt (kosher or sea)

fresh ground black pepper
1 to 2 red onions,
 sliced $\frac{1}{4}$ inch thick
8 fresh black mission figs
4, 6-ounce Chilean bass fillets
4 ounces unsalted butter

1. Place a 1-gallon sauce pot over medium heat. Add a tablespoon of olive oil and the yellow onion. Sauté until onion is translucent.

2. Add minced garlic; cook another 3 to 5 minutes.

3. Add lentils and stir until lentils are coated with the onion/garlic mixture. Add red wine, salt, and pepper. Bring to a boil, then simmer for 1 hour, stirring every 15 minutes. Lentils should be cooked at this time. Set aside.

4. Place red onions on a plate and brush olive oil on both sides. Salt and pepper both sides. Grill each side of onion for 3 to 5 minutes.

5. Once onions are grilled, place in a bowl and cover with plastic wrap. The onions will continue to cook for fifteen minutes.

6. Slice figs lengthwise and place flesh side up on a plate. Brush with olive oil. Salt and pepper the flesh side. Carefully place on the grill for 2 to 3 minutes. Set aside.

7. Brush olive oil onto sea bass; season with salt and pepper. Grill each side 4 to 5 minutes. The fish should feel very firm when done.

8. Heat lentils over medium heat. Once hot, add butter and stir until melted.

9. In four bowls, evenly place lentils on the bottom of the bowl. Place fish on top of lentils. Place grilled onions on top of fish and place grilled figs on top of the onions. Garnish with Italian parsley. Serve.

# Panzano
## 909 17th Street, Denver, 303-296-3525

## Tuna Carpaccio
*1 serving*

3 ounces sushi-grade
  yellowfin tuna
2 tablespoons olive tapanade
1 teaspoon chopped thyme
  and oregano, mixed
1 teaspoon finely chopped
  lemon zest

1 tablespoon balsamic
  vinegar reduction
salt & black pepper
6 baby arugula leaves
4 artichoke chips
1 tablespoon extra virgin olive oil

1. Using a razor-sharp knife, slice the tuna loin paper-thin on the bias to get pieces that you can see through. Slice a total of 8 pieces of tuna, enough to place around the edge of a chilled, 7-inch serving plate, to form the carpaccio base of the dish.

2. Prepare a tuna tartare mixture by chopping the remaining tuna finely.

3. Place the chopped tuna in a small bowl and combine with 1 tablespoon olive tapanade, $1/2$ teaspoon thyme-oregano mixture, $1/2$ teaspoon lemon zest, $1/2$ tablespoon balsamic vinegar reduction, and salt and pepper to taste.

4. Place the arugula leaves, stems in, in the center of the plate to cover the bare spot.

5. Place a small amount of the tuna tartare on top of the arugula, and top with an artichoke chip, repeating three times to build a tower. Sprinkle the remaining tapanade, herbs, and lemon zest evenly over the tuna carpaccio, followed by a drizzle of the remaining olive oil and balsamic vinegar reduction, and a sprinkle of salt and pepper to finish.

### Olive Tapanade

1 cup pitted kalamata olives
1 cup sun-dried tomatoes
1 cup extra virgin olive oil

1 tablespoon chopped garlic
$1/4$ cup capers
$1/8$ cup anchovies

Chop all the ingredients very small and mix together.

### Artichoke Chips

1 large artichoke
peanut or canola oil
salt

1. With a paring knife, peel the artichoke all the way down until all that is left is the heart. It is important to remove all the green from the bottom of the artichoke because otherwise it does not cook well and will not become tender.
2. Place the artichoke heart in lemon water to prevent oxidization.
3. Slice the artichoke in paper-thin circles with a mandolin. The first slices will be ring-shaped, and as you get deeper into the heart, the slices will be solid round pieces.
4. Fry these slices right away in 300-degree peanut or canola oil until light golden brown and crispy.
5. Drain the slices on toweling to remove any excess oil, then season with salt while they are still hot so the salt will stick.

### Balsamic Reduction

2 cups high-quality balsamic vinegar
1. Reduce the vinegar in a small saucepan until it is condensed to about ⅔ cup.
2. Allow the very concentrated reduction to cool before using sparingly.

## Lemon Rosemary Gnocchi with Oven-Dried Tomatoes, Niçoise Olives, and Grilled Zucchini in a Lemon Olive Oil Broth

*4 servings*

Gnocchi translated from Italian means "dumplings" usually cooked in water or broth. There are two principal forms of gnocchi—potato or semolina dough. The former is usually made in the northern regions and the latter in Rome and the south. Some people believe gnocchi originated in Piedmont where recipes have been found that date back to 1801. (Gnocchi is also the name for a small, rippled dried-pasta shell.)

### Lemon Rosemary Gnocchi

10 pounds Yukon Gold potatoes
7 eggs
2 pounds ricotta cheese
1 pound flour

¼ cup chopped rosemary
⅓ cup lemon zest
salt & white pepper

1. Bake the potatoes until soft. While the potatoes are still hot, peel them with a knife and rice them. It is important to do this while they are still hot so the gnocchi do not get overly starchy.

2. Put the riced potatoes on a mixing board or clean counter and form a well in the center of the potatoes. Add all the remaining ingredients into the well and mix in the potatoes with your hands just until everything is incorporated. Taste mixture and add salt and pepper.

3. Working with a small portion at a time, roll out the mixture on a floured surface to shape 1-inch diameter logs. Cut the logs on the bias (at an angle) into 1-inch pieces, periodically dipping your knife in flour to avoid sticking, and place the pieces on a baking sheet.

4. Bring salted water to a boil in a large, low pot with a lot of surface area. Decrease the temperature of the water so it simmers gently.

5. Drop the gnocchi into the simmering water and cook until they float. Skim them out gently and shock them in ice water.

6. Coat a sheet tray with olive oil, and place the gnocchi on the tray when cool.

### Olive Oil Broth

| | |
|---|---|
| 1 cup shallots | chicken stock |
| 1/4 cup garlic | 4 ounces butter |
| 2 sprigs fresh thyme | 2 ounces extra virgin olive oil |
| 1 tablespoon white peppercorns | zest of one lemon |
| 1 cup lemon juice | 1 teaspoon chopped fresh thyme |
| 1 cup white wine | salt & pepper |

1. In a small sauce pan, sauté the shallots and garlic until translucent.

2. Add the aromatics (thyme sprigs and white peppercorns) and deglaze with lemon juice. Let this reduce until dry.

3. Add the white wine and reduce until dry again.

4. Add the stock and cook down by half.

5. Strain the liquid through a fine chinois into the blender. Turn the blender on and add the butter, olive oil, lemon zest, chopped thyme. Season with salt and pepper to taste, and set the sauce aside in a warm place, away from direct heat.

### Gnocchi Garnish

| | |
|---|---|
| 1/4 cup pitted niçoise olives | 1/4 cup oven-dried tomatoes |
| 4 grilled zucchini, sliced 1/2-inch thick on the bias | 2 tablespoons garlic chips |
| | 1 teaspoon chopped rosemary |

### Oven-Dried Tomatoes

10 roma tomatoes, sliced in half
   lengthwise with seeds removed
¼ cup olive oil

1 teaspoon kosher salt
½ teaspoon black pepper

1. In a mixing bowl, toss all the ingredients together so the tomatoes are evenly coated.

2. Place the tomatoes, cut side up, on a baking rack with a sheet tray underneath to catch the juices in a 250-degree oven for 2 hours to dry.

3. When done and cooled, cut dried tomatoes into ½-inch strips.

### Garlic Chips

1. Use a paring knife to slice whole cloves of garlic lengthwise as thin as possible.

2. Place the garlic slices in a pan with enough room-temperature olive oil to deep fry.

3. Heat on the stove to bring the garlic and oil up to temperature together. (By starting the garlic in cold oil, you will come out with perfectly golden chips.) The garlic will crisp up in minutes, then remove it from the oil and drain on a towel.

### Assembly

As four portions, prepare this dish in two batches, so as not to overload the pan. Overloading the pan will cause the gnocchi to stick.

1. In a hot 12-inch sauté pan, add 1 ounce of olive oil. When the oil just starts to smoke, add the gnocchi and shake the pan gently.

2. Add the tomatoes, zucchini, and olives all at once to warm. Sprinkle the rosemary all around and season with salt and pepper to taste. (Use discretion when adding the salt since the olives are very salty.)

3. Place 2 ounces of the lemon olive oil broth in the bottom of a soup plate and gently spoon the gnocchi in the center. Garnish each portion with garlic chips and a sprig of rosemary.

## Chocolate Velvet Crostada

*10 servings*

### Paté Sucre

1 pound butter
12 ounces sugar
3 egg yolks

1½ ounces heavy cream
½ teaspoon vanilla extract
1½ pounds pastry flour

1. Combine the sugar and butter in the mixer with a paddle and cream well. Add the egg yolks, cream, and vanilla extract. Mix ingredients thoroughly, making sure to scrape down the bowl.

2. Add the flour and mix again until just incorporated. Do not over mix. Remove dough from bowl and cover with plastic wrap. Refrigerate for at least 2 hours. (Making this days in advance is great.)

3. To make the shell, remove the dough from the refrigerator and roll out to a $\frac{1}{4}$-inch thickness and a circumference of 1 inch larger than the tart mold. Line a 12-inch drop bottom tart pan with the rolled out dough, cover the dough with parchment paper and place pie weights in the pan.

4. Bake at 300 degrees for 15 minutes or until a light golden brown.

### Chocolate Pot de Crème Filling

| | |
|---|---|
| 2 vanilla beans | 12 ounces chocolate, melted |
| 3 cups heavy cream | $1\frac{1}{2}$ cups sugar |
| 2 cups milk | 8 egg yolks |

1. Cut the vanilla beans in half lengthwise and scrape out the inside of the bean into a pot with the cream and milk.

2. Bring liquid to a boil, then turn heat off and whisk in the melted chocolate.

3. Mix together the sugar and yolks in a stainless steel bowl, and slowly add the scalded cream and milk mixture. This filling can be made days in advance.

### Banana Caramel Sauce

| | |
|---|---|
| 2 cups heavy cream | 1 cup water |
| 1 banana | 4 ounces butter |
| 2 cups sugar | |

1. Steep the cream and banana together in a saucepan.

2. In a separate pot, heat the sugar and water until the mixture turns rich brown in color.

3. Remove the sugar-water mix from the heat and stir in the cream mixture and the butter, making sure you use a pot that has plenty of room because the caramel will foam up to three times its volume when you add the cream and butter.

4. Strain the sauce through a chinois.

### Caramelized Bananas

Slice a ripe banana into $\frac{1}{2}$-inch discs. Sprinkle slices liberally with granulated sugar and burn with a blowtorch or place in a broiler to caramelize.

### Assembly

1. Spread $\frac{1}{3}$-cup creamy peanut butter all over the bottom of the pre-baked tart shell.

2. Pour in the chocolate pot de crème mix until it comes $\frac{1}{4}$ inch from the top of the shell.

3. Place crostada on a baking sheet and cook in a 275-degree oven for approximately 40 minutes, or until it sets up in the center.

4. Let cool in the refrigerator for at least 1 hour.

5. Cut the crostada into 10 pieces and lay 6 pieces of caramelized bananas on each slice.

6. Decorate a chilled dessert plate with 2 ounces of the banana caramel sauce and lay a slice of the crostada on top. (Optional: Garnish with whipped cream.)

# Papillon Café
## 250 Josephine Street, Denver, 303-333-7166

## Yellow Curry Pork with Apples and Spinach

*3 servings*

### Yellow Curry Sauce

| | |
|---|---|
| 1 tablespoon garlic | 1 ounce ginger |
| 1 ounce yellow curry paste | 1 ounce Galanga |
| $1\frac{1}{2}$ ounces butter | 2 ounces green apples |
| $\frac{1}{2}$ ounce shrimp paste | 3 each lime leaf |
| $1\frac{1}{2}$ teaspoon coriander seed | $\frac{1}{2}$ bunch cilantro |
| $\frac{1}{2}$ large onion, sliced thin | $\frac{1}{2}$ ounce tumeric |
| 2 large carrots, sliced thin | 1 can coconut milk, unsweetened |
| 2 large celery stalks, sliced thin | 1 pint heavy cream |
| 2 lemongrass stalks | |

1. In a large sauce pot, sauté garlic and curry paste (do not brown) 1 minute in the butter.

2. Add shrimp paste and coriander seed. Add all the other vegetables, apples, and dry ingredients. Sweat with cover for 10 minutes. Do not allow the bottom to burn.

3. Add all the wet ingredients. Simmer 15 to 20 minutes on low heat.

4. Remove from heat and allow to steep for 1 hour.

| | |
|---|---|
| 9, 2-ounce pieces of pork tenderloin, pounded thin | 9 thin wedges Granny Smith apples |
| salt & pepper | 6 ounces blanched spinach |
| flour | salt, pepper, and sugar to taste |
| 3 ounces white port | sliced oranges |

5. Season pounded pork tenderloins with salt and pepper, dust with flour.

6. Sauté the pork and reserve for later.

7. Deglaze pan with a white port.

8. Add apple wedges and 6 ounces of yellow curry sauce. Simmer for 1 minute.

9. Add spinach; toss. Adjust seasoning with salt, pepper, and sugar. Garnish with sliced oranges.

10. Shingle pork on plate, pour remaining sauce over the top.

## Jumbo Sea Scallops with Spicy Peanut Sauce

*6 servings*

### Peanut Sauce

| | |
|---|---|
| 1$\frac{1}{2}$ tablespoons of whole coriander seed | 2$\frac{1}{2}$ tablespoons sweet soy sauce |
| 2 tablespoons peanut oil | 1 tablespoon soy sauce |
| 2 tablespoons garlic chili paste | 7 tablespoons rice wine vinegar |
| 3 tablespoons Madras curry powder | 2 tablespoons brown sugar |
| 1 can unsweetened coconut milk | 13 ounces smooth peanut butter |
| | salt & black pepper |

1. In a small sauce pot, lightly brown coriander in peanut oil.

2. Add chili paste and curry powder. Then add coconut milk, soy sauces, vinegar, and brown sugar.

3. When the mixture is warm, add to blender and run on medium speed. Add peanut butter and blend until smooth. Add consistency with warm water. Adjust seasoning with salt and black pepper. Keep warm.

### Scallops

| | |
|---|---|
| 24 jumbo sea scallops | white pepper |
| peanut oil | flour |
| kosher salt | 6 servings cooked jasmine rice |

1. Remove muscles from side of scallops; place scallops on paper towel and let dry.

2. Heat 2 medium sauté pans hot with peanut oil.

3. Season scallops with salt and pepper. Dip scallops in flour, shake off excess, and place in hot sauté pan. Brown on 1 side, then brown the other side. Remove scallops and place on paper towel.

4. Ladle desired amount of peanut sauce onto serving platter or individual plates. Place scallops on sauce and serve with jasmine rice.

# Radex
## 116 East 9th Avenue, Denver, 303-861-7999

### Black Olive Pesto (Tapenade)

| | |
|---|---|
| 10 large cloves garlic, peeled | 6 cups olive oil |
| 1, 10-ounce can black olives, drained | 1 tablespoon squid ink |
| | 1½ pounds Parmesan cheese |
| 8 cups kalamata olives, checked for pits | ¼ tablespoon white pepper |
| | 2 cups walnuts, chopped |

1. Put garlic and olives in food processor and chop fine.

2. Add olive oil and squid ink until well combined.

3. Add cheese, white pepper, and chopped walnuts.

4. Combine well and store in proper container.

### Risotto

*12 servings*

| | |
|---|---|
| 3 leeks, chopped to fine dice | bouquet garni (parsley, lemon thyme, basil, and rosemary) |
| 1 yellow onion, fine dice | |
| 2 tablespoons garlic, fine dice | 1 pinch chili flakes |
| 6 cups risotto | 1 tablespoon paprika |
| 1½ gallons vegetable stock | 2 tablespoons butter |
| ¼ cup tomato paste | ¼ cup cream |
| 3 cups white wine | 4 tablespoons mascarpone |

1. Sweat leeks, onion, then garlic. Add risotto. Sauté risotto until coated with oil evenly. Meanwhile, in separate sauce pan, heat vegetable stock and tomato paste. Keep very warm.

2. Add white wine, bouquet garni, chili flakes, and paprika to risotto.

3. Add heated stock until risotto is covered. Cook slowly on low heat. Stir occasionally.

4. When risotto is a little past al dente, finish with butter, cream, and mascarpone.

5. Place on sheet tray and cool.

# Rose's Café
### 1515 Madison Street, Denver, 303-377-7649

## Vietnamese Seafood Delight
*Per person*

| | |
|---|---|
| 2 to 3 shrimps | crab legs (optional) |
| 2 to 3 sea scallops | sesame oil |
| 6 black mussels | garlic |
| 3 clams (steamed open) | minced lemongrass |
| 3 to 4 pieces firm fish | fish sauce |
| squid rings | light stock or water |

1. In a 12-inch sauce pan, sauté all seafood in sesame oil with garlic and minced lemongrass.

2. Add a splash of fish sauce and enough light stock or water to barely cover seafood.

3. Cover and steam until fish is done and mussels open.

4. Finish with oriental chili paste to taste. Serve in shallow bowl with side of steamed rice.

## Swordfish or Tuna Sicilian Style
*Per person*

| | |
|---|---|
| 1 teaspoon capers | breadcrumbs |
| 2 to 3 anchovy filets | olive oil |
| fresh or dried rosemary | extra virgin olive oil |
| ½-inch thick swordfish or tuna steak | lemon juice |

1. Mince together capers, anchovy filets, and a healthy pinch of rosemary.

2. Spread mixture over both sides of fish and then lightly press onto plate of breadcrumbs.

3. Sauté in cast iron skillet in olive oil 3 to 4 minutes per side (or until both sides are brown and fish is cooked.) Plate and drizzle with extra virgin olive oil and squeeze of lemon juice.

# Sam's No. 3
## 2580 South Havana Street, Aurora, 303-751-0347

## Vegetarian Green Chili
*6 servings*

⅛ pound margarine or butter
½ onion, sliced (white, yellow, or red)
½ large tomato, diced
½ tablespoon salt
⅛ tablespoon minced garlic
⅛ tablespoon black, rolled pepper
¼ tablespoon dried oregano
¼ tablespoon ground mustard

1¼ cups black beans, precooked or canned, drained, and rinsed
1½ cups frozen corn
1½ ounces diced green chilies (adjust to taste)
1¾ ounce diced tomatoes
⅛ to ¼ gallon of water, depending on desired thickness

1. In large stockpot over medium-high heat, combine margarine or butter, onion, and tomato. Sauté until soft.

2. Add salt, garlic, pepper, oregano, and mustard. Sauté, covered, for 1 minute. Immediately add black beans and corn. Stir in well.

3. Add chilies and tomatoes. Stir well; let cook for 3 minutes.

4. Add water to desired thickness, stir; heat through and serve.

## Meatloaf
*20 servings*

10 pounds ground beef
1 tablespoon salt
1 tablespoon cumin
1 tablespoon chili powder
1 tablespoon minced garlic
1 tablespoon ground mustard

1 medium yellow onion, diced
5 ounces Heinz 57 sauce
1 tablespoon Lawry's seasoning salt
8 raw eggs (no shells)
1 cup uncooked oatmeal

1. Mix all ingredients completely.

2. Grease bread pans and cook at 350 degrees until done.

## Sam's Famous Homefries

1. Wash desired amount of #1 Idaho potatoes. Leave jackets on!

2. On high heat, steam until cooked through, with lid of steamer on. Leave a little escape in lid; cook for approximately 45 minutes to 1 hour.

2. With spoon, peel jackets off potatoes and remove all poor markings (bruises, eyes, etc.). Let sit out until they reach room temperature.

4. When potatoes have cooled, put in refrigerator and cool at least 5 hours. When completely cooled, slice to desired thickness (preferably about ³⁄₁₆ inch).

5. On 400-degree grill, grill with margarine until golden brown. Try adding onions, chives, ham, bacon, cheese, hot sauce, etc.

# Tante Louise
### 4900 East Colfax Avenue, Denver, 303-355-4488

## Porcini Mushroom Bisque
*16 servings*

2 teaspoons garlic, chopped
½ cup shallots
1 pound frozen porcini
  mushrooms
1 pound crimini mushrooms

2 cups Cognac
2 gallons mushroom stock
1 quart heavy cream
salt & pepper to taste

1. Sauté garlic, shallots, and mushrooms. Deglaze with Cognac.

2. Add mushroom stock and reduce by ¼.

3. Add cream, blend and strain. Season with salt and pepper.

## Roasted Five-Spiced Half Duck
*12 servings*

1 orange
2 onions
10 cloves garlic

2 pounds salt
12 star anise
1 pound brown sugar

| | |
|---|---|
| 3 ounces ginger, sliced | $\frac{1}{4}$ cup five spice |
| $\frac{1}{2}$ cup soy sauce | 1 gallon ice |
| 2 gallons water | 6 whole ducks |

1. Bring sliced orange, onions, garlic, ginger, soy sauce, water, salt, star anise, brown sugar, and five spice to a boil.

2. Add ice. Let ice melt and refrigerate brine.

3. When cool, add whole ducks and submerge completely in brine overnight or 18 hours; then remove from brine.

4. Roast duck in 325-degree oven for 1 hour. Take out, let it rest for 30 minutes. Cut into half ducks and place under a broiler until crispy.

### Wild Rice Pilaf
*6 servings*

| | |
|---|---|
| 2 teaspoons garlic | 1 cup Indian harvest |
| 4 teaspoons shallots | wild rice blend |
| 1 leek, chopped | $\frac{1}{2}$ cup chopped hazelnuts |
| $\frac{1}{4}$ teaspoon butter | 2 handfuls fresh spinach |
| $2\frac{1}{4}$ quarts chicken stock | 2 teaspoons fresh thyme |

1. Sauté garlic, shallots, and leek in butter together until leek is soft.

2. Add chicken stock and rice; bring to a boil.

3. Cover and simmer over low heat for $\frac{1}{2}$ hour.

4. Add remaining ingredients, salt and pepper to taste, and toss to mix.

# 240 Union
## 240 Union Boulevard, Lakewood, 303-989-3562

### Thai-Style Beef Salad
*2 servings*

| | |
|---|---|
| 3 tablespoons fresh lime juice | 4 cups thinly sliced romaine lettuce |
| $2\frac{1}{2}$ tablespoons vegetable oil | 6 radishes, trimmed, thinly sliced |
| $1\frac{1}{2}$ tablespoons oriental sesame oil | 4 green onions, thinly sliced |
| 2 tablespoons Thai fish sauce | 1 large carrot, julienned |
| (nam pla) | 2 tablespoons minced mint |
| 2 teaspoons grated lime peel | 2 tablespoons minced cilantro |

8 ounces cooked sliced roast beef,
    cut into thin strips (about 2 cups)

1. For dressing, whisk first 5 ingredients in small bowl to blend. Season dressing with salt and pepper.

2. Combine beef, lettuce, radishes, green onions, carrots, mint and cilantro in a large bowl; toss with enough dressing to coat.

3. Divide salad between 2 plates.

4. Serve, passing any remaining dressing separately.

## Tuna Summer Vegetable Salad

*2 servings*

| | |
|---|---|
| 12 ounce tuna steak,<br>    $1\frac{1}{2}$ to 2 inches thick | $\frac{1}{2}$ cup cannelini beans, cooked<br>1 lemon, juiced |
| 1 cup arugula or baby spinach | 3 to 5 assorted tomatoes, |
| $\frac{1}{2}$ cup corn kernels, cooked | cut into different shapes |
| $\frac{1}{2}$ cup red onion, sliced thin | $\frac{1}{4}$ cup olive oil |
| $\frac{1}{2}$ cup green beans, blanched | salt & pepper to taste |

1. Drizzle a little oil on tuna and season with salt and pepper.

2. Preheat a sauce pan or grill to medium-high heat. Sear tuna about 2 minutes per side.

3. Combine remaining ingredients in a mixing bowl. Toss to mix well and season with salt and pepper.

4. Mount mixture into the center of serving plates. Slice tuna into 6 to 8 slices and place on top.

# Vasil's Euro-Grille
### 7340 South Clinton Street, Englewood, 303-799-3600

## Almond-Crusted Diver Scallops

*9 servings*

| | |
|---|---|
| 36 diver scallops | 1 cup plus 2 tablespoons flour |
| 2 cups honey | $1\frac{1}{2}$ pounds almonds, ground |
| 1 cup soy sauce | |

1. Rinse and blot scallops on a dry cloth.

2. Mix honey and soy together.

3. Flour each scallop, dip in the honey/soy mixture and then in the ground almonds.

4. Sear, almond side down, until golden brown.

5. Turn over, and cook on medium heat for 10 to 15 minutes.

## Apricot Mustard Crusted Colorado Lamb Chops
*9 servings*

| | |
|---|---|
| 1½ pounds dried apricots | ½ cup honey |
| 1 quart chicken broth | salt & pepper to taste |
| ¼ cup Dijon mustard | 8½-pound rack of lamb |
| ¼ cup grain mustard | 1½ cups Lavender bread crumbs |
| 1 cup rice wine vinegar | |

### Lavender Bread Crumbs

1 cup and 2 tablespoons bread crumbs

2 tablespoons dried Lavender      salt & pepper to taste

1. Cook apricots for 15 minutes in chicken broth or until tender.

2. Cool for 30 minutes. Drain chicken broth and discard it.

3. Chop apricots and blend with both mustards and vinegar. Add honey and blend until smooth. Add salt and pepper as desired.

4. Cut lamb chops into 2 bones per chop, 2 chops per person. Preheat oven at 400 degrees and roast chops to internal temperature of 115–120 degrees for medium rare (use meat thermometer).

5. Top with apricot mustard and Lavender bread crumbs.

## Black Forest Cheesecake with Pistachio Crust
*9 servings*

### Crust

| | |
|---|---|
| 3 cups finely chopped pistachios | ½ cup sugar |
| ½ cup brown sugar | ½ cup butter, melted |

Combine and mix, set aside.

### Filling

3 cups brandied cherries

Drain and place between paper towels. These can be purchased in the specialty section of the grocery store. If you can't find them, use black cherries.

**Cheesecake Batter**

*Note:* All ingredients should be at room temperature.

| | |
|---|---|
| 1 pound ricotta cheese | 3 large eggs |
| 2 cups sour cream | 3 tablespoons pastry flour |
| 1 pound cream cheese | 3 tablespoons cornstarch |
| 1½ cups sugar | 5 tablespoons vanilla |
| ½ cup butter, melted | 5 tablespoons lemon juice |

1. Combine ricotta cheese and sour cream in mixing bowl.

2. Beating slowly, add cream cheese, sugar, and butter.

3. Increase speed to medium and add eggs, flour, cornstarch, vanilla, and lemon juice. Beat on highest speed possible without splattering for 5 minutes.

4. Spray spring-form pan with oil. Press pistachio crust into pan.

5. Pour in cheesecake batter until pan is ¾ full. Place cherries evenly on top of batter and then add the remaining batter.

6. Bake in preheated oven at 350 degrees for 1 hour. Turn off heat and leave in closed oven for 1 more hour.

7. Place in refrigerator until cool (overnight, if possible).

# Yanni's
## 2223 South Monaco Parkway, Denver, 303-692-0404

## Grape Leaves Stuffed with Rice, Dill, and Walnuts
*Makes about 33*

Plain yogurt would go well alongside this classic Greek appetizer.

| | |
|---|---|
| 1, 16-ounce jar grape leaves | 1 cup chopped parsley |
| 8 cups water | ¼ cup finely chopped walnuts |
| 1 pound long-grain white rice | ¾ cup chopped fresh dill |
| 2 teaspoons salt | 1 teaspoon ground black pepper |
| 1 cup olive oil | 2 cups crumbled feta cheese |
| 1½ pounds onions, chopped | (about 8 ounces) |
| (about 4⅓ cups) | ½ cup fresh lemon juice |
| 4 large garlic cloves, minced | lemon wedges |

1. Place grape leaves in large bowl. Cover with water. Let soak while pre-paring rice filling, separating leaves occasionally.

2. Bring 4 cups water, rice, and 1 teaspoon salt to boil in heavy medium sauce pan over high heat. Reduce heat to low, cover and cook until rice is tender and water is absorbed, about 20 minutes. Uncover; set aside.

3. Heat $\frac{1}{2}$ cup oil in heavy large pot over medium heat. Add onions and sauté until beginning to turn golden, about 15 minutes. Add garlic, sauté 1 minute. Remove from heat. Stir in parsley, walnuts, dill, pepper, and remaining 1 teaspoon salt. Cool slightly. Mix in cheese, then rice. Cool completely.

4. Preheat oven to 375 degrees. Place 1 large grape leaf, vein side up, on work surface. Cut off stem. Patch or overlap with pieces of other leaves if necessary to form about 5- to 6-inch surface area. Spoon scant $\frac{1}{4}$-cup rice filling in center of leaf. Fold bottom of leaf over filling. Fold in sides. Roll up to enclose filling in leaf. Arrange seam side down on baking sheet. Repeat with enough grape leaves to use up remaining rice filling.

5. Line bottom of two 13×9×2-inch glass baking dishes with any remaining grape leaves. Divide stuffed grape leaves between prepared dishes, arranging seam side down in rows in single layer.

6. Mix remaining 4 cups water, $\frac{1}{2}$ cup oil, and lemon juice in medium bowl to blend. Pour enough lemon-oil mixture over stuffed grape leaves in each dish to cover. Cover dishes with foil.

7. Bake until lemon-oil mixture is absorbed and flavors blend, about 1 hour. Uncover; cool to room temperature. (Can be prepared 4 days ahead. Cover and refrigerate. Let stand at room temperature 1 hour before serving.) Arrange stuffed grape leaves on platter. Garnish with lemon wedges.

## Classic Roast Leg of Lamb

*8 to 10 servings*

| | |
|---|---|
| 6 to 8 garlic cloves | $1\frac{1}{2}$ cups olive oil |
| 8- to 10-pound lamb leg, trimmed | 2 quarts water |
| salt & freshly ground pepper | strained, fresh juice of 6 lemons |
| 1 tablespoon mustard | |

1. Preheat oven to 500 degrees.

2. Finely chop garlic cloves. With a sharp knife, make $\frac{1}{2}$-inch slits all around leg of lamb, and stuff garlic, salt, pepper, and mustard inside each slit.

3. Rub lamb with $\frac{1}{2}$ cup olive oil, 1 chopped garlic clove, salt, pepper, and mustard.

4. Place lamb in baking pan and add water, 1 cup olive oil, and lemon juice.

5. Bake for approximately $2\frac{1}{2}$ hours or until lamb is tender and slightly rare.

6. Baste every 20 minutes with pan juices.

## Garides Tourkolimano
## (Jumbo Shrimp in Tomato Feta Sauce)

*8 to 10 servings*

$1\frac{1}{2}$ pounds crushed tomatoes
$1\frac{1}{2}$ pounds tomatoes, diced
2 tablespoon tomato paste
1 cup lemon juice
1 cup olive oil
3 cups red wine

1 tablespoon black pepper
2 tablespoons sugar
4 pounds jumbo shrimp,
   tail on, deveined
1 pound crumbled feta cheese

1. In a soup pot, add 2 quarts of water and add all ingredients, except shrimp and feta, bring to a rolling boil. Simmer for $1\frac{1}{2}$ hours.

2. In two large sauté pans, add 2 pounds shrimp to each and sauté in olive oil. Evenly add sauce from soup pot while shrimp is cooking.

3. Add $\frac{1}{2}$-pound crumbled feta to each pan and stir lightly until a nice orange color.

# Index

ABC television, 136
ACF Culinarians of Colorado, 120
Adirondacks, 143–144
Aiello, Inc., 158
Al Fresco, 26
Albalone, 48
Albany, the, 82
Albert, 12
Allen, Fred, 58
Allen, Woody, 46
Allison candy, 149
Allphin, Bob, 113
Almond-Crusted Diver Scallops, 230–231
Alpine Village Inn, viii, 3–5, 82, 170
*America's Dining and Travel Guide,* 120, 129, 139
Amethyst Room, 39
Amole, Gene, ix, xi, 136–137, 148, 150, 177–190
Andretti, Mario, 46
Andurlakis, Nick, 46
Andy's Smorgasbord, 167
Appetizers (recipes), 218–219, 232
Apple Tree Shanty, 5–6, 82, 175
Apricot Mustard Crusted Colorado Lamb Chops, 231

Arcade Restaurant Company, 37–38
Archuleta, Joe, 152
Argonaut Hotel, 99, 121–123, 130
Arizona Biltmore, 175
Armatas, Sam, 150–151
Armatas, Spiro Sam, xi, 147–150
Art Institute of Colorado, xii
  Garlic and Rosemary Roasted Leg of Lamb, 205–206
  Huckleberry Pie, 208–209
  Red Chard Casserole, 206–207
Artichoke Chips, 218–219
Ashe, Arthur, 46
Asher, Jane, 124
Atler, Larry, 75
Aviation Country Club, 17

Bainter, Jeffrey, 46
Baker, Ray, 116
Balsamic Reduction, 219
Banana Caramel Sauce, 222
Banjo Club, 93
Barolo Grill, 51
  Braised Duckling with Black Olives, 192

Lamb Shank "Osso Buco Style," 191–192
  Semifreddo di Limone, 192–193
Barrett, Marjorie, 30, 153
Barros, Joe, 154
Barthes, C., 2
Baskerville, Vernon, 117
Bastien, Bill, 115–116
Baur, Clara, 13
Baur, John Joseph, 13
Baur, Otto, 13–16
Baur, Pauline (Kohler), 13
Baur, Thusnelda, 13
*Baur's Beacon,* 13, 175
Baur's Chocolate Torte, 190
Baur's Restaurant, 13–17, 77, 149
Beck, Frank, 28–29
Becker, Maxine N., xi
Beebe, Lucius, 156
Ben Cook Plumbing and Supply, 63–64
Bennett Coffee Shop, 164
Bertoni, James, 93
Best Fares, 139
Bibelot, 40–41
Billy Wilson Trio, 115–116
Bisset, Jacqueline, 46
Black, Helen, 4

Black Forest Cheesecake with Pistachio Crust, 231–232
Black Olive Pesto, 225
Black Orchid bar, 149
Blankenship, James, 63, 113
Bleu Cheese Dressing, 141
Blue Front shoe repair, 149
Blue Parrot Inn and Restaurant, 64, 164, 166
Blythe Restaurant, 92
Boat, Jaydee, 162
Boccalino's, 165
Bocuse, Paul, 49
Bodegas Olarra winery, 161
Boggio's Rotisserie, 165
Bon Vivant, 158
Bonfils, Helen, 4
Borra, Fred, 171
Boston, the, 11
Boston Lunch, 147
Boulder Hungry Farmer, 171
Bourgougnon, Mr., 2
Braised Duckling with Black Olives, 192
Braised Oxtails, 31
Bramhall, Fred, 49
Brando, Marlon, 128, 132
Braque, Lucien, 99
Brasel, Sean, 41
Bread and sweet breads (recipes), 179–180, 189–190, 203–204, 210, 214, 231
Breed, George T., 2
Brick Oven Beanery, 18–20
Brisket with Gravy, 181–182
British Hotel Corp., 36
Broadmoor, 42
Broadway Theater, 64
Broker Restaurants, 145, 169–173
Brooke, Cindy, 46
Brooke, Romana, 46
Brooks, Max, 150

Brooks Brothers, 149
Brooks Tower, 80
Browder, Randy, 52
Brown, Jean, 117, 122
Brown Palace Hotel, 64, 96–97, 119, 129, 156
Bruno's Italian Bistro
  Gangster Chicken, 194
  Tuscan Lamb Shank, 193–194
Brunswick, the, 11
Buchwald, Art, 38
Buckhorn Exchange Restaurant, 164
  Famous Bean Soup, 195
  Lavender Pepper Duck Breast with Raspberry/Red Zinfandel Sauce, 195–196
Bunn, Ken, 43
Burg, Frankie, 23
Burgess Bill, 46
Burkhard, Cecil, xi
Burr, Raymond, 43, 83
Business Radio Network, 129, 139
Business Talk Radio, 139
Byers, William, 92

Café Bonaparte, 48
Café Franco, 165
Café Giovanni, 25–27, 43
Café Promenade, 28–31, 40
Calhoon, Curtis, 46
Calhoun, Patricia, 155
Callaway, Charles, 28, 30
Capitol, The, 62
Caramelized Bananas, 223
Carlton, Michael, 39, 43, 153
Carnes, Del, 135
Carpenter, Crista, xi
Carter, Nell, 46
Casa Bonita, 153
Caston, Saul, 4
Castro, Fidel, 139
Centennial Racetrack, 114, 130
Central Bank, 150
Chagall, Marc, 34

Charpiot, Fred, 1
Charpiot, Louis, 62
Charpiot's hotel, 73
Chase and Chucovich, 97–98
Chat and Chew, The, 168
Chateau Lafite, 102
Chateau Pyrenees, 34–36
Chateaubriand of Buffalo, 47
Chesapeake, the, 11
Chesterton, G. K., 158
Chevalier, Maurice, 128
Chez Michelle, 120
Chez Thoa, 165
Chez Walter
  Crème Caramels, 197–198
  Roesti (Potatoes Swiss Style), 197
  Sliced Veal Zurich Style, 196–197
Chianti's, 48
Child, Julia, 139
Chile-Concarne, 86
Chili. See Soup or chili
Chili Sauce, 188–189
Chin, Jimmy, 74–75
China Café, 168
Chinese Noodles, 87–88
Chinook Brule, 200
Chinook Tavern
  Chinook Brule, 200
  Stuffed Port Chops with Red Onion Marmalade, 198–199
Chives, 51
Chocolate Pot de Crème Filling, 222
Chocolate Velvet Crostada, 221–223
Chop Suey, 87
Choucroute Alsacienne, 187
Clark, Nancy, xi, 174
Clark, Walter, 117
Classic Roast Leg of Lamb, 233–234
Clemens, Bill, 148
Cliff Young's, 39–44

Filet Mignon of Tuna with Sweet Soy and Ginger Butter, 44
Coffee, Joe, 59
Cole's Hall, 62
Colorado College, 42
*Colorado Connection,* 138
*Colorado Gourmet Gold,* 162
Colorado Mine Company, 45–47
Colorado Public Radio, 138
Colorado Soccer Camps, 112
Colorado State University, 107
*Colorado Sun,* vii, 8
Colwell, James, 14–16
Conder, Jim, 138
Continental Broker, 48
Cook, Kenneth, 78, 80
Cook, Marvin, 63–65, 78–80
Cook, Michael, 78–80
Cook, Tony, 78–81
Cook's Plumbing, 79
Cooper, Jackie, 46
Cooper Building, 77
Cordillera's Picasso Room, 175
Cork and Cleaver, 46
Cory Hotel, 83
Cosmopolitan Hotel, 74–75
Country Kitchen, 170
Craig Morton's, 48
Crawford, Dana, 28, 30
Crawford, Morris, xi, 117
Creamerie, 11
Crème Caramels, 197–198
Crider, Ron, 139–140
Crosby, Cathy Lee, 46
Crowther, Dick, 121
Cruise, Robin, 153
Cruse & Co. Bordeaux, 107
Cucumber Red Onion Relish, 212

Cuisine, early Denver, 85–88
Culinary Institute of America, 83
Culinary Program, 120
Cunard Cruise ships, 119, 129
Curtis, Jamie Lee, 36
Cygnar, Claudia, 159
Cygnar, Tom, xi, 159

Dambach, Pauline, 4
Dambach, Ray, 4, 170
Damone, Vic, 46
Daniels, Bill, 117, 133
Daniels and Fisher, 149, 167
Dante Bichette's, 41
David, Elizabeth, 90
Davidson, Saul, 46
Davis, Al, 128, 131–132
Davis, Marvin, 173
Day, Judge Edward C., 4
de la Renta, Oscar, 43
de Salle, Mike, 168
Debuyzer, Duco, xi
Delbec, Andre, 99
Demi-glace, 211–212
Dempsey, Jack, 60–61
DeNiro, Robert, 36
Denver, James William, 92
Denver, John, 46
Denver Broncos, 131–132
Denver Burglar Alarm Co., 41
Denver City Dining Room, 2
Denver County Club, 83
Denver Dry Co., 149
Denver Dry Goods Tea Room, 17
*Denver Epicure,* 162
Denver French colony, 11
*Denver Post,* x, 63, 89, 100, 135, 137, 144, 156, 158
Denver Public Library, x, 91, 146
*Denver Republican,* 37
Denver Tech Center, 49

*Denver Times,* 32, 55, 71, 85
Dessert (recipes), 106, 142, 190, 192–193, 197–198, 200, 201–202, 202, 203, 208–209, 215–216, 222, 221–223, 223, 231–232
Diamond Cabaret, 42
*Dining in Denver,* 162
Doc, 87–88
Doc's place, 88
Dolly Madison ice cream, 150
Donaldson, Max, x, 21–22
Douglass, Corky, 102, 108, 168
Dove, The, 42
Duckling Bigarrade, 140
Dudley's, 49–51
Duesenberg, 24, 41, 43
Dumas, William, 136
Dumplings, 179–180
Duncan Hines, 153
Dutchman, 169–173
Duval, Miss, 36

Eagles, The, 46
Eastwood, Clint, 46, 128
École Hotelier de Lausanne, 129
Eddie Ott's Sherman Plaza, 17
Eden East, 50
Edelweiss Café, 162–163
Edelweiss Restaurant, 164
Edwards, Vince, 134
Effie, the Blonde Tigress, 122
Eggplant Stuffed with Clams, 141
Eisenhower, Mamie, 117
Eisenhower, President Dwight, 116–117
Ekberg, Anita, 117, 128
Elephant Corral, 1
Elgar, Edward, 182
Elitch Theatre, 83
Ellis, Mrs., 85
Emerson Street East, 168

Empire Bakery, 2
*Empire Magazine,* 154, 173
Enberg, Dick, 132
Enigma, 182
Ernie Capillupo's Restaurant and Lounge, 182
Espresso Chocolate Torte, 215–216
Eugene's, 48
European Hotel, 92
Everett, Jeannie, x
ExServicemen's Club, 130

Famous Bean Soup, 195
Fashion Bar, 148–149
Faye, Alice, 117
Federal Reserve Bank, 77
Fennel Potato Cake, 212–213
Figaro's European Coiffures, 130
Fike, Al, 23
Filet Mignon of Tuna with Sweet Soy and Ginger Butter, 44
Fine, Clark, xi
Fink, Thoa, 165
Fish and seafood (recipes), 44, 67, 127, 142, 209–210, 212–213, 216–217, 217, 218–219, 224–225, 226, 226–227, 230–231, 234
Flagstaff House Restaurant
   Hot Valrohna Strudle with Cocoa Sorbet, 201–202
   Kalamata Olive–Crusted Rack of Colorado Lamb with White Polenta and Ratatouille Vegetables, 200
Flaherty, Jack, 151
Fletcher, Selmon, 130
Fleurie's, 50
Focaccia Croutons, 214
Footers, 168
*For Gourmets Only,* 133

Fort, The
   Gonzales Steak, 202–203
   Negrita, 203
   Pumpkin Walnut Muffins, 203–204
Forum of the XII Caesar, 36
Fotinos, Pete, 152
Four Seasons, 36
Fourth Story Restaurant
   Porcini Mushroom and Bacon-Infused Beef Consommé, 204
   Strawberry Soup, 205
French, J. B., 49
French Restaurant, 1
*Friday Feast,* 136–138
Frog's Legs Sauté à la Provençale, 105
Frommer, Arthur, 139
Fuji Inn, 168

"Gabby Gourmet," 18, 49
Gaiety, 82
Gandi Dance, 93
Gangster Chicken, 194
Gardner, Charlie, 169
Garides Tourkolimano, 234
Garlic and Rosemary Roasted Leg of Lamb, 205–206
Garlic Chips, 221
Garnish. *see* Sauce or garnish
Gart's, 149
Gazetta, Rich, 148
George V, 36
Georgia Boys Bar-B-Que, 175
Gerstle, Heinz, viii, 99–103, 119, 129, 133–135, 138
Gerstle, Irmgard, 99–100
Gevens's, 12
Glendinning, 11
Gnocchi Garnish, 220–221
Gobel, George, 168
Golden Lantern, 165
Golden Ox, 52–54

Goldsmith, Jack, 40–41
Gonzales Steak, 202–203
*Good Life,* 140
Goodwill, 132
Gotham Hotel, 63, 79
Goto, Leo, 74–75
*Gourmet Cooking,* 136
*Gourmet* magazine, 181
Grain Exchange, 23
Grape Leaves Stuffed with Rice, Dill, and Walnuts, 232
"Grapevine" program, 138
Greatest Bouillabaisse, 67–68
Greeley Gas Co., 133
Green, Bobby, 46
Green Gables Country Club, 63, 78
Green Onion Buerre Blanc, 213
Grilled Chilean Sea Bass with Red Wine Lentils, Grilled Figs, and Grilled Red Onion, 217
Groen, Aileen, xi
Grusin, Dave, 84

Halper Gail, xi
Hamblin, Ken, 139
Hamilton, Joe, 113
Hamilton, Scott, 36
Hanna, Pat, 4, 52, 123, 153
Hans Brinker's, 24
Harrington, Maureen, 100
Harris, Phil, 117
Harvey, Fred, 23
Have U E 10, 22
Hawkins, Bud, 168
Hawkins, Vic, 99, 113, 122
Hawthorne, Jim, 136–137
Hayden, John (Luke), 123
Hayden, Mrs., 123
Heinsohn, Marvel, 167
Heinsohn, Sally, 167
Henderson, Joann, 158

Henrici's Golden Barrel Supper Club, 28, 158
Hensel-Phelps, 138
Herb Crusted Fallow Venison Loin with Salsify Purée and Huckleberry Mint Sauce, 210–212
Herman's pawn shop, 149
Herrmann, Christopher, 108–109
Herrmann, Karen Michelle Wolfe, x, 103–105, 107–110, 120, 125
Heston, Charlton, 36
Hi-Spot, 147
Hilton Hotel, 36, 130
Hoagland, Ed, 20
Holladay, Ben, 92
Homard (Lobster) au Court-Bouillon, 67
Hopkins, R. T., xi
Hopper, Frank, 34
Horseradish Cream, 210
Hotel Metropole, 64
Hot Valrohna Strudle with Cocoa Sorbet, 201–202
House of Delmonico, 2
Huckleberry Pie, 208–209
Hucko, Peanuts, 96
Hudson, Colonel, 170
Hudson's, 39
Hughes mansion, 101
Hulse, Heavy, 114–115
Hummel, Max, 136
Hummel's, 168
Hungry Dutchman, 174
Hungry Farmer, 169–173
Husted, Bill, 43, 139, 144, 165, 168

*Intermountain Jewish News,* 60, 75
Inverness Hotel & Golf Club
Herb Crusted Fallow Venison Loin with Salsify Purée and

Huckleberry Mint Sauce, 210
Seared Prosciutto-Wrapped Ahi Tuna with Cucumber Red Onion Relish and Fennel Potato Cakes, 212–213
Smoked Salmon with Quinoa Waffle, 209–210
Ireland, Attorney, 123
Ireland, Gail, 123
Ivory's Piano Bar, 83–84

Jackson, Bill, 117
Jackson, Stew, 41
Jacob Schueler confectionery store, 14
Jacobs, John Henry, 13, 16
Jacobs, John Joseph, 16
Jagger, Mick, 42
Jail House Bar, 93
Janse-Kok, Kees, xi
James Cella's Restaurant & Oyster House, 2
Javits, Jacob, 131
Jax, 41
Joe "Awful" Coffee's Ringside Lounge, 59–61
Joe's Place, 162
John R. Thompson Co. of Chicago, 156, 158
Johnson, Donna, xi
Johnson, Magic, 36
Johnson, Pat, 20
Johnson, Ross, 19–20
Johnson, Van, 128
Johnson, Wayne, xi
Jones, Rebecca, 124
Jordan, Eddie, 115
Jordan, Tom, 50, 138
Jordan Winery, 50–51, 138
Joshel, Lloyd, 122
Joshel, Suzanne, 122–123, 129
Joslins, 149

Jumbo Sea Scallops with Spicy Peanut Sauce, 224–225

Kalamata Olive–Crusted Rack of Colorado Lamb with White Polenta and Ratatouille Vegetables, 200–201
Kalin Bourgogne, 42
Kaskela, John, 46
Katz, Alan, 39
Kaye, Richard, 123
KDEN-1240 radio, 129, 138
Kessler, John, 153
KFML Radio, 133
Khayyám, Omar, 95
King Farouk, 28
Kinkel, Father Robert J., xi
Kllanxhja, Tish, 28–29
KLMO 1060 AM, 140
Kludge, Rudolph, 93
Kludge Restaurant, 93
KMGH-TV, 138
Knauss, Edwin, 101
Knauss, Emma, 101
Knight, Orville, 49
KNUS radio, 139–140
KOA radio, 116
KOA-TV, 136
Kreck, Dick, viii, xi, 2, 63
KRMA-TV, 133, 135–136
Kuehl, Pat Hanna, xi
Kuner, Jacob, 15
Kuner, Marie, 15
Kuner-Empson Company, 15
Kuner Pickle Company, 15
KVOD radio, xi, 29, 138

L.A. Raiders, 131
La Flecke, Jacques, xi
La Pyramide, 104
Laffite Restaurant, 63–68, 79

Greatest Bouillabaisse, 67–68
Homard (Lobster) au Court-Bouillon, 67
Lagasse, Emeril, 139
Lalli, Mario, 28
Lamb Shank "Osso Buco Style," 191–192
Lambatos, Jimmy, 46
Lambetis, Pete, 152
Lande's of Denver, 69–70, 165
Lao-tse, 178, 185
Larimer, Gen. William, 91
Lathrop, Mary, 98
Lavender Bread Crumbs, 231
Lavender Pepper Duck Breast with Raspberry/Red Zinfandel Sauce, 195–196
Le Profile, 39, 43, 78–81. See also Profile Room
Leach, Robin, 137
Leighton, Terry, 42
Lelands, 2
Lemmon, Jack, 83
Lemon Dill Vinaigrette, 210
Lemon Rosemary Gnocchi with Oven-Dried Tomatoes, Nioise Olives, and Grilled Zucchini in a Lemon Olive Oil Broth, 219–220
Leonard, Benny, 61
Leone, Jack, 25
Leone, Jan, 25, 27
Leo's Place, 74–77, 82–83
Leppek, Chris, xi, 60, 74
LeRoy, Warner, 161
Les Jardins, 49
Levys, 148
Liberal Church Mission, 92
Library, 168
Limbaugh, Rush, 139
Lithgow, William, 77
Little Angel Collection, 112
Liverling, 86–87

Lloyd's Furs, 123, 149
Lobster Newburg, 127
Locke, Sandra, 46
Loews Giorgio Hotel Espresso Chocolate Torte, 215–216
Porcini Mushroom Risotto, 215
Tuscan Warm Summer Salad, 214
Lombardo, Guy, 128
Long, Don, 59
Loop Market, 149
Lopez, Greg, 126, 132
Los Dos, 78–81
Louis, Joe, 61
Lou's Restaurant & Bar, 93
L'Ousteau de Baumaniere, 107, 108
Lowry's Prime Rib, 80

M. & K. Restaurant, 162
Macaulay, Rose, 168
Magic Pan, 24
Mailand, Ann, xi
Mailand, Larry, xi
Malden, Karl, 128
Mama Mia, 42
Manhattan Café, 82–84
Manhattan Restaurant, vii, 89–90, 164
Mapelli, Sonny, 123
Mapelli, Senator, 123
Mapelli meats, 150
Marciano, Rocky, 61
Mario's of Aspen, 28
Markham, 73
Marti, Hans, 101
Martial, 20
Martin, Ira, 113, 117
Martino, Tom, 139
Marvelous Marv's, 80
Marv's Folly, 80
Masala, Joe, 28
Master, Charles, 51
Master, Janie, xi, 49–51
Master, Mel, xi, 48, 49, 51
Master Chef Cooking School, 49
McCartney, Linda, 124

McCartney, Paul, 124, 130
McCarty, Michael, 143–144
McCrary, J. N., 85
McEncroe, Donna, 136
McFarland, Will, 17
McGaa, William, 91
McGaa, William Denver, 91
McGaa Street Restaurant, 91–93
McGee, Mickey, 116
McGill, Gary, 173
McNasser's Restaurant, 2
McPherson, Karen, 143
Meadows, Audrey, 117
Meat (recipes), 5, 31, 47, 105, 106, 118, 126, 127, 140, 141, 180–181, 181–182, 182–183, 183–184, 184–185, 191–192, 192, 193–194, 194, 195–196, 196–197, 198–199, 200–201, 202–203, 205–206, 210–212, 223–224, 227–228, 228–229, 231, 233–234
Meatloaf, 183–184, 227–228
Meet the Boys in the Band, 137
Meier, Theodore L., 15
Mel's Restaurant and Bar, 48, 51
Grilled Chilean Sea Bass with Red Wine Lentils, Grilled Figs, and Grilled Red Onion, 217
Mussels "La Cagouille," 216–217
Menu collecting, 21–24
Merman, Ethel, 117
Messenger, Helen, 156
Midway Hotel, 92
Mikawa, Fred, 171
Miller, Bryan, 153
Miller, Pat, xi, 18, 49

Miller, Roy, 162
Miller Stockman, 148
Miss USA, 36
Mon Petit, 43
Monkees, The, 46
Moonlight Ranch, 162
*Morning,* 177
Morrison, Barry, 89, 153–154
Morrison, Pinky, 153
Moulin de Mougin, 49
Muftar, Fred (a.k.a. Fred Thomas), 28–29
Murphy, Audie, 117
Murphy, Franklin G., xi
Murphy, Tom, 45
Murray, Mark, 137
Mussels "La Cagouille," 216–217
My Friends in Evergreen, 24

Namath, Joe, 46
Nation, Carry, 85
Navarre Restaurant, vii, 17, 96–98
NBC, 132
Negrita, 203
Nelson's Restaurant, 12
Neusteter, Mrs., 123
Neusteter, Myron, 123
Neusteter's, 168
New Wyoming Hotel, 92
*New York Times,* 83, 137
New York University, 101
Nichols, Charles, 91
94th Aero Squadron, 23
Noisettes of Lamb à la Quorum, 126
Normandy French Restaurant, 23, 99–106, 108–109, 119–120, 129, 132–133, 138
Frog's Legs Sauté à la Provençale, 105
Potato Pancakes, 106
Veal Scallopini Marsala, 106
Zabaglione, 106
North Side Spicy Meatballs, 182–183

Northwoods Inn, 82, 170, 174
Novak, Ed, xi, 119, 145, 171

Oakland Raiders, 131
Obrey, Terry, 136
O'Brien, Kathleen, xi
Ohle, Bob, 112
Ohle, Debbie, 112
Ohle, Ernst, 110–112
Ohle, Ernst Jr., 112
Ohle, Esther, 110–112
Ohle, Ila, 112
Ohle, Martye, 112
Ohle's Deli-Restaurant, 110–112
Ohle's Gifts, 112
Old Heidelberg, 164
Old Lighthouse, 21
Old Mexico, 147
Olive Oil Broth, 220
Olive Tapanade, 218
Opera House, 11
Ostrow, Joanne, 137
Ott, Eddie, 17
Ott, Johnny, 17, 96
Outrigger, 74–75
Oven-Dried Tomatoes, 221
Oxford Hotel, 12, 30

Pacific pawn shop, 149
*Pack Your Bags,* 138
Page, Patti, 46
Palace Arms, 129
Palatial Restaurant, 37–38
Palm, The, 42
Panzano
Chocolate Velvet Crostada, 221–223
Lemon Rosemary Gnocchi with Oven-Dried Tomatoes, Niçoise Olives, and Grilled Zucchini in a Lemon Olive Oil Broth, 219
Tuna Carpaccio, 218–219

Papillon Café
Jumbo Sea Scallops with Spicy Peanut Sauce, 224–225
Yellow Curry Pork with Apples and Spinach, 223–224
Parisian Turkey, 141
Parisienne Rotisserie Inn, 162
Parsons, Tom, 139
Pasoe, Steve, 46
Patio Lamaze, 63, 113
Patio Restaurant, 75, 99, 113, 119, 121, 123, 125, 129–130, 133
Pierre's Steak Diane, 118
Paupietees de Boeuf, 127
Peacock Tavern, 168
Peanut Sauce, 224
Peck, Gregory, 36
People's Restaurant, 1
Pepin, Jaques, 139
Perlmutter, Abe, 4
Peters, Dave, 19
Peterson brothers, 173
Petit, 168
Pfister, James, 40
Phelps, Joseph, 138
Piccadilly, 78–81
Pie Crust, 209
Pierre's Quorum. *See* Quorum Restaurant
Pierre's Steak Diane, 118
Pig on a Bun, A, 147, 149
Pinhorn, Richard, 89
Plaza Athenee, 36
Polenta, 201
Porcini Mushroom and Bacon-Infused Beef Consommé, 204
Porcini Mushroom Risotto, 215
Port Wine Sauce, 199
Pot Roast, 180–181
Potato Pancakes, 106
Pourdard, Frank, 168
Presley, Elvis, 46
Pressey, Mark, 84
Professional Book Center, xi

Profile Room, 39, 41, 78, 81, 101, 123. *See also* Le Profile
Prudhomme, Paul, 139
pti restaurant, 169–173
Pumpkin Walnut Muffins, 203–204

Q's, 41
Quelland, Carroll, 113
Query, Dave, 41
Quinn, Anthony, 128
Quinoa Waffles, 210
Quorum Restaurant, viii, 75, 81, 99–100, 107, 114, 117–119, 121–132, 134, 137
  Lobster Newburg, 127
  Noisettes of Lamb à la Quorum, 126
  Paupiettes de Boeuf, 127

Radex
  Black Olive Pesto, 225
  Risotto, 225–226
Ramon's, 48
Ratatouille, 200–201
Rathskeller, 11
Rattlesnake Club, 43, 143–144
Red Chard Casserole, 206–207
Red Slipper, 65
Redford, Robert, 43, 46
Rehn, Lou-Jean Holland, x, 1
Reichl, Ruth, 153
Reithmann, John J., 1
Relish (recipes), 187–188, 212
Restaurant
  early Denver history, 1, 8–12, 55–58
  failures, 48
  liquor licenses, 94–95
  slang, 32–33
  theme, 169–173
Restaurant De L'Opera, 2
Restaurant Edelweiss, 146
Restaurant Hall of Fame, 119

*Restaurant Show, The,* 138
Reynolds, Debbie, 83
Rialto theater, 149
Rice (recipes) 229
Richards, Stan, 39
Richlow Manufacturing Company, 92
Richman, Phyllis, 153
Richthofen Castle, 102
Rifkin, Bobby, 42
Risotto (recipe), 225–226
Roasted Five-Spiced Half Duck, 228–229
Roasted Garlic, 214
Roberts, Jimmy, 66
Robineau family, 4
Robinson, Sugar Ray, 61
Rockefeller, John D., 156
*Rocky Mountain News,* x, 53, 62, 92, 101, 108, 123–124, 126, 132, 135, 137, 139, 143, 177
Rocky Mountain Oysters, 47
Roesti (Potatoes Swiss Style), 197
Rogers, Ginger, 46
Rolling Stones, The, 46
Romig, Joe, 169
Roncetti's, 168
Rooney, Andy, 145
Roosevelt Grill, 82
Rosemary Jus, 201
Rosenfeld, Saul, xi
Rose's Café
  Swordfish or Tuna Sicilian Style, 226–227
  Vietnamese Seafood Delight, 226
Ross's Lounge, 93
Roth, Jack, 4
Roth, Kaye, 4
Roth, Marc, 40
Rotterdam of the Holland-American ship line, 83
Roundtree, Richard, 46
Ruby's nightclub, 39, 41
Rucker, Ellyn, 84
Russell, Green, 91

Saddle Rock, 2
Salad (recipes), 229–230, 230, 214
Salad dressing (recipes), 81, 141
Sam Joe Yang's restaurant, 12
Sam's Famous Home-fries, 228
Sam's No. 3, 147–152
  Meatloaf, 227–228
  Sam's Famous Home-fries, 228
  Vegetarian Green Chili, 227
Samsonite, 148
Santa Fe Railroad, 23
Satan's, 93
Sauce or garnish (recipes), 188–189, 195–196, 199, 210, 211–212, 213, 218, 220–221, 222, 223–224, 224, 225
Savalas, Telly, 46
Savre, Marilyn, xi
Savre, Robert, xi
Schaeffer, Heinz, 130
Schafbuch, Jim, 136
Schmidt, Jimmy, 143–144
School of Hotel and Restaurant Management, 101
Schueler store, 16
Schwalbe, Henry, 121
Schwalbe, Thelma, 121
Schwartz, Arthur, 153, 155
Schwayders, 148
Schwayder, King, 123
Scotch 'n' Sirloin, 78–81
Scotch 'n' Sirloin Salad Dressing, 81
Scott, Buck, viii, xi, 45–47
Scott, Cindy, xi, 45, 47
Seafood. *See* Fish and seafood
Seafood Curry Bengal, 142
Seared Prosciutto-Wrapped Ahi Tuna

with Cucumber Red Onion Relish and Fennel Potato Cakes, 212–213
Seattle Fish, 82
Sedaris, David, 144
Seeley, John E., 2
Semifreddo di Limone, 192–193
Senate Lounge, 99, 122
Senor Pico, 75
17th Avenue Grill, 39
Shaner's, 168
Shank, Paul, 156
Sheraton, Mimi, 137, 153
Shotgun Willie's, 42, 167
Side Line, 11
Sileo, 93
Simic, Thirza, 128, 130
Simic Dolph, 128
Simms, 24
Sliced Veal Zurich Style, 196–197
Slumgullion or Boeuf Bourguignon, 184–185
Smaldone, Checkers, 114, 149–150
Smaldone, Eugene, 114, 149–150
Smaldone, Francis, 114, 149–150
Smith, Kenny, 23
Smith's Restaurant, 12
Smoked Salmon with Quinoa Waffle, 209–210
Smythe, Pete, 133
Soapy Smith, 168
Soltner, Andre, 73
Soufflé (recipe), 27
Soup or chili (recipes), 67–68, 186, 195, 204, 205, 220, 227, 228
Spedding, Doug, 41
Spedding Chevrolet, 41
Speer, Mayor, 98
Sperte, Greg, 63–64
Sperte, Joseph, viii, 63–66, 78–79, 113, 136
Sperte, Roger, xi, 63–65, 79

Sperte, Shannon, xi, 63
Spicy Meatballs, 182–183
St. Charles Company, 91–92
St. James Hotel, 73
St. John, Bill, 108
Stanley Plaza, 63, 79
Stanley Plaza Apartments, 78
Starry Night, 114–115
Stein, Gertrude, 177
Stephanino, 78–81
Sterling, David, 158
Stew Jackson Burglar Alarm Co., 41
Stewart, Jimmy, 117
Stockdorf, Julius F., 13–14
Stokowski, Leopold, 156
Stonescape Restaurant, 24
Stouffer Food Corporation, 159
Strawberry Soup, 205
Street, Della, 43
Strings, 168
Stromberg, Al, 168
Strombergs, 43
Stuffed Port Chops with Red Onion Marmalade, 198–199
Stuffing a turkey, 177–178
Suhatsky, Charles, 146
Super Bowl Soup, 186
Sweet 'n' Sauer Holiday Relish, 187–188
Swordfish or Tuna Sicilian Style, 226–227
Sylling, Jean, xi
Sylling, Ron, xi
Symes, Judge J. Foster, 150

T. Michael's Le Profile, 80
Tabor barber shop, 149
Tabor Grand, 149
Tally Ho Supper Club, 116
Tante Louise, 102, 108, 119, 228
  Porcini Mushroom Bisque, 228

Roasted Five-Spiced Half Duck, 228–229
  Wild Rice Pilaf, 229
Tappan Ranges, 136
Taylor, Blair, 49–51
Taylor, Liz, 42
Taylor, Robert, 128, 132
Taylor Supper Club, 23
Tel Autograph, 17
Terrace Restaurant, 169
Thai-Style Beef Salad, 229–230
Thally, Don, 117
"The Good Life," 120
Theme restaurant, 169
Thomas, Fred. See Muftar, Fred
Thomas, Louis, 104
Thunderbird night club, 158
Tiffin, The, 156–158
Tiffin Inn at Writers' Manor, 156
"Tin Cup Colorado" show, 133
Tivoli Brewery, 143
Top of the Hub, 159
Top of the Park, 168
Top of the Rockies, 23, 159–161
Top of the Sixes, 159
Torgove, Howard, 75
Tortoni's, 12
Touch, 41–42
Town Club, 101
Trader Vic's, 75
Traubel, Helen, 156
Trinkaus, Appollonia, 34
Trinkaus, Conrad, viii, xi, 34, 36
Trio's Enoteca wine company, 30
Troisgros Brothers, 49
Trophies and Engraving, 112
Tuna Carpaccio, 218–219
Tuna Summer Vegetable Salad, 230
Turn of the Century, 42
Turner, Frank, 65
Turner, Ted, 36

Tuscan Lamb Shank, 193–194
Tuscan Warm Summer Salad, 214
Tweed, Jo, xi
240 Union
Thai-Style Beef Salad, 229–230
Tuna Summer Vegetable Salad, 230
235 Fillmore, 48

University Building, 149
University Club, 28
University of Colorado, 169
University of Denver, 119
University of Southern California, 169
Ustinov, Peter, 128

Van Dyke, James, 41
van Horne, Harriet, 51
Vasil's Euro-Grille
Almond-Crusted Diver Scallops, 230–231
Apricot Mustard Crusted Colorado Lamb Chops, 231
Black Forest Cheesecake with Pistachio Crust, 231–232
Veal Scallopini Marsala, 106
Vegetable (recipes), 106, 141, 197, 200–201, 206–207, 212–213, 221, 228
Vegetarian Green Chili, 227
Verge, Roger, 49
Victoria Station, 168
Victory theater, 149
Vienna Café, 2
Vietnamese Seafood Delight, 226
Vino Vino, 41

Wade, Frank, 133
Wagner, Gail, 169
Wagner, Kyle, 155
Waiters, 71–73
Waldorf-Astoria Hotels, 101
Walker, Emory C., Jr., x
Wallace, Billy, 46
Walton, Barbara, 1
Warwick, Dionne, 83
Wellshire Inn, 75
Western Art Museum, 97
Westman Commission Company, 146
Westword, 155
White Genoise Cake, 202
White Spot, 148
Wienerschnitzel, 5
Wild Rice Pilaf, 229
Wilde, Oscar, 7
Wilscam, Tom, xi, 169–173
Wilscam Enterprises, 171, 173
Wilscam's, viii, 169–173
Windsor Hotel, 92, 164
Wine Company, 161
Winter, William L., 96
Wise, Thom, 49–50
Wiseman, James R., xi
Witham, Sally, 41
Witulsky, Dorothy, xi
Wolf, Marcia A., xi
Wolf, Roger, 45–46
Wolfe, Andy, 152
Wolfe, Jean, x, xii, 17, 44–45, 75, 96, 110, 119–120, 125, 130–131, 136, 167
Wolfe, John, 29
Wolfe, Pierre, viii, xii, 45, 75, 96, 102–103, 107–108, 114, 117, 119–120, 128–129, 131, 133–139, 152, 177

recipes, 5, 27, 31, 47, 105, 106, 118, 126, 127. 140, 141, 142
Wolfe, Ronald Pierre, x, 103, 105, 110, 125
Wolhurst Country Club, 115
Wolhurst Mansion, 24
Woman's Exchange, 11
Woods, Teddy, 169
Woody Herman Band, 41
Wootten, Uncle Dick, 24
World of Foods, A, 136
World of Food and Fine Dining, 129
Wright, Larry, xi, 82–84
Writers' Manor, 156

Yan, Martin, 139
Yangas, Sandra, xi
Yanni's
Classic Roast Leg of Lamb, 233
Garides Tourkolimano, 234
Grape Leaves Stuffed with Rice, Dill, and Walnuts, 232
Yellow Curry Pork with Apples and Spinach, 223–224
Yellow Curry Sauce, 223–224
Young, Cliff, viii, xi, 39, 41–42, 78
Young, Sharon Gomez, 42
Yutang, Lin, 175

Zabaglione, 106
Zolo Grill, 41
Zotazar, 149
Zucchini Nut loaf, 189–190